Praise for *Parenting at the Intersections*

"*Parenting at the Intersections* is a book about *belonging*. Belonging in the face of disconnection, migration trauma, colonial wounding, and neurodivergence. Belonging in ways that are not always comfortable for caregivers of all kinds to engage in and around. Jaya and Priya invite the reader of this book to re-remember the beauty of difference and the necessity of how to foster and curate our childrens' differences. **They speak of parenting our neurodivergent children of color as an act of liberation from systems of oppression.** This book is a love letter and a form of disruption—this is my favorite kind of rebellion: one rooted in decolonial love."

—**Jennifer Mullan, PsyD**, author of *Decolonizing Therapy*

"Illuminating and endlessly compassionate, this book validates the myriad ways in which those parenting at the intersections are pressured to help their children conform to societal expectations and 'typical' developmental milestones, while offering up insights and education that make it not just possible to—but impossible *not* to—better understand and honor each child's unique journey, experience, challenges, and strengths. This is **an invaluable, nuanced, and deeply needed guide to parenting diverse children** as we move, together, toward a future in which all brains and bodies are supported—and belong."

—**Jessica McCabe**, How to ADHD

"This book is chock full of insight, lived experience, and richly earned wisdom. **No parent at the intersections will feel alone as they read it.** It exudes a spirit of generosity toward parents of challenged children that is a healing balm."

—**Patty Wipfler**, founder of Hand in Hand Parenting and coauthor of *Listen: Five Simple Tools to Meet Your Everyday Parenting Challenges*

"*Parenting at the Intersections* is what can happen when the primary relationship of parents and children is witnessed with complexity, care, and dignity. . . In these pages we are welcomed into a dynamism of cultural humility and lived authority. **Priya and Jaya built for us a space of inquiry where conscious community can show up for every kind**

of family, where every family can be supported to hold every child in the way each child needs to be held—and where collectives can choose resilient grace, reliable vitality, and committed connection over simple perfectionism. As they examine the ways in which ableism, adultism, racism, economic injustice, and other layers of oppression press in to interfere with authentic relationship, they guide us to bold efficacy in countering these forces in the most immediate zones of our lives. This is a work of courageous creativity and joy."

—**Dr. Leticia Nieto**, author of *Beyond Inclusion, Beyond Empowerment*

"*Parenting at the Intersections* is a wonderful contribution to literature and very needed. Focused on parents raising BIPOC neurodivergent children, **the book and its authors invite parents in to experience, connect, and grow**. There is a pleasing warmth and relational quality that **will surely resonate and empower parents and others** who read this book. There is much to learn about intersectionality in neurodivergence, and this book is a welcome contribution to the knowledge base. The authors cover a lot of ground, and the book includes several lived experience contributions. What a pleasing and informative book to review! I would recommend it to any parent and any professional working with BIPOC neurodivergent children."

—**Dr. Robert Jason Grant**, creator of AutPlay Therapy,
author, and neurodiversity advocate

"This is a must-have book for any caregiver or mental health professional standing at the crossroads figuring out how to support a child navigating the complexities of neurodivergence and color. **The authors masterfully educate the reader, while simultaneously showing how it is possible to parent and guide from the heart.** The result is a beautiful invitation to look deep within in order to help a child understand, discover, and embrace who they are."

—**Lisa Dion, LPC, RPT-S**, creator of Synergetic Play Therapy
and author of *Aggression in Play Therapy:*
A Neurobiological Approach for Integrating Intensity

"*Parenting at the Intersections* offers an impressive discussion on the complexities of parenting neurodiverse children of color. **Through poignant stories and friendly analysis, readers are invited to come together and reflect on both the challenges and the joys of their parenting journeys amidst systems and institutions that often do not center their children.** I've never seen a parenting guide like this that threads together community building, racial literacy, and neurodiversity. Coauthors Ramesh and Saaral unpack our very notion of 'difference' from a social justice framework, and welcome more light, joy, presence, and love into the parenting process. Essential and utterly new, this book offers compassionate wisdom and thoughtful strategies for parents and adults who love the full variety of BIPOC children."

—**Dr. Anu Taranath**, professor, speaker, racial equity consultant, and author of *Beyond Guilt Trips: Mindful Travel in an Unequal World*

PARENTING AT THE INTERSECTIONS

RAISING NEURODIVERGENT CHILDREN OF COLOR

JAYA RAMESH
PRIYA SAARAL

CHICAGO

Published by Parenting Press
An imprint of Chicago Review Press Incorporated
814 North Franklin Street
Chicago, Illinois 60610
ISBN 978-1-64160-889-3

Land and Labor Acknowledgments

This book was written on the unceded and stolen land of the First peoples of Seattle, and we dedicate this book to the Duwamish, Stillaguamish, and Coast Salish peoples, and to all Indigenous peoples of Turtle Island, past and present, and honor with gratitude the land itself and the tribes.

We also acknowledge that this country was built by the stolen labor of enslaved peoples of Africa, the labor of Indigenous peoples who had stewarded these lands for thousands of years, and the forced and voluntary immigrant labor from which we benefit today. We thank and honor the contributions of all survivors and subsequent generations that have paved the way for us.

Library of Congress Control Number: 2023948753

Cover and interior design: Jonathan Hahn
Cover photo: Baldube / Shutterstock
Author photos: Maxine Tu Yip
Interior art: Ujjayini Sikha
Ujjayini Sikha is an Indian-born artist based in San Francisco. An erstwhile engineer turned artist, she specializes in doing portraiture in all its variable forms. Her artistic adventures can be found on Instagram @ujjayinisikha.

Printed in the United States of America

We dedicate this book to the many storytellers who took the time to share their lives with our readers so they may feel less alone. And to all of the unique and quirky children out there who inspire us to imagine and work towards another world.

Jaya

To my children, Rohan and Taejas: Thank you for teaching me to really *see* the world, to keep playing, to stay curious, and to lead with compassion—you are my reasons.

To my husband, Ravi: Thank you for being a true partner and for believing—what a gift to be known and loved by you.

To my parents, Lakshmi and Ramesh: Thank you for showing me the way—I am forever indebted.

Priya

To my Ahir, who calls me *amma*: Thank you for breathing life into me and guiding me. Your playful spirit, humorous wisecracks, and fierce determination are my love and joy.

To my Vibha, who lovingly calls me *peima*: Thank you for teaching me to dance with abandon.

To my *amma* and *appa*, Lalitha and Swaminathan: Thank you for breathing life into me, first. And for sprinkling my childhood and Maya's with lots of play and laughter.

CONTENTS

Part III: Relating to the World Outside

Part IV: Building a Better World

FOREWORD

It's that time of year again, and Kyah is a happy little boy.

He darts around the room—like a white rabbit who has an appointment to catch—worrying about whether he's on Santa's naughty list and whether we've put out the cookies and the glass of milk. "Santa loves cookies and milk!" he exclaims to me for the umpteenth time today, and then drags the fluffy white blankets off the bed and plucks off the three neatly folded white towels on the end-of-bed bench, hauling them out of the room. Exhausted, I follow him to the living room where he has gathered other towels, blankets, and irregularly cut shapes of white paper—anything white, really—to create a massive pile of white things in the center of the parlor.

Around the heap, sticking out of its many creases, are Kyah's toy things: a noisy plastic sleigh with four perpetually smiling Lego-like occupants pulled by a reindeer he isn't quite convinced is actually a reindeer ("It's probably just a Christmas cow," he told his mother last week); a made-in-China choo choo train with wobbly tires decorated with festive green and saccharine red colors; and the less fortunate side of a cardboard box that he's cut up into the iconic shape of a Christmas tree, painted green, and dotted with red splotches ("Christmas trees need red baubles!"). Poised on the sofa, watching the whole proceedings, is a snowman made of a white pillow tucked and massaged appropriately to fit the billing. His eyes are made of the chocolate chips Kyah had excavated from his favorite cookies; a canoe drawn on notebook paper by his sister Alethea stands in for the snowman's smile. The nose is a red pen.

I leave Kyah's wild celebrations for a while to take delivery of an Amazon parcel at the door. He doesn't know it yet, but the parcel contains a brand-new Santa costume we had ordered three days ago. I hide the parcel away, wondering whether the sellers thought our order to be rather peculiar, and return to the white heap and its wild shaman dancing around it. "Merry Christmas, Dada! Is Santa coming today? Is Santa going to come?"

"I want Santa to be here."

"I want Santa to be here."

"I want Santa to be here."

Through a tired smile, I mutter the words I said yesterday, and the day before that, and the day before that . . . "Yes, my love. Santa will come today, and if he doesn't come today, maybe he'll come when he is ready."

"OK."

He flashes me a five-year-old smile, and then begins to sing, "Jingle bells, jingle bells, jingle all the way." A few feet away, our window opens out into a warm Hamburg day. Not quite sunny but warm enough for small buzzing critters—frozen still during winter—to float through the crack, bringing greetings and glad tidings of a different sort.

It's April.

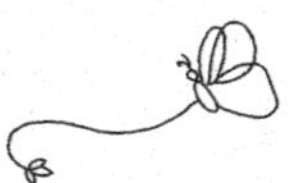

At one time, I tried to convince our dear Kyah that it wasn't Christmas after all by telling him "Christmas" referred to a specific day of the year, a day that only came around once in a long while. "It isn't Christmas; today isn't Christmas," I said. I was frustrated, a bit exhausted with answering his endless questions about Santa, about his littering elves, about the vagaries of the North Pole, about the snickering antics of Santa's archnemesis, the Grinch, and about whether the jolly old woodsman was finally going to ride his eternal sleigh into our home, bearing gifts. It was hard work picking up after him, bending every morsel of our everyday lives to fit within the thematic confines of yuletide. Kyah, however, shrugged off my rationalizations: "But it is Christmas!" he said.

I spoke to a friend about Kyah's autism, his obsessions with Christmas, and my concerns that I was "gentrifying" him by trying to drag him into my sense of time. He offered feedback I already knew but was awfully glad to hear: "Kyah senses temporality differently; he doesn't locate time along linear trajectories as you've learned to do. For him, time always begins. Why don't you forge agreements with him? Tune into what he's doing with time."

Those words were a beautiful reversal of the dominant gestures of inclusion, therapy, and pity that trailed his diagnosis. Instead of trying to correct his fixations with Christmas, I was being invited to lean into the monstrous calendar-queering crack that enlisted his little body in how it came to matter. What if it was Christmas? What if Christmas wasn't merely the isolatable date on the calendar? What if Christmas had a stranger virtuality that its pixelated actuality, nailed to the twenty-fifth day of Decembers, could not acknowledge? A processual fugitivity only an autistic body could pattern? Was there something to Kyah's persistent and unironic celebrations of Santa?

Was there a way to meet him in the middle?

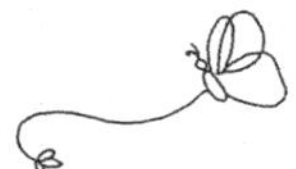

As the African father to an Afro-Asian autistic boy, I worry about him. A lot. It is one thing to parent a minoritarian child—already a matter of exclusions and effacements—but then quite another to parent a disabled minoritarian child. I worry that he'd never be on time in a world calibrated to ableist notions of punctuality. I worry he'd either be too late or too early, that the train would leave without him. I worry he might not even notice and that he'd be stuck to a pile of white things somewhere. Then I worry that I often get in his way and lament my incapacities to accompany him in his crip-ontological dis/avowal of normative cartographies of embodiment.

However, in small glimpses of the exquisite, in how he notices patterns, in how he points out things I miss, in how he looks at my impoverished attempts to capture time and tether it to the Procrustean clock, in how he insists that there's more—I wonder if it isn't the other way around: I wonder if he is worried about me.

This book is the heartfelt acknowledgement that there is more. It's hard to see it—especially for those of us who must keep our hands at ungreased levers, cranking the machine against its algorithmic desires to produce for dominant others. It's hard to slow down because our intergenerational bodies are calibrated to the grime in the hull of the ship. It's hard to listen to the strange ethereal sounds emanating from our little ones because we are too busy screaming at the pearly gates, wanting to be let into whatever city of power we've been denied entry into.

But then, what if disability is not the inadequacy it is popularly articulated as? What if a strange excess, a spillage, a corporeal refusal to abide the terms of an established order, blossoms in the cracks of crip-bodies? What if we are seeing the world too straightforwardly? What if clarity is getting in our way of noticing the promiscuity of the world?

"At the heart of this book," Jaya and Priya write, with a profound vulnerability that stresses the nonlegibility of the worlds they seek to herald through their careful inquiry, "is a belief that parenting our neurodivergent children of color is an act of liberation from systems of oppression that does not have to be done alone." They suggest that "parenting our differently wired children of color in this world offers us an immediate and profound opportunity to disrupt our socialization and conditioning on what it means to be 'normal.' In doing so, we invite you to view our children's differences as the medicine the world needs, and our role as parents as the midwives of an unarticulated future."

Kyah is a time traveler whose notions of temporality address the anxious urgency within climate discourses, as well as the racialized scarcity of the clock and its mechanical preferences for White cosmologies. In our children, in our disabled children, in Kyah, a sidling logic flashes up that distresses the economy of relations we are incarcerated within. In this book, you'll find kind companions who sense that the thing to do, as White stability hollows out the politics of our moment, must go beyond the critique of oppressive paradigms, leap into the extraordinary ordinariness of parenting, and dwell beside the liminal cracks of neurodivergence.

Jaya and Priya follow Kyah's parallaxed gaze: they sneak between the lines and sniff out the curious life-forms that inhabit peri-feral worlds. Unwilling to settle exclusively for grand gestures, they write in small doses, naming practices, sitting by our tables, picking up littered toys along with us, placing their hands on our backs when we sigh with frustration, nodding us closer to the crack, urging us to revisit the heap in our living rooms—the crude contraption of white on white creases—and beckoning us on to take a closer look. This time with slanted eyes. I hear them say to you, to me, along with Kyah, kneeling by that magnanimous pile:

"See? It really is Christmas."

Báyò Akómoláfé, PhD
Author, *These Wilds Beyond our Fences: Letters to My Daughter on Humanity's Search for Home*

Dr. Báyò Akómoláfé—a philosopher, psychologist, professor, and poet. He is a teacher and public intellectual renowned for his unconventional views on global crises, activism, and social change.

PREFACE

RELATIONSHIPS MATTER IN PARENTING.* They breathe life into the mundane day-to-day of packing lunches, driving carpool, advocating for your child's education, picking up medicine refills, and walking the dog. Our relationships with our children, our partners, our friends, or even ourselves can be a source of healing. So when we began this book, we intentionally committed to prioritizing our most significant relationships—between us, with our children, and with other important people in our lives. Meaningful relationships remind us of what has real value and can be lighthouses that help us come back to shore safely. Even though we may never meet you, we value the relationship we are entering into with you, dear reader, and in that spirit we begin by telling you a little bit about ourselves and the process of writing this book.

When we were asked to collaborate on this project, we instinctively felt drawn to it while simultaneously asking ourselves, *Who are we to write this book?* This question, at the surface, may simply call to mind impostor syndrome.† However, the internal question of who we are to be taking up space is an invitation to unpack the historical conditioning and the structural inequalities that give rise to this doubt. The question is not just *Who are we?* but *Who are we as Brown, neurodivergent*

* Throughout the book, we use *parenting* interchangeably with *being a caregiver*. We recognize that not all of us with children in our care are in traditional parenting roles.
† Impostor syndrome is a feeling that you are not as good as others around you, first described by Dr. Pauline Clance.

women, without social media followers, to write this book? In grappling with *this* question, we have come to understand that we are the people to write this version of this book in this way—the way only we could.

We come from a set of experiences: Indian immigrants with caste privilege, women of color in the context of the United States, mental health therapists with attention-deficit/hyperactivity disorder (ADHD), and mothers to children who teach us another world is possible with their play, curiosity, and tender hearts. We engage with the world through dominant modes of communication, including speaking and writing. Oh, and we are dog lovers. Emerging from our lived experiences is a desire to uplift the stories relegated to our society's shadows. We also believe other books should be written by those embodying experiences different from ours. There is room for all of us at this table.

In writing this book, I, Jaya, learned more of how my brain works. I thrive when I can create some structure in my day. My creativity comes as a burst, and the fear of losing momentum often propels me to hyperfocus for a while. This inevitably leads to needing downtime to regroup, often as a nap in the day. My husband often jokes I am a high-performing race car that needs pit stops to retune. I think big and often miss details, which you can see in all the furniture I have assembled in our home. In writing this book, I am grateful for our editors!

For me, Priya, in a world that has appeared to spin too fast, I naturally rebelled and retreated, finding solace in the motto "Slow and steady wins the race." I found myself chuckling that I, someone who struggles with attention, reading, and writing, decided to coauthor a book. This process has challenged my long-held negative belief about my ability to create meaningful things because of my comfort with slowness, my hyperfocus on dotting the *i*'s and crossing the *t*'s, and my innate talent for procrastination. Writing a book places incredible demands on executive functioning, and discovering the novel ways in which my brain has stretched and twisted in service of creation has been affirming and rewarding.

Despite our colorful individual differences, we discovered gifts that have complemented each other and helped us to grow. While we naturally fit as collaborators in our personalities and our work processes, it would be untruthful to say we did not also push each other beyond our respective comfort zones that resulted in some big feelings. In service of our relationship, we created time to attend to each other's inner emotional landscape; deep and soulful listening was instrumental to the alchemy of this book. Making time to listen has to be an intentional practice in modern times, when life races by. We made it a sacred aspect of our book-writing process. In doing so, we honored our different emotional experiences, and this has been healing, because it allowed us to tap into our internal wisdom more clearly.

Throughout this book, we worked to reclaim the concept of time: we committed to take, make, and honor each other's relationship to time, but also our own. Many books written by two authors have taken much less time, but that isn't *this* book. This book was not just an intellectual exercise. Instead, it has been intentionally simmered with love, enriched by holding space for our ADHD, and navigated through a few gazillion more neural networks than necessary.

In hindsight, we also worked hard to reclaim the concept of labor and ownership in writing this book. Initially, we started engaging in teamwork through the traditional capitalist divide-and-conquer approach. This inevitably led to frustration, guilt, comparison, a sense of unfairness, etc. When we returned to listening to each other, something unexpected transpired. We were able to break down manufactured walls around labor and lean more into a collaborative process that was not focused on ledger keeping of how much the other produced. When we oriented to holding production and contributions more expansively, we could release ourselves from relating to each other transactionally. We are both in awe of the unintentional ways in which the process of writing this book has been such a healing and transformative journey for both of us, helping us grow with one another as writers and bringing us closer and tighter in friendship.

At the core of this book is a desire to build community with and for parents, and this requires accountability. To hold ourselves accountable to the parents who shared their experiences and to our larger communities, we asked four wise people from our communities to be members of an elder council. They met with us and offered listening, championed our work, provided constructive feedback, and gave invaluable counsel. An example of what emerged from meeting with our elders is the decision to provide pseudonyms for our parent participants and to edit out specific, revealing information to protect children's privacy and confidentiality. We wanted to honor that children may have different levels of comfort with owning or being out with this particular intersection of their identities as they grow into adulthood. Our heartfelt appreciation to Leticia Nieto, Agnes Kwong, Jamie Pearson, and Janne Mayes for holding us with love and care.

We are deeply indebted and grateful to all the parents who offered their time, stories, and wisdom for the greater community. These parents reminded us that love is an action, a verb, rich with curiosity, courage, and a fierce commitment to the liberation of our children. To express our gratitude and to begin building community, we created a space for parents to meet via an online call. The conversation spanned many topics, but mainly being together, even across screens many miles apart, created a deep kind of emotional safety and kinship that is hard to qualify. The experience reminded us that we do not have many safe spaces for parents raising Black and Brown neurodivergent children. We hope this will change.

For you, dear reader, we hope that the voices included in this book offer a lovely reminder of our interconnectedness, though we may never meet. We hope these stories from parents across the country will inspire, offer reassurance, and provide a sense of belonging. Together let's continuously reimagine a better world for all of our children.

A NOTE ON LANGUAGE

It was important to us as authors to ensure that our writing is accessible to our readers. Wanting to be connected with you, we begin by explaining some terms and how we use them in this book.

BIPOC

You will notice that we interchangeably use terms like *BIPOC* (Black, Indigenous, or person of color) and *POC* (person of color), understanding that these are imperfect terms. The word *BIPOC* is a nod to centering the racial assault and dehumanization that Black and Indigenous communities face that is markedly different than other communities of color. Similarly, *Latinx*, *Latine*, *Latino/Latina*, and *Hispanic* also stem from various responses to particular cultural and political conditions. We recognize that not all who are from or have Latin American heritage identify with these terms.

Many such broad descriptors are used in the cultural milieu; they all risk collapsing diverse communities into a single umbrella without noting the different experiences these communities endure. These linguistic conveniences end up perpetuating the very thing we are critiquing—that the structures of oppression we live under minimize and blur the distinctive lived experiences of our various communities. At the same time, these terms also exist to communicate the connectedness of our liberation. We recognize this tension and sit with the complexity of our times. We only use these broad terms when the context calls for it. Wherever possible, we will name the specific identity and location of the people we refer to and how they want to be identified.

Neurodivergence

We also call attention to the word *neurodivergence*, which, simply put, refers to a human variance in which the brain is wired to think, learn, and communicate differently from the typical population, where "typical" is informed by a socially constructed "norm." We will unpack where this idea of a norm comes from in the coming chapters. What constitutes neurodivergence is evolving. We experienced this evolution as we wrote the book. When we began, we included the following conditions: autism (including nonspeaking); ADHD; giftedness; learning challenges such as dyslexia, dysgraphia, and dyscalculia; intellectual disabilities; OCD; and Tourette's syndrome. In our learning process, we came to understand that for some, other conditions such as bipolar, complex post-traumatic stress disorder, and personality disorders also fall under this roof. However, when we put out a call seeking parents to interview, we used the initial definition and received responses from parents speaking about those experiences.

We recognize that the term *neurodivergent* itself centers on the neurotypical experience. It is antithetical to the notion of this book that is written to center the voices of the divergent. Once again, we are faced with the limits of the current language and wish to use the term *neurodivergent* to communicate clearly.

Furthermore, we situate neurodivergence as a disability, while honoring that some neurodivergent individuals may not identify as disabled. As such, we interchangeably use *disability* and *neurodivergence*. We also want to acknowledge that within the disability community, there is a difference in how people identify. Some people use identity-first language, like "an autistic person," and others prefer to be referred to as "a person with autism." Here again, we honor how people wish to identify themselves when sharing their stories, but when it comes to our language around collective identity, we will be using identity-first language as preferred by many self-advocates in the disability community. Lastly, we move away from terms like *high-functioning* and *low-functioning* and use terms like *high and low support needs* to reflect the conditions of the social environment rather than focus on the individual. Most recently in this field, the word *profound* has also been used synonymously with *high support needs*.

The neurodivergent experience is vast and deep. Being neurodivergent positions people outside of the dominant structure. But not everyone's experience within this community is the same. Some within the neurodivergent community are further marginalized by their race, type of disability, sexuality, and class, for instance. In addition, as speaking members of this neurodivergent community, we hold the privilege of being able to participate in the dominant communication modes, and this privilege limits our ability to know the lived experiences of those who are nonspeaking entirely. Recognizing this, we have worked to learn from parents with children with various access needs and communication differences and are grateful to include some of their stories here. Furthermore, while we have included some experiences of parenting nonspeaking children, we recognize that the book has a limitation in that it privileges the spoken word, and the suggestions we offer may not readily cater to all communication needs and may need parents to adapt these suggestions to suit their child's unique strengths, communication and learning needs, and relationships.

Ultimately, there is no getting around the fact that writing a book privileges a particular way of knowing the world. As much as the book is about trying to disrupt, by the very nature of being a book, it ends up reifying ableist and supremacy* culture (raising one type of communication over another and glorifying the written word). So even though we are writing a book about how these structures cause harm, by the act of writing, we are reinforcing the very system we are critiquing. We sit in the uncomfortable liminal space of knowing something is problematic and not yet having the means to entirely disentangle from it.

Supportive Needs but Special Education

We intentionally avoid the term *special needs* when referring to children with disabilities. The term is simply inaccurate—there is nothing special

* When we use the term *supremacy*, we are referring to many different types of supremacy, including White supremacy, caste supremacy, patriarchy, and ecological supremacy. Sometimes we are specifically discussing the impacts of White supremacy and as such name that. Ultimately, all forms of supremacy are linked, and examining them as individual artifacts is counterproductive.

about the fundamental needs that our children have as humans. This term perpetuates ableism and distances our children further from nondisabled children. Instead, we use the term *supportive needs* to describe the services that our children receive to meet their physical, emotional, and intellectual needs. You will notice we use the term *special education* in some chapters, but this is in reference to an educational program designed for children with disabilities to ideally receive an equitable education. Therefore, in this context we use the term to refer to the program.

INTRODUCTION

We are not alone in our struggles and never have been. Somos almas afines [We are related souls] and this interconnectedness is an unvoiced category of identity.

—Gloria E. Anzaldúa

At the heart of this book is a belief that parenting our neurodivergent children of color is an act of liberation from systems of oppression that does not have to be done alone. What we mean by this is that parenting our differently wired children of color in this world offers us an immediate and profound opportunity to disrupt our socialization and conditioning on what it means to be "normal." In doing so, we invite you to view our children's differences as the medicine the world needs, and our role as parents as the midwives of an unarticulated future.

Some of us parents may readily see the connection that systems of oppression have to our parenting, and some of us may find this idea novel or altogether overwhelming. Whatever your response to this statement, we see you. Parenting our children of color with neurodivergence can often be a lonely and disorienting experience. We can feel like we have done something wrong, or worse, that something is wrong with our child. We get it is hard to see through the haze of our day-to-day existence, spanning the gamut of shuttling between school, doctor's appointments, and laundry. Our offering in this part storytelling, part self-inquiry book is to situate parenting children of color with neurodivergence within various interlocking oppressive structures, such as White supremacy and ableism. We know these are hefty topics—don't worry, dear reader, we break them down in chapter 2!

In this book, you will find a chorus of expert voices, in which parents and caregivers sing alongside researchers and writers. With this, we hope to offer an antidote to dominant narratives of how parenting should look and what parenting can be. Holding space is what we do best as mental health therapists (and parents), allowing voices to be heard and stories to come through, and in doing that, we reveal the patterns and themes interwoven in the fabric of our lives. The stories you will read in this book are from parents of color on their journeys, and they surface the tension of parenting within the context of these systems while also challenging it. By making the connection explicit between how these systems of oppression inform and shape our parenting, we offer an invitation to parents to slow down and reflect on their parenting journeys. We believe that when parents can be given the space to listen to their inner wisdom and their children's voices, and the time to find connection with others, it is the most radical way to disrupt systems of oppression.

Ultimately, we hope that this book will normalize parenting experiences at the multiple intersections of lived experiences that our children and parents hold. We hope it will celebrate the various ways to parent and help parents feel less alone in their struggles and joys. We hope it widens your lens and helps you to appropriately contextualize how you are parenting. Part of the offering of this book is an invitation to be comfortable with not fully knowing, and to find our way together on this journey of parenting children with neurodivergence. To not fully arrive.

Who Is This Book For?

This book is for parents in the trenches of parenting children at the intersection of race and neurodivergence. We recognize that parents are at different junctures in making sense of this experience. Some parents have newly diagnosed children. Some are wondering if their child is neurodivergent and what that means. And some have been doing this for a while. We welcome all of you with open arms.

We also want to offer a fair warning. This is not your typical parenting book. You will not be offered steps and protocols, and we imagine this might be unsatisfying if at this time you are in need of quick answers. But we trust that parents can arrive at their own solutions through reflection, and we believe that there is no singular way to parent correctly. On our parenting journeys, we often receive advice on what to do about many things, including sleep, feeding, tantrums, schools, etc. It's easy to get caught up in the voices out there. We believe parenting is about listening to those voices *and* returning home to our own. As such, rather than telling you how to parent, this book offers you ways to think about parenting. The ideas in this book are emerging from a politicized lens, and we invite you to take what fits at this moment and leave what does not. We think this book might be most satisfying to those who have begun to question and investigate the impact of the systems of oppression on their parenting and children.

If you are not a parent of a BIPOC neurodivergent child, we still invite you to read this book. The times we live in need you to understand the experiences of your neighbors, your students, your patients, and your niblings.* Community matters, and many of the parents we spoke to for this book wished the people around them had more of an understanding of what it means to parent neurodivergent children of color. Maybe the wisdom shared here will also invigorate your thinking about parenting, support, and care for *all* children.

More so, we can understand that some of you, especially those new to these experiences, may wish for a happy ending or stories that capture a triumph of good over evil. We understand that it may be hard to stay with the trouble as you read stories of confronting systemic oppression. But the reality for too many parents at this intersection is that the triumph is in their staying power to get up the next day and do all of it again and to find joy in the most unexpected places.

We imagine that reading stories that either mirror your reality or feel foreign may provoke some feelings. We encourage you to notice what is stirred in you and tend to it. What brings you to your knees? What makes you want to look away? This book is an invitation to unpack, disentangle, and reimagine. We invite you to explore the caverns of your mind, wander through the attic of intergenerational inheritances, and surrender to the magic and wisdom our children offer.

---

* A gender-neutral term for nieces and nephews.

Why Now?

Parenting can be challenging enough without also having to contend with navigating complex systems such as those involving extended family, education providers, medical institutions, law enforcement, mental health, pharmaceuticals, nonprofit industrial complexes, and technology. However, raising a Black, Brown, or Indigenous and neurodivergent child while negotiating these systems multiplies the level of complexity and danger that has been unrecognized for too long. We believe parents who are raising BIPOC and neurodivergent kids will see themselves reflected in these stories. Still, we also think that there is something universally human in this particular struggle and triumph.

We are writing this book because, as parents from different cultural and racial locations, we found no examples of parenting books that spoke to our experiences, talking about the joys and struggles of raising our neurodivergent children in these spheres. As mental health therapists, we see too often with our clients the anxiety and depression that emerge from not being reflected by the larger culture. As neurodivergent and BIPOC folx,* we do not see our stories being told.

When there are stories that mirror our realities in some way, we can feel deeply known, acknowledged, validated, hopeful, and less alone. There is room for possibility, love, and spaciousness—another world where there is radical acceptance of the many ways to be. We know that books that tell our stories matter; representation matters. But representation is not enough; including differences does not transform structural oppression and injustice. We are painfully aware of this, yet we also believe that naming that diversity in stories that account for a broad range of human experiences is part of that transformational process. For representation to move beyond inclusion—and, often, inclusion into dominant ways of being—an analysis of the structures of settler colonialism, White supremacy, ableism, and capitalism is needed. Ultimately, we believe that stories that are multiple and multidimensional can disrupt the continued dehumanization of bodies and minds that are disabled and neurodivergent.

* A gender-inclusive alternative for *folks*.

How to Read This Book

Think of the contents of this book as a house. In part 1, we give you a look at the foundation and the frame of the house. These chapters provide the reader with a way to think about parenting and to expand the context in which we parent beyond family and schools. The chapter on child development offers an antidote to usual development models that do not center on the experiences of our children. Part 2 gives you a tour of the various rooms within the house. These are topics related to parenting that happens within the framework we explored in part 1, including chapters on play, adolescence, and technology. Part 3 explores the surrounding neighborhood: the outside systems we encounter in our parenting, including school, medical, and legal systems, and our communities. Part 4 brings it all together to make the house a home, offering a vision for parenting neurodivergent children of color.

Throughout the book, you will hear from parents living at our intersections every day. Additionally, you will learn from some research and reflect on your journey through reflective prompts. As a political act, we have intentionally relied on information that comes from lived experiences, academic research, news articles, podcasts, and even our journal entries.*

You are welcome to read this book in any order. Skip chapters to what calls you most, and return to those chapters that you need to sit with more. You have full permission to dance with this book as you desire. We invite you to use the stories as a portal to self-discovery.

Reflection Questions

Throughout the book, you will notice reflection prompts. As you dive into these questions, be gentle and compassionate with yourselves, and please take all the time you need. There is no urgency to complete them in one sitting, and there is no right way to answer them. Maybe you write

---

* We want to acknowledge that many of the academic research and sources we cite were produced within a Western context solving a particular cultural problem and not all answer questions specific to our communities. Yet we have included them because of what is largely available thus far. We are in the process to disentangle and be in right relationship with knowledge stemming from a White-centered context. It is our hope that this work becomes a part of a larger body of work that reflects the changing tides.

it down, sing about it, or draw it out. The important thing is to reflect. The more we reflect, the more we know ourselves, and the more we know ourselves, the better attuned we can be for our precious children.

We think reflection can be done both individually and in community. While for some, journaling and drawing are supportive processes, we find that talking with a trusted friend, close family member, or your pet can also be useful. As you reflect, notice the information your body offers. Some things we find helpful to pay attention to include the temperature, sensations like tightness and tingling, and what your body is needing to do, whether it is to shake or shrink. As you notice, there is nothing to do but take in the information the body reveals. Allow it to move through you. This returning to the body is a grounded practice in disrupting supremacy and productivity cultures, which depend on our disconnection.

PART I

THE FOUNDATIONS OF THE HOME

1

THE FRAMEWORK

Early in the process, we received a question about whether our project would center the voices of neurotypical parents in raising their neurodivergent kids. Implicit in this question was whether we would once again perpetuate ableist ways of knowing, being, and parenting in the world. We sincerely hope not! Even though we identify as women of color and neurodivergent, we know that we also have internalized ableism and are committed to the long, sometimes painful, soul-healing work of disentangling from these messages. This is generational work, and even with this commitment, we know we will falter and write or say something that reflects these systems' hold on our being. May we all hold each other with love, grace, and gentleness.

So that we orient in the direction of liberation from systems of oppression, we have relied on several analytical lenses as our compasses. They are, in no particular order:

- Intersectionality.
- Disability justice.
- Neurodiversity paradigm.
- Attachment.
- Developmental approach.

Intersectionality

Emerging from critical race theory,* the term *intersectionality* was first popularized by professor Kimberlé Crenshaw. But even before the term entered the mainstream, revolutionaries such as Sojourner Truth, Angela Davis, and the Combahee River Collective all gave voice to the experiences of living at the intersections of race, gender, and sexuality. Crenshaw based her understanding of the concept in her observations as a lawyer, seeing that race conversations privileged Black men and gender conversations focused on White women, thereby missing the unique experiences of Black women. As she writes, "Because the intersectional experience is greater than the sum of racism and sexism, any analysis that does not take intersectionality into account cannot sufficiently address the particular manner in which Black women are subordinated." That is, there is an unparalleled experience of being both Black and a woman that can't simply be understood by a lens that only addresses race or gender. While it was originally relegated to the legal context, today intersectionality is employed in activism, education, and other sectors to illustrate the complexity in experiences of both privilege and oppression of our multiple identities.

At the heart of this book is the idea of intersectionality: we propose that parenting a child of color with neurodivergence creates a unique set of joys and challenges. While we specifically focused on the experiences of raising children at the particular intersection of race and neurodivergence, we would be remiss if we did not acknowledge other identities such as class, sexuality, gender, religion, immigration status, and so on. As such, without compromising the privacy of our participants, we showcase how various identities play into particular experiences.

Disability Justice

Another framework that profoundly influences our work is disability justice. Created by Black, Brown, and queer people, it emerged in response to the disability rights movement, which was a single-issue approach to addressing the ways disabled people were being left out of the larger cultural

* Critical race theory holds that race is a social construct and that racism is upheld through societal institutions and policies.

conversation, including politics, health care, the workforce, and other institutions in society. Patty Berne, a cofounder of Sins Invalid, writes:

> The Disability Rights movement simultaneously invisibilized the lives of disabled people of color, immigrants with disabilities, disabled people who practice marginalized religions (in particular those experiencing the violence of anti-Islamic beliefs and actions), queers with disabilities, trans and gender non-conforming people with disabilities, people with disabilities who are houseless, people with disabilities who are incarcerated, people with disabilities who have had their ancestral lands stolen, amongst others.

Berne goes on to make the connection between ableism, colonial conquest, capitalism, and White body supremacy and how these systems of oppression feed off each other. A disability justice framework is built on intersectionality (the first principle) and sees everybody, every mind, as having value and a place in our world. It affirms that our productivity does not decide our worth. As Berne states,

> A disability justice framework understands that:
> - All bodies are unique and essential.
> - All bodies have strengths and needs that must be met.
> - We are powerful, not despite the complexities of our bodies, but because of them.
> - All bodies are confined by ability, race, gender, sexuality, class, nation-state, religion, and more, and we cannot separate them.

Neurodiversity Paradigm

A neurodiversity paradigm articulates that brain and neurocognitive functioning diversity is akin to gender and racial diversity. It rejects notions of "normal"—often standardized based on White, cis-het, nondisabled males—and shifts away from pathologizing behaviors, feelings, and thoughts. Like an ecological model applied in biological sciences, a neurodiversity paradigm approaches diversity as critical to the survival of our larger cultural, political, and environmental ecosystem. As queer, autistic scholar Dr. Nick Walker states, "Neurodiversity is a natural and valuable form of human diversity. . . . The idea there is one 'normal' or 'healthy' type of brain or mind, or one 'right' style of neurocognitive functioning, is a culturally constructed fiction, no more valid (and no more conducive to a healthy society or to the overall well-being of humanity) than the idea that there is one 'normal' or 'right' ethnicity, gender, or culture."

Beyond the inherent value in diversity, a neurodiversity paradigm examines the social and political forces that problematize differences. It considers what it means to live under toxic and oppressive structures and challenges societal institutions and cultural ideologies that perpetuate ideas of normativity.

Attachment

Attachment is a long-standing bond between caregivers and children that grounds children and helps orient them to who they are and how safe they are in the world. This bond is not a binary switch; it is not just there or not. So much of the work we do as mental health therapists is about building secure attachment in sessions with couples, parents, and children. So it is no surprise that we would orient toward an attachment framework here too.

For a child to form a healthy, secure attachment with their parent and other caregiving figures, their bond needs to be consistently nurtured and nourished with *love deposits* in their attachment bank. Being with your child through a cry, providing gentle care when they're sick, being a loving witness while holding a limit, and delighting in them even if you can't stand their video game are examples of love deposits. When a child's attachment bank is full of love deposits, they learn that their needs matter, and they learn to trust with confidence in their caregiver's unwavering source of safety and support. When infused with necessary structure and warm limits, a child can now fearlessly explore their world, knowing they have a secure base to return to for their next deposit of love. In learning to attach to a parent or caregiver, they are learning to connect to self. This early imprinting of attachment offers the template for future relationships with others.

How children develop is partly nature and partly nurture. We know children are wired for love—they are ever so ready to receive it, even if they may not always be ready to show it or to acknowledge receipt and return their love in conventional, neurotypical ways. When parents engage in the radical offering of love, again and again, with enough warmth, fluidity, and flexibility, they are engaged in a sacred dance that not only teaches a child their first and most important lesson in love but also creates new neural pathways in the brain, directly impacting their development. And beyond the great significance of early attachment, ongoing, sustained nurturing and support can help children grow, heal the hurts, and build resilience and confidence in life.

The significance of attachment between a parent and child goes well beyond the early years of childhood into the nurturing and strengthening of the parent-child emotional bond throughout the years. Research shows that the ongoing connectedness between a parent and child is protective as children emerge into adulthood. Widening our understanding of the impact of attachment beyond the early childhood years gives us hope and confidence that as parents, it is never too late to lean into our children, especially if our early bonding years were rocky.

It is also worth pointing out that attachment is not always about the parent-child bond. Much mainstream understanding of attachment theories stems from White researchers who have focused their research largely on White, North American and European, nondisabled families. There has been more research done to determine the validity of attachment theory across cultures. We know that in collectivist cultures, a whole village is often available to care for a child, not just the parents, making their secure base much richer. Another unique feature of collectivist care is that care geared toward secure attachment is also geared to primarily promote social harmony, whereas in Western societies, the primary function of attachment care is to promote autonomous functioning.

We also believe that living under oppressive systems impacts attachment patterns. Neuroscience helps us understand that unresolved trauma of oppression gets passed down to future generations by impacting the psychobiology of parents and caregivers. The toxic stress of parenting in the face of the ever-present systemic barriers impacts parents' ability to be present and attuned enough over our children's formative years, compromising parents' ability to consistently protect and defend the attachment bond.

Developmental Approach

When we think about the parenting dynamic, the dance is between a parent and child, each with their own stories, wiring, perceptions, beliefs, and behaviors, all in constant flux within an oppressive world. So to understand our parenting dynamic, we seek to understand both our parent self and our child through a developmental lens.

Conventionally, when we think about development, it is in the context of understanding how children grow into adulthood. These frameworks, normed against White and neurotypical kids, privilege a linear progression with very specific timelines for meeting development markers. We will talk more about how these development frameworks fail our children's process in chapter 3, but often when children do not meet these milestones, a *behaviorist* approach is used to get kids "caught up" or to "fix" a behavior. Behaviorism focuses on the surface of our human experience, asking *What is the undesired behavior?* and *How do I get my child to stop this behavior?* But these questions address just the visible tip of the iceberg and ignore what is submerged. This way of thinking about development centers the adult's agenda for children's behaviors without taking account of our children's needs.

Rejecting notions of linear progression and shaping behaviors, we reimagine an approach to child development that is equivalent to seeking the deepest, most affirming truth there is. We caution against using development models as checklists to assess where our children should be. Our children will progress at their own pace, which may include returning to earlier stages of development as needed (conventionally referred to as *regression*), and each phase will bring forth different needs and build or strengthen different skills. This orientation also instructs us to move closer to the root of a behavior and to see the behavior as something to be understood, rather than fixed. The questions that consume us are *Why is my child exhibiting a particular behavior? What needs are they communicating through this behavior?* and *How can I meet those underlying needs?*

This approach, using a developmental lens to understanding behavior, is more child centered, anti-oppressive, strength based and therefore more humanizing, focused on meeting children's core needs and trusting in their ability to grow and bloom in the ways just right for them. As our children change, at whatever pace they do, we are then invited, as parents, to grow and change so we can meet them right where they need us to. Just when we become more comfortable changing diapers in the middle of the night, we find that we must adjust to potty training. Parenting is living at the edge of mastering a skill long enough to fall back into being a beginner, continuously moving from competence to incompetence.

And as parents of neurodivergent children of color, our shifts in response to the needs of our child will also differ from societal norms. Ideally, we are able to respond to the evolving needs of our children, ensuring that the connection between parent and child remains uninterrupted. However, the reality is that for some of us, adapting to our children's needs on cue is made harder by the trauma of living under systems of oppression. So even though as parents we love our children, how we show our love is complicated by how we think and feel about our race, gender, ability, class, and immigration status, to name a few factors. Time and space are stolen by the pressures of working to survive on the capitalistic treadmill, the obligations and demands placed on us by current conditions of our society. Some of us are so busy surviving, that it is hard to even notice the changes in our children, let alone take the invitation to meet them where they are. Some of us are trapped by our own internalized oppression, making it harder sometimes to empathize with our child's struggles and see the function of our child's emotional explosion, their resistance to new foods, or their insistence on wearing the same shirt every day. Seeing parenting from a developmental lens, too, would implore us to not blame or shame ourselves for the darker shades of our parenting but instead help us ask ourselves: *Why am I struggling in my parenting? What needs are my behaviors communicating?* and *How can I meet my underlying needs?*

As we parent our children through the terrains of race and neurodivergence, our responses to their needs are informed by our own comfort with these identities, as well as the environment and context we inhabit. Consider this parenting experience:

Jillian is a cis woman of color who does not identify as neurodivergent. She is raising a boy who has ADHD. Jillian is at a school event with her son. The other kids all sit quietly in their seats waiting for the program to start while her son runs up and down the theater aisles. Aware of the teacher's exasperation and the quiet whispers of parents around her, Jillian quickly becomes flustered and wishes her son would just comply. She hurriedly gets up and pulls him out of the theater. She does not want to be that parent, and she certainly does not want her entire racial group to also be portrayed negatively through this incident. Fear of unfair judgments propels her to harshly criticize her son. He looks up at her confused and scared. In that moment, she feels the distance between her and her child. On cue, shame takes over Jillian.

Now imagine these alternatives. What if Jillian entered this school event with a group of friends and family who celebrated not only her son but also her? What if the school was a place that welcomed movement and provided different ways to show up? What if there was an expansion of what it means to be present at an event? At the very least, what if her son's behavior did not have to be an assassination of her parenting or her racial group? And if there were no changes systemically, what if Jillian could soothe herself in the moment and place her rightful anger onto the school system and intolerant parents instead of her child?

We imagine that Jillian would be less stressed, feel more spacious in her responses to her son, and be able to meet him where he is, resulting in a stronger connection between the two of them. We also imagine that her son would feel supported and affirmed in his needs.

Jillian's story shows us that as parents, how we feel about ourselves can be shaped by our investigation of systems of oppression, which can support our ability to shift from *Something is wrong with me (or my child)* to *Something is wrong with the system*. We recognize that such an internal shift is dependent on an ongoing practice of self-inquiry that calls for our time and capacity in the very context of systemic oppression that does not award us the luxury of these resources. So even though we can lean into our children's needs at times and under certain conditions, it is understandable that we revert back to strategies focused on keeping ourselves safe. We say this to normalize wherever you may be in your parenting journey.

In this book, you will hear from parents all across the board. Some vocalize a celebration of their children. Others name their worries and grief about their children. Yet others hold a difficult complexity, attempting to reconcile their personal parenting values with what the system awards them and their children. We hold all these stances with love and spaciousness. We hope that these stories make you feel less alone, connected by an invisible thread to a larger community of parents like you across the North American continent. We see you and we celebrate you. We are all doing the best we can in any given circumstance, together.

2

STANDING AT THE INTERSECTIONS

The Contexts We Parent In

Another world is not only possible, she is on her way. On a quiet day, I can hear her breathing.

—*Arundhati Roy*

THERE ARE NO LOUSY PARENTS, only human ones. We want to be there for our children, especially when our children need us the most. But when we are overscheduled, we find our patience stretched thin when our child wants yet another bedtime story. We see our immense love for our children fading behind a fog when our child screams bloody murder because a cookie breaks. Even when we recognize our depleting resources, we often cannot find the time to nourish our needs. That kind of time is often a privilege. We are pushed to keep our heads down to survive in the here and now, dealing with a school suspension, medical appointments, a probation charge, or seeking support and community—which speaks to the insidious and potent nature of oppression that many parents and children endure.

The various structural forces that shape our parenting remain hidden in the background of our lives. To demystify and strip them of their power, this chapter unveils those forces. As one wise parent, Sophia, an Afro-Indigenous-Latina mom of two multiracial kids, told us during our writing, "We need to name the enemy to fight it." So this chapter will dig into White supremacy, ableism, capitalism, adultism, and settler colonialism and make the connection that while these systems are big and unruly, they utilize parenting to replicate their oppressions.

Ultimately, these systems have shaped hardworking parents, making parenting against them a relentless act of resistance. There is a throughline between these systems, the messaging we have received, and our parenting. It is just hard to see it clearly, and that is intentional. We are not here to tell you to fix these systems as a parent and add more *shoulds* to your to-do list. You are doing a lot—we see you.

Yet we see parenting as a path to liberation for our children and ourselves, and for future generations. Even though these systems feel impossible to counter, we think that increasing our awareness of the connections between these systems and our parenting allows us to consciously choose how we relate to our children, our expectations, what we teach them, and how we want to engage with the various institutions in our lives. Therefore, we hope this framework provides you some validation for your life as a parent, fuels you to rightfully claim what your child needs at the next IEP (individual education plan) meeting, motivates you to seek community, or reminds you to be a little less hard on yourself for shortcomings.

In writing this book, we noticed so many ways these systems live in us as authors too. We struggled with our ideas around productivity, urgency, and perfectionism. Some of these struggles resulted in debilitating migraines for one of us. Our bodies know before our minds. Noticing the grip of these forces on our minds and bodies allowed us to release some of the shame, guilt, and not-enoughness these systems impose on us (to release all of it is the work of a lifetime!). In those moments when we could take a deeper breath, we could be in a different relationship with these systems of oppression; we could ground into our power. We share this vulnerability with you to say, *We are in this with you.*

When we noticed how these structures of oppression played out in the micro moments of our lives, we got to make informed choices about how we wanted to engage and respond. It was a small but powerful way that we practiced chipping away at these systems, while also having to live within them.

This is our wish for you.

Body Check

We know these are charged concepts, and you may want to put the book down now or skip this chapter. And that is OK. We trust you will return when it feels right to you. Alternatively, you may find it helpful to read this chapter a section at a time, consider the reflection questions for each one, and then return. As always, you are in the driver's seat.

If you are staying, let's take a collective breath before moving on. We find it helpful to feel our feet on the ground beneath us. We also find that looking around our environment can orient the body to the present moment. Before we begin, we invite you to get something that is comforting, like a warm drink, a blanket, a journal, or anything else that is a resource on this journey of uncovering.

What's *Normal* Got to Do with It?

> *Everyone is subject to oppression. You don't have the isms, they have you.*
>
> —*Leticia Nieto*

There is a passionate commitment to "normal" in our society. The standards of this normal are intentionally crafted descriptions that decide socially acceptable behaviors. Molded by these standards, we can spend a lot of time and energy fitting into a world not created with all of us in mind. Think of a moment in your life when you wished to look different or be someone else. Maybe you wanted your eyes to look different or perhaps you wished you had lighter skin. We all compare ourselves to this mythical norm that upholds Whiteness as the paragon of humanness and, as a result, feel not enough or broken. This is the intention.

Our schooling into this idea begins early. We are taught through our storybooks with White princesses, the media coverage that focuses disproportionately on Black crime, schools that punish learning differently, and the playground where certain kids are excluded, just to name a few.

Unfortunately, we are even taught this in our families, when Grandma casually says, "Oh she is not that pretty; she is too dark." It is everywhere.

These same standards are used on our children. Let's take a minute and imagine a chubby-cheeked little boy with blond hair and blue eyes eating an ice cream cone in the middle of a park. We can see drippings of chocolate staining his shirt, and the brown liquefied ice cream around his mouth obscures the redness of his lips. Imagine a passer-by chuckling and cooing at the child's focus on the quickly melting dessert. This scenario reveals what the world possibly sees as the ideal. It is an ideal that represents what a child should look like, how they should behave, and what they should inspire in the world.

It is no mystery why a child of color that is neurodivergent is treated as less than. When someone sees our children, the thing that gets noticed first is the color of their skin. And with that comes a whole set of perceptions, ideas, and stereotypes, conscious or not. And then on top of that, when they discover our child is neurodivergent, a host of other biases comes into play, which reflects ableist mindsets presuming neurotypicality as the norm.

As adults, we know what these perceptions can mean, and many of us have experienced the harsh reality of being seen as the other. We have also experienced this othering in the indictments of our parenting. We know that to be seen as less than can mean being judged, condemned, criminalized, exoticized, stereotyped, attacked, and erased. So naturally, we worry about how the world will interact with our children.

We all get pulled into the aspiration toward this mythical normal, whether we want to or not. As parents, we have digested these norms because that is what *our* parents taught us, which they learned from their parents. Conforming is one of the most strategic acts of survival. But it does not have to be the only way. Some of us seriously question the relevance of these norms, and some even dare to live against them. To understand how normal came to be, come with us as we look at the structures operating in the background, like soulless puppeteers directing a show we never agreed to be a part of. By explicitly naming them, we have the opportunity to step outside of the prescribed roles and liberate ourselves from normal.

While we present these structures of oppression separately, it is essential to note that they all work together to bolster the impacts they have on us. Furthermore, the intersectionality of our lived experiences complicates their effects. For instance, as South Indian parents, we face discrimination and oppression, but our experiences differ from those of Black parents, almost all of whom had ancestors who were brought over on slave ships and continue to face the brutalization of these systems. In the name of collective liberation, we do not want to suggest a universal experience, and as such, we give voice to these differences to underscore that our unique identities shape our interaction with these systems.

Breaking free is all of our work. And we cannot do so without awareness.

Let's Breathe

One breath in, one breath out.
Scan your environment.
Remember, it is OK to pause and return later.

White Supremacy

things are not getting worse, they are getting uncovered.
we must hold each other tight and continue to pull back the veil.
—*adrienne maree brown*

Let's talk about White supremacy. We use this term because it requires us to shed notions that racism is about a few bad apples. It requires us to confront that White supremacy, both historic and current, lives in all of our systems, from economics and the military to education and religion. These institutions create and uphold advantages for White people and intentionally create barriers for Black and Brown people. It lives in our institutions, in the cultural stories we tell, in our relationships with others, and even in our own beliefs.

White supremacy is irrevocably tied to the pursuit of continuous wealth accumulation, which requires human labor that is either free or cheap. To achieve this, people were categorized across socially constructed racial lines, determining who is good, beautiful, safe, trustworthy, intelligent, and worthy of protection—and who is not. Sonya Renee Taylor writes about how White supremacy indexes people on an invisible ladder, placing some bodies higher than others. White people are placed at the top of this ladder. And their continued status there requires the systematic denigration and dehumanization of Black people, a process known as *anti-Blackness*. This same ladder metaphor can be used to illustrate how people are ranked across gender, class, disability, and so on.

The assignment of White bodies to the top of the ladder is connected to the development of race sciences that appropriated the logic of the biological sciences that emerged during the seventeenth century. During this time, the European Enlightenment philosophers based their ideas on secularism and scientific study and categorized the natural world into hierarchies. It was not a far stretch, then, to take the learnings from biological sciences and apply them to groups of people. Encoding these narratives into institutions, policies, and social practices was and continues to be instrumental to extracting free and cheap labor and sanctioning systematic erasure, violence, and cruelty toward people of color.

An evil and monstrous institutionalization of race science was the field of eugenics, which argued that only those with desirable traits should reproduce. Proponents championed the notion of breeding out anything that signaled non-Whiteness, including criminality, mental illness, disabilities, and poverty, from the gene pool. The massacre of the Jewish people under the Nazis is an example of eugenics in action. The forced sterilization and menstruation management of disabled women and girls to address unwanted pregnancies is another example.

Therefore, "white supremacy is not a shark; it is the water," as spoken artist Kyle "Guante" Tran Myhre says. It is not *just* about viewing White people as superior but also about the perception that Whiteness sets the standard for humans. In the United States, White supremacy is inextricably linked to other systems of oppression and seeps into our cultural landscape. We refer to the work of Kenneth Jones and Tema Okun, who have plainly laid out the characteristics of White supremacy culture. Here we list a few:

- *It looks like seeking perfectionism:* We are afraid to make mistakes in our efforts and believe that our end products must be blemish free. It strips us all of our humanity, which is beautifully flawed. Think of the birthday parties and holiday dinners and the stress of getting everything just right.

- *It looks like valuing scientific objectivity:* We find it hard to accept other ways of looking at the world. We are taught to center logic and devalue the expression of emotions or paying attention to our bodies. A message you might have grown up with is to not be too emotional, to stop crying, communicating that our emotional landscapes are an inconvenience.
- *It promotes black-and-white thinking:* White supremacy sees the world as good vs. bad and has little tolerance for complexity. An example of this might be how our children's behavior is seen as an indication of bad parenting or a reflection of their poor character.
- *It encourages urgency:* Everything needed to have been done yesterday and time for processing is not valued.

Reflection Questions

- How do you succumb to urgency in your parenting?
- How are you embodying perfectionism in your parenting?
- Are there times you have found yourself thinking that your way of doing things is the only way? What impact did it have on your relationships?

Ableism

All freedom is relative—you know too well—and sometimes it's no freedom at all, but simply the cage widening far away from you, the bars abstracted with distance but still there, as when they "free" wild animals into nature preserves only to contain them yet again by larger borders.

—*Ocean Vuong*

Ableism is prejudice, bias, and discrimination toward those with disabilities, including neurodivergence. Like racism, ableism works at the ideological, institutional, and interpersonal levels. Based on society's construction of normalcy, different bodies and minds are deemed unworthy and deficient. Implicit in the discrimination is that those with disabilities are broken and need to be fixed. An ableist society organizes around the needs and experiences of those without disabilities. Policies, infrastructures, and institutions serve those without disabilities. And when disabled folx cannot function, perform, or live in this context, they are problematized.

Ableism is linked intimately to White supremacy and capitalism. White supremacy deems who is acceptable and deserving in our society through race science's faulty and dangerous mechanisms. And capitalism is built on profits and resource extraction, so it needs bodies that can be subjugated to be overworked but has no time for bodies that cannot produce under the regime of its system. Ableism thus prizes competence, high IQ intelligence, productivity, and efficiency. Here are some ways ableism shows up:

- *In our language:* The terms *lame*, *dumb*, or *spaz.*
- *In our attitudes:* Seeing disability as a personal failing. Saying, "You can overcome this if you just put your mind to it."
- *In our interactions with people:* Presuming we know better and thinking something is wrong with another person because of their disability.
- *In our infrastructure:* Buildings and sidewalks that do not accommodate wheelchair accessibility. Spaces that assault the senses with strong perfumes and loud noises. Virtual spaces that do not allow for text enlargement or screen readers or provide captioning.
- *In companies:* Companies that do not hire because of the worry that a person with a disability might not be a productive worker. Job descriptions that require lifting or travel when not actually necessary.
- *In our media:* People with disabilities are seen as strange, innocent, dangerous, or needing to be rescued.

Ableism is threaded into all aspects of our lives, and the impacts are catastrophic on people's lives at these intersections.

Reflection Questions

- When it comes to noticing your child's concerns or struggles, are there times you want to fix them? What do you hope for in fixing them?
- Think of times when your child's need or ability has fallen out of the accepted standard. What did it provoke in you?

Capitalism

But only when everything hurts
May everything change.
—*Amanda Gorman, "Hymn for the Hurting"*

Capitalism is an economic system that promises that if one just works hard and has the proper motivation, one can achieve great heights. While it makes no guarantee that everyone will partake in society's riches, it is predicated on the erroneous belief that we live in a meritocracy and that everyone is provided equal opportunities to attain wealth. As such, we can't talk about capitalism without acknowledging that it is intertwined with White supremacy and ableism. Supremacy dictates that the more a group of people are seen as "other," foreign, dangerous, or less, the more the state, in conjunction with private entities, can leverage the labor of that group to transform land and resources into private commodities. As noted antiracism scholar Ibram X. Kendi states, "Racism and capitalism emerged at the same time, in 15th-century western Europe, and they've reinforced each other from the beginning."

Capitalism and ableism also reinforce each other, by sorting out those who do not produce for the system.

Here are some of the characteristics of capitalistic culture:

- *Growth:* Progress in the form of *bigger* and *more* is valued. At the heart of this is consumption: we are told in many ways that what we buy and own corresponds to how well we are doing.
- *Scarcity:* We are told that there is never enough. A simple example is commercials that tell us some product will sell out, exploiting a fear that might not even have existed before. Scarcity motivates people to compete against each other, but more important, it normalizes stepping on others to get what we want.
- *Exploitative labor:* Labor is taken from minoritized and poor communities and funneled up to fatten the pockets of a few at the top.
- *Productivity:* Promotes, glorifies, and rewards those who work hard. The rewards, of course, enable further participation in the capitalist and supremacist culture. The titles, the bonuses, and the perks at work, such as free lunches, are all designed to keep people working even harder. Those who can't work at this pace or choose to value relationships instead are less valuable.

- *Striving:* An emphasis on productivity conditions us to constantly strive. We are told we need the next big thing, whether the house, the vacation, or the gadget. We are promised that consumption will address the not-good-enough-ness we feel living in this system. Unfortunately, the treadmill we are on goes nowhere, and the pause button is impossibly hard to find.
- *Rest devalued:* In conjunction with striving, we are told to work harder and faster and never stop and rest. Rest is also commodified, and in an ironic twist of capitalism, our ancestral practices are sold back to us.
- *Self-reliance:* Those who need more support from the system are seen as a burden.

Reflection Questions

- Where are the places in your parenting in which you think more is always better?
- How has comparison slipped into your assessment of your parenting or your child's ways in the world?
- What are the ways you rest? What do you notice in yourself when you try to make time for rest? Whose voices are in your head?

Let's slow down. There is no rush. These pages will wait. How is your heart? How is your body?

Adultism

Not everything that is faced can be changed, but nothing can be changed until it is faced.

—James Baldwin

Within the very narrow definitions of "normal" constructed by White supremacy and capitalism, being a child is a powerless experience. As adults, we are entrusted with much power and authority to parent and teach our children—that is by design. On behalf of our developing children, we decide whether they will get vaccinated or medicated, whether we will raise them with religious family values, and when they will get their first cell phone. On behalf of our neurodivergent children, we may have more decisions to make. How we discern what is best for them in these moments rests on the assumption that we know best through our own experiences and judgment. As such, sometimes we protect them when we are afraid and push them when they are scared; we feed them until we are full and layer them up until we are warm. We ask them to conform so we can fit in. When we assume that we know better and demand more respect because of it, we risk slipping off a precarious edge and misusing our power in ways that hurt our children. We call this *adultism*—when adults consciously or subconsciously oppress children, diminishing their voice and agency, intentionally or unintentionally. Adultism at its core centers on the adult agenda: our abilities, our perspectives, and our lived experiences.

We believe that all of us parents try our best to show up responsibly for our children with no intention to power over them. Sadly, the reality is that when external oppressive forces bog down our judgment and good thinking, we become fearful, and we unknowingly channel the oppression we experience onto our kids.

But adultism is also alive and kicking in the outside world—at the dentist's, at school, at the grocery store, at the park. For a neurodivergent child of color, the grip of an adultist world oriented toward ableism and racism can be crushing. A tantrum in public to a sit-down with a cop, hyperactivity in the classroom to being caged like a zoo animal, an innocent game with a toy gun to a life lost in seconds. These are the heavy truths of children's powerlessness under adultism in the world outside.

The following are some ways in which adultism shows up in our daily lives. Before we present this list, we pause, breathe, and remind you (and ourselves) that finding your parenting moments on this list is not a reflection of your personal failure; it is the success of systemic oppression. We name these aspects to shed light on our humanity and that of our children. Awareness is the first step toward healing and change.

- *Be dismissive, critical, and shaming:* "What do you know, you are only nine!" "Act your age!" "Use your words!" "I told you so!" We talk over them, down to them, and sometimes talk around them, as if they're not there. We don't consider their interests, opinions, or solutions seriously.
- *Remove choice and control:* We decide what they wear, what and how much they eat, and what they should do. We do not consider whether they want to be touched (we pull them in for a hug, pinch their cheeks, tickle). We do not accept their chosen identities around gender, sexual orientation, disability, etc. We force our solutions on them, such as making them share or apologize against their will.
- *Set unreasonable expectations and limits:* We consider respect a one-way street, bottom-up. No back talking is allowed. We set limits and consequences that don't center our child's true needs but our own. We use military-style discipline at home: "Do as I say or else." "Go to your room!" "You're in time-out!" And at school: "Single file, keep hands to yourself." "Sit up straight." "No talking!" "Detention!" We hold very high expectations of their abilities and success, expecting perfection and obedience. Or we hold low expectations of their abilities and success, with a sense of apathy or giving up, "They will never get it, why try?"
- *Abuse:* Physical discipline. Sexual violations. Neglect and/or silent treatment.

Reflection Questions

- How does control show up in your parenting?
- What makes it hard to listen to your child's wishes and opinions?
- What behaviors of your child make you uncomfortable? Are these moments an opportunity for you to set a limit with your child, or is this an invitation for you to be curious about your own discomfort?

Body Check

We have made it this far. Let's take a breath.
Let's return to the body.
A small exercise we like to do is to slowly tighten and release parts of our body from head to toe.
We invite you to try it now, if it feels right.

Settler Colonialism

The first thing you likely did this morning was set foot on stolen Indigenous land.

—*Kay Holmes*

We feel the weight of White supremacy, ableism, capitalism, and adultism when we write about them—they are massive and seem impenetrable. It is helpful to see these systems instead as middle-level managers in a company. They perform at the request of a bigger and more powerful system: settler colonialism. Think of it as the ultimate boss, one who wears many disguises and lives burrowed deep underground, making it hard to know how it operates. Often, we are made to believe that because it is out of sight and out of mind, it is a relic of the past. To continue to build our awareness muscle, we uncloak settler colonialism and lay bare its tactics.

Settler colonialism is colonialism that occupies and transforms Indigenous lands into a commodity by erasing Indigenous communities. This is enacted via genocide, unequal land treaties, and forced cultural assimilation. To continuously take land and erase Indigenous communities oils the machine of White supremacy and capitalism and breathes life into ideas like individualism and scarcity. As a result, everything from food, dress, and power structures (how decisions are made and who makes them), to land-use practices and approaches to relationships are erased and reconfigured. Settler colonialism has no end; it is a continuous and ongoing project, and the colonizer never leaves.

Promoting the story that colonialism is something of the past is instrumental in protecting and promoting the innocence of settlers today.

Though we all varyingly benefit from this system, it allows those of us who are not Indigenous to look away, to not acknowledge our complicity in upholding the nation-state project, a goal of settler colonialism. It dupes us into believing that the nation's promise of belonging and security is meant for all of us. Unfortunately, when we see something as an artifact of the past, it is hard to know its shape, contours, and texture. It makes it even harder to connect it to our parenting.

Taking over the land, extracting resources, and erasing people because they are "unworthy" and "savage" has irrevocably harmed Indigenous communities, who are suffering indignities and living with the trauma of having their evolving ways of life erased. Resmaa Menakem, an antiracist author and trauma therapist, states that the system's impact is not only historical but also intergenerational, persistent, and personal. As racialized people of color, who are diasporic settlers, we find it is not appropriate for us to give voice to the lived experiences of Indigenous communities. Instead, we surface the tenets of settler colonialism and the shape it takes today. Additionally, we hope that for those who are not Indigenous, we can examine how we are accountable for upholding this system, given our complex social identities.

Here are some of the devices of settler colonialism.

- *Separation:* Separating people from their land fuels other separations, including from ancestry, resiliency practices, and communities, which results in deep intergenerational trauma. It is worth reiterating that the actual severing of people from their lands is particular to the Indigenous communities of North America. An outcome of this violent occupation has been the normalization and proliferation of the belief that land, community, and ancestry are valueless. This ethos of disconnection occupies all our minds and bodies. When we have internalized separation from each other, the land, and our cultures, it is no wonder we think something is wrong with us rather than the forces that produced these conditions. Some of us may struggle with parenting in these conditions; we may find it hard to connect that loneliness, guilt, and worry are a product of something more historical and intentional. We may end up thinking that we are bad parents.

  Cutting down the way of life that tethers people to the universe is done systematically and intentionally. In the past, it looked like criminalizing cultural and resilience practices like the Ghost Dance.* Today, separation looks like the government policies that tear children away from their parents at the US-Mexico border. It looks like breaking up Black and Brown families through incarceration. Our attachment to our communities and our families is oxygen. Starving us of this has left so many communities of color disoriented.

- *Doubt:* When we are disconnected from our ancestors and our ways of life, we can turn to so-called experts to appease our doubts. We seek answers, but ironically the wisdom that these experts peddle comes from our various lineages. Think of swaddling the baby or carrying the baby on the back. Think of the advice given to parents about incorporating mindfulness into their days. Furthermore, by devaluing traditional ways, not only are we sold back our ancestral wisdom through the capitalistic machine, but also the practice of seeking the counsel of trusted elders within our circles is interrupted. It is no wonder we feel alone.
- *Individualism:* The colonizers believe that their individual desires and interests are paramount over those of the existing Indigenous communities and the land. Inherent in this belief is an entitlement to personal freedoms over communal welfare. Today, this looks like people pushing back on universal health care, critiquing social welfare programs like SNAP, opposing tax levies that will fund schools, and shirking masks in a pandemic. Individualism rejects reliance and interdependence.
- *Accumulation:* Predictably, when we do not live in sync with nature, and when we do not privilege living communally, we inevitably become fearful. This fear that we do not have others to depend on leads us to accumulate and hoard. A striking example is when during the early days of the COVID-19 pandemic, people around the country stocked up on masks to the extent that there was a shortage of PPE for frontline workers. A

* The Religious Crimes Code of 1883, not repealed until the 1970s, made the Ghost Dance and Sun Dance of Indigenous communities illegal. According to the teachings of Wovoka, a shaman from the Paiute tribe, performing the Ghost Dance would end the westward expansion of the colonizers and reunite the spirit and living worlds.

powerful antidote to this was the mutual aid practices within the disability community.

- *Transactional relationships:* Being out of sync with ancestral ways, our relationship with nature shifts. We treat the land and water as expendable resources to serve the human kingdom. We are conditioned to use the same approach with people, especially those unlike us. As a result, many of our relationships are transactional. The question that centers on whether we connect is *What can you do for me?* We can see this play out with corporations and businesses that build relationships with communities because it serves their profit margins.
- *Standardization and conformity:* To move fast, continuously conquer, and accumulate wealth, we're conditioned to discard difference, complexity, and nuance. Sold a "one size fits all" paradigm of existence, we are left with unrealistic binaries and overly simplistic storylines. We are assured that conformity to these standards will result in belonging and safety.

Reflection Questions

- Are there times you have kept or collected resources without sharing them with others? What was going on, and how do you think this served and cost you?
- How do you doubt yourself as a parent? Are there times you have felt confident? What felt different between these experiences?
- Do you sometimes find it difficult to connect to your intuition? What has made it hard to do so?

Parenting Love Ethic

Allow systems to be hospitalized. To be composted. To die, and to die well.

—Dr. Báyò Akómoláfé

We discuss these structures of oppression not to discourage you but rather to affirm that neither you nor your child is broken. Navigating these systems with and for our neurodivergent children of color is a herculean task. But once we've recognized the connections between the systems and our parenting, what then?

While we are not here to tell you what to do or how to do it, we do find it helpful to see parenting as a long, drawn-out act of healing and growth, if we allow ourselves to be open to it. When we welcome this opportunity, we cannot but see our children as a portal to illuminate our healing. Our healing impacts them; their healing depends on ours. Suddenly, the stakes of parenting have become much higher. It isn't just about the diapers or the piano lesson. It is about the opportunity to make parenting therapeutic. What we mean by this is that in our immediate sphere of influence, we can practice releasing what we have been taught to fear and what we have internalized as the truth. It is not fear then that drives therapeutic parenting but love.

A sense of deep love for our children begins at home and within ourselves. So much of how we show up for them is held in the external spaces that challenge us, trigger us, and exhaust us. When we lose ourselves in these spaces, we take parenting personally (*how could we not?*), and we often get subconsciously transported to old hurts in our life and act in ways that are not helpful to our children, in ways we often regret. So how do we find our bearing when we get lost in chaotic waves? By cultivating a practice of love to anchor us.

Black feminist author and activist bell hooks talks about a *love ethic*, one that "presupposes that everyone has the right to be free, to live fully and well." But, she adds, "to bring a love ethic to every dimension of our lives, our society would need to embrace change." Adapting this framework to parenting, we have a *parenting love ethic.* We propose that a parenting love ethic begins with our inner child and our parent self. We cannot love our children well and unconditionally until we are open to caring for and loving ourselves. Loving ourselves comes in packages deeper than manicures, and it is a practice. We call them *practices* because the process is ongoing, and there is no destination. It is a way of being. And how much we do and how these practices look can be diverse. For some, regular therapy to process childhood wounds is possible. For others, using the car ride from work to take five minutes to be with our feelings might be what is available at this moment. No judgment and no shame. Do what you can and when you can. These practices are not linear, and there is certainly no one way to do it!

- *Love is a practice of* ***giving care:*** A parenting love ethic means cultivating a practice of giving gentle care to self so that we can offer the kind of care we want to for our children. Holding ourselves with gentleness looks like
    - Accepting ourselves as imperfect human beings who are bound to mess up (and have capacity to repair!).
    - Being conscious of the shoulds we place on ourselves that get in the way of our acceptance of self and generate fear.

  Giving care to ourselves helps us move from fear to spaciousness and allows us to hold our children with the gentle care they deserve.
- *Love is a practice of being* ***responsible:*** A parenting love ethic means taking responsibility for our own story and unhealed childhood wounds. We make time regularly to notice and reflect on our thoughts, feelings, and struggles (triggers, rigidities, etc.) and meet them with gentle curiosity. Tending to our wounds, no matter how late, affirms that we are all good and deserving. Being responsible for our own healing in this way can allow us to be more present for our children's.
- *Love is a practice of a* ***willingness to (un)learn:*** We investigate our relationship to the systems of oppression within which we parent so that we can unpack ideas and values that our inner child and adult parent self have internalized. To do this we acknowledge and question the grip of systems of oppression on us and find small ways to deliver ourselves from its suffocating hold.
- *Love is a practice of showing* ***respect:*** We listen to our children deeply and lean in, committing to seeing them as worthy, whole, and competent. We take the bid when our children call us into their world, whether through nonsensical babbles, repetitive play, or long-winded storytelling. To join them in what perceivably looks incoherent may actually illuminate the path forward.

At its core, the parenting love ethic, then, is a committed practice of stepping in and answering the call that comes from our children's voices, examining our intergenerational and cultural inheritances, understanding our relationship to systems of power, and coming home to ourselves all in the service of collective liberation.

Resources for Deeper Understanding

Machado de Oliveira, Vanessa. *Hospicing Modernity: Facing Humanity's Wrongs and the Implications for Social Activism*. Berkeley, CA: North Atlantic, 2021.

Soundararajan, Thenmozhi. *The Trauma of Caste: A Dalit Feminist Meditation on Survivorship, Healing, and Abolition*. Berkeley, CA: North Atlantic, 2022.

White Supremacy

Kendi, Ibram X. *How to Be an Antiracist*. New York: One World, 2019.

Menakem, Resmaa. *My Grandmother's Hands: Racialized Trauma and the Pathway to Mending Our Hearts and Bodies*. Las Vegas: Central Recovery, 2017.

Ableism

Piepzna-Samarasinha, Leah Lakshmi. *The Future Is Disabled: Prophecies, Love Notes and Mourning Songs*. Vancouver: Arsenal Pulp, 2022.

Wong, Alice, ed. *Disability Visibility: First-Person Stories from the Twenty-First Century*. New York: Vintage, 2020.

Capitalism

hooks, bell. *Where We Stand: Class Matters*. New York: Routledge, 2000.

McGhee, Heather. *The Sum of Us: What Racism Costs Everyone and How We Can Prosper Together*. New York: One World, 2021.

Adultism

Fletcher, Adam. *Facing Adultism*. Olympia, WA: CommonAction, 2015.

Settler Colonialism

Dunbar-Ortiz, Roxanne. *An Indigenous Peoples' History of the United States*. Boston: Beacon, 2014.

Hopkins, John P. *Indian Education for All: Decolonizing Indigenous Education in Public Schools*. New York: Teachers College Press, 2020.

3

THE MAP IS NOT THE TERRITORY

Understanding How Our Children Develop

Oppression interrupts a process of development that has liberation as its natural end.

—Leticia Nieto

"He is a year and a half and still not picking up food!"

"My six-year-old still needs to use a nighttime diaper."

"Every other kid seems to read chapter books. Why is my daughter struggling?

"My teen is having a hard time making friends, but my cousin's kids have no problems."

It is normal to notice how other children are developing, and maybe even more so to compare their development to our own children's progress. To notice means you are a highly attuned parent—and the comparison just means you are human.

But we think it is worth pausing and asking where we get these ideas about what our children should be able to do at any given time, and how those standards may or may not be useful. We all rely on various models and frameworks to understand the world around us. For instance, we may use a map to navigate our environment. However, the map only offers a model of reality—not reality itself. Like navigating a new place, parenting calls on us to pick up figurative maps. We hope to locate where we are with our children and what direction we need to head toward. These maps then tell us when our child is "off course."

Conventional wisdom states that children develop through various stages and should meet certain cognitive, emotional, and physical milestones at certain times. Multiple factors, including nature and nurture, influence the trajectory of child development. While we often consider genetics, environment, hormones, biological sex, nutrition, housing, and exercise, we think less about socially constructed categories such as race, ability, gender, sexuality, and socioeconomic class.

Ideally, these socially constructed identifiers would not affect how our children develop. However, the reality of raising children with multiple minoritized identities is that these factors do have an impact, which can provoke challenges for parents. When we are parenting at the intersection of race, neurodivergence, and other social identities, we only vaguely know where we're going, and the only "maps" we have are collections of assorted wisdom glommed together from our own lived experiences in a family system, naturally inherited cultural beliefs, the predominant culture of our physical locations, and, simply, our intuition. The reality is that these maps we receive for our parenting journeys do not reflect the cartographical realities of raising a BIPOC child who is neurodivergent. To not find ourselves on this map or to stray away leaves us feeling lost, confused, and hopeless.

How, then, do we find our way?

We propose that parents of children at the intersection of race and neurodivergence are mapmakers. When faced with frameworks that do not always fit us, sometimes we need to craft new ways to charter the development journey with our children. We are invited to look at the maps we have been given and courageously step outside their boundaries. We follow our children's lead. In this chapter, we join you in this mapmaking process by sharing how we think about the various aspects of child development.

Role of Safety and Stress in Child Development

The experience of safety is essential as children grow. All human beings have the innate ability to perceive and respond to threats. Brain science tells us the amygdala, located in the base of our brain, acts like the alarm system in a house that alerts us to intruders. Responses can include either running away (flight), confronting (fight), hiding (freeze), or making the intruder feel better about themselves (fawn). All of these are survival responses designed to ultimately keep us safe.

But safety is not all about these far and few between incidents of physical threats. Safety is the felt sense of existing in the day-to-day, feeling comfortable, knowing what to expect, trusting, and dropping into our authentic selves. All of us during the COVID-19 pandemic experienced a lack of safety to varying degrees, the intersection of our identities determining how safe we felt during this time. The pandemic and its related impacts have disproportionately affected vulnerable populations, including children of color and children with disabilities, in all ways: physically, emotionally, financially, and academically.

Wanting to feel safe again after experiencing something frightful is built into all of us. To regulate their emotions, an adult may go for a run or paint, or talk to trusted friends and relatives and share their feelings. Children, however, are wired to depend on their caregiver for emotional regulation—"borrowing" their parents' nervous system to regulate, known as *coregulating.* Lisa Dion, founder of Synergetic Play Therapy Institute, reminds us that regulation is not the same as calm; it is simply a means to have a mindful moment of connection to oneself in the midst of a perceived challenge. According to her, when a parent is regulated, they are better able to "rock the baby"—that is, help a child come to a state of regulation.

We can celebrate the innate wisdom we all have, neurodivergent people included, to regulate our own nervous system. Among neurodivergent people, the many ways of regulating, include averting eye contact, pacing up and down, talking out loud, echolalia,* breathing, bouncing, rocking, curling up in fetal position, hand flapping, spinning, shaking, or stimming. These behaviors are important ways in which the body naturally seeks regulation. Sadly, in our culture, they are judged harshly, as we privilege the neurotypical ways of regulation that embody social politeness and social engagement—aspects that are attributed to someone who is well adjusted.

For our neurodivergent children of color, neurodivergent regulatory behaviors are not the only aspect under unforgiving scrutiny. White

---

* *Echolalia* is the repetition of another person's words where sometimes the words have no specific meaning.

supremacy, ableism, and adultism make the world unsafe for our children. They do not have the power to distance themselves from these pressures, despite our best efforts to protect and support them. The far-reaching tentacles of these systems penetrate the psyche of our neurodivergent children of color and viscerally and tangibly weigh them down, impacting how safe they feel. And then the strategic adaptations our children use to navigate the world are deemed unacceptable.

Through advances in brain research over the last two decades, we now know that the persistent forces of oppression, such as racism, poverty, and family or community violence, create a consequential level of constant stress for individuals. This type of prolonged and pervasive stress is known as *toxic stress*. Under conditions of toxic stress, our bodies do not find relief from stressors. Stressors generally are anything that produces a spike in hormones such as adrenaline and cortisol. When our bodies do not get a break from stressors, we live in a heightened state of survival—the "intruder" never leaves! This results in increased cortisol production. High levels of cortisol are connected to decreased overall well-being.

Because the brain is still developing, children are more vulnerable to the effects of toxic stress. It can cause changes in brain chemistry and structure. In the short term, toxic stress affects how children learn, play, connect, or even receive love. In the long run, exposure to toxic stress increases the likelihood of mental health struggles such as depression and anxiety. Furthermore, children can have an increased chance of physical health complications in the future, such as diabetes and heart disease. Nadine Burke Harris, founder of the Center for Youth Wellness, links childhood trauma to triple the risk of heart disease and a twenty-year difference in life expectancy in later life. Children are also more vulnerable when protective factors are unavailable to help mitigate its effects. Unfortunately, toxic stress is hard to identify.

The very nature of the oppressive forces our children experience from their immediate environments means there is no relief from toxic stress, and no way to separate its effects from the developmental process. Ignoring this context can lead us to slip into seeing behaviors solely as a manifestation of the individual makeup. Understanding toxic stress, then, helps us to contextualize our children's developmental path and to disrupt singular stories of development.

A Neurodiversity Approach to Development

We affirm that regardless of differences in development, the inability to participate in psychological meaning-making or communicate thought processes does not make an individual any less worthy. In the absence of frameworks that capture variation as the norm, we find value in refocusing the lens we use to think about development.

One way we reorient our view is by relying on the approach of the neurodiversity movement: "A central premise of the neurodiversity movement is that variations in neurological development and functioning across humans are a natural and valuable part of human variation and therefore not necessarily pathological." Therefore, a diversity approach does not presume that there is a norm from which bodies and minds deviate. Instead, variation is the norm. Instead of seeing a child who is not speaking by a certain age or who is engaged in repetitive movements to self-soothe as *different from others*, we see it as *variations* in adaptations.

Using limiting frameworks only leads to seeing behaviors such as rocking and tics, sensitivities to textures, and difficulties with sustaining attention as concerning. Rigid developmental frameworks lead to people with disabilities being met with the assumption that they are not capable when they are. The neurodiversity-centric practice assumes that all brains can grow and learn beyond the initial formation years, the concept that is called *neuroplasticity*.

In contrast to the medical model, which sees the deficit, a neurodiversity paradigm and developmental approach looks at child development from a strengths-based perspective.* We pause here to note that a strengths-based lens means that there is richness and possibility amid the variations in human minds. It does not mean that focusing on strengths or "superpowers" is a way to bypass the lived realities of those who are neurodivergent. Sadly, in our culture, we swing from problematizing to idolizing people. This pendulation leaves no room for complexity. So when we say strengths-based, we think of the internal resources, like outside-the-box thinking, available to neurodivergent people. We see them as distinctive and adaptive strengths needed to navigate oppressive systems.

---

* We dig into this more in chapter 8, on navigating the medical system.

Our approach to strengths also views growth as nonlinear, which means we believe in refocusing our view of what is typically perceived as regression. A return to earlier developmental steps may actually be the child's innate intelligence choosing to revisit earlier adaptations that helped their growth so that they can reorganize and step into the next task with more resources.

Furthermore, we think this approach also encourages us to examine what we value as strengths. In our society and cultural upbringing, we regard skills like playing an instrument and academic achievement as strengths to be celebrated. However, we can fail to consider that a child's ability to daydream, bring friends together in a made-up game, and express their raw emotions on the grounds of a park are also assets. When we're consumed by valuing productivity, it is difficult to notice the offering embedded within the fantasy worlds our child builds in their head. When we buy into the dominant ideology of normal, we may miss the invitation to lay on our backs with our children in the middle of a park and hear the sky gods whisper.

We adopt the theory of *asynchronicity* as a lens to think about development for all neurodivergent children. Based on observations with gifted children, asynchronicity is defined as a mismatch in cognitive, emotional, psychological, and physical development. For instance, a gifted seven-year-old child might excel in mathematics but continue to need support with eating and have explosive tantrums. In other words, while one milestone on a developmental chart has been reached, others are ahead or behind that marker. The development is not synchronized in all areas.

Asynchronicity provides a spacious and generous framework for navigating differences in the abilities of our neurodivergent children. It normalizes that a child might excel and struggle in many different, seemingly contradictory ways. It normalizes that a child may need more support in one area than another. It normalizes that a child may revisit a developmental stage, an occurrence that often happens when trauma or a stressor is experienced. We invite this expansive and strengths-based way of thinking about all our children. What if we saw a six-year-old who continues to suck their thumb as innately wise for knowing how to self-soothe? Ideally, such a way of seeing our children will eventually allow us to see the beauty and wisdom within their behavior, however they show up.

In addition to seeing variation in development as the standard, we also find alignment with the less stigmatizing *theory of multiple intelligences* by psychologist Howard Gardner. An alternative model challenging the concept of general intelligence, Gardner's theory states that every human has seven intelligence areas and that individuals can be more robust in some areas. They are spatial, linguistic, logical-mathematical, bodily-kinesthetic, musical, naturalist, interpersonal, and intrapersonal. If nothing else, something is appealing about an approach that is pluralistic and expansive. But also, such a model affirms the diversity of strengths our neurodivergent children possess and deems all types of intelligence equally worthy.

The disability justice and neurodiversity movements teach us that a liberatory approach is possible. It encourages us to wonder if, contrary to the dominant cultural values, these differences are not inherently unfavorable. What if the fault resides in the design of our societies and the reliance on limited ideas around intelligence and cognitive development? What if these attributes, perceived as glitches, are what is necessary for evolutionary adaptations and possibilities? Our disabledness reminds us that we are interconnected and, as such, meant to depend on one another for care, companionship, and growth. An evolutionary perspective encourages us to ask, *What if the disability is not a problem but the answer?*

With this question in mind, we consider the cognitive, emotional, identity, and sexual aspects of the development of our children.

Embracing Variability in Cognitive Development

Cognitive development is how children think, learn, process, and use information and reasoning. When we go to the doctor for a well check, our child's provider is using well-defined milestones to assess whether our children are on track along these domains. In our schools, teachers and administrators rely on similar frameworks to assess children's learning. Instead of describing the frameworks used, which center on neurotypicality anyway, let's unpack the context in which they were developed and the reasons for them.

These models were developed by White men at a time of rapid industrialization and colonial occupation across the world. The demands placed by economic growth and development and the desire for wealth accumulation meant that many people were leaving extended family systems in rural areas and moving as nuclear families to urban centers. At the same time, in response to the needs of the expanding workforce, universal schooling was standardized. If factories needed obedient and hardworking workers on the assembly lines, then the school could be a place to begin training in compliance and work ethic.

In this context, nuclear families solely shoulder the responsibility for creating the ideal child, and schools oversee producing efficient workers. A "normal" child is required for the sustainability of capitalism. Developmental models, then, offer a quick and streamlined way to rank normal and to sort out who will place a burden on the system. The standardization of normal led to labeling children who were seen as needing more intervention as *problems*. The responsibility to address the needs of these children who were not meeting these established milestones was delegated to parents, especially mothers.

Simply put, the desire to have our society expand and gain more power in the world resulted in universal schooling, smaller family units, and the development of standards that would help determine which children could be trained to contribute to these efforts. The responsibility for producing future workers and consumers fell squarely on the shoulders of parents.

Today, our medical and educational institutions flag a child who is not babbling by a certain age or is not inclined to sit still during class time. We are told that something is wrong with our child and are given a list of providers and services to follow up with. Standards were normed against White neurotypical children, and practitioners use these narrow measures to determine who is atypical.

We know the differences in our kids are the variation that is evident in any species. For instance, some variations can be attributed to brain structure. Magnetic resonance imaging (MRI) shows that the hippocampus, amygdala, and cerebellum vary in autistic brains and can be smaller in those with ADHD. Some brains also have variations in the amount of dopamine and serotonin. As a result of variability in structure and neurochemistry, differences can very well mean a child expresses cognitive development differently. It is no surprise then that if we rely on models that do not account for variability, we will see these differences as divergent.

An example of a specific metric used to judge and label children is the intelligence quotient. IQ was initially intended to measure "general intelligence" based on verbal reasoning, working memory, and visual-spatial skills to address the needs of students with various learning profiles. IQ and personality tests were also used to determine the parameters of normalcy so that people could do well in the military and the workplace. Weaponized by the eugenics movement, IQ measurement defended the segregation, sterilization, and institutionalization of disabled people of color. While it is no longer explicitly used to support eugenics, psychologists today still question the validity of the IQ test and the validity of the concept of general intelligence. The notion that one metric can comprehensively assess all aspects of intelligence in human beings and distill it into a number is simplistic and dangerous.

Ultimately, employing these development standards on children who do not fit them predictably produces a troublesome feedback loop. Criteria normed against children who are not neurodivergent are used to confirm that children who are neurodivergent are atypical. This map is frustrating and provokes anxiety for many parents. Many of our children will not progress through all the stages. Some will stay longer in one. Others may revert or go back and forth. Even though the map we have was not meant for our children, our children are still judged against it, and it does not take away from the varying emotional experiences parents go through when they see their child not following the prescribed trajectory.

Given that the cognitive frameworks do not fit neurodivergent children, we encourage you, again, to create your own maps. You know your child. Give yourself and your child permission to move in the direction and pace that they need. Your child may take some time in developing a skill and may need to revisit a phase—all of this is OK.

Individuating: Identity Development at the Intersections

One of the most important psychological aspects of growing up is figuring out who we are. But knowing oneself is not just a cognitive process, nor solely an emotional or spiritual one. Fundamentally, knowing yourself is a regulatory process of the nervous system—it is a felt sense experienced as returning home to yourself. The more our children can feel and know themselves, the more they can rely on their internal resources and be at choice about how they want to respond to the world around them.

Identity development, then, is a lifelong process that contributes fundamentally to the internal confidence that human beings hold in navigating their world. Studies have shown a strong correlation between identity development and self-esteem.

Identity formation begins with an attachment to self. Starting as early as birth (think of a baby playing with their own hands), it features prominently in toddlerhood (a child asserting their right to refuse with a *No!*) and later again around the preadolescence phase. The more a child connects to themselves, the more they can *individuate*, or psychologically become their separate person. Separation, then, is necessary to have healthy relationships with others. Identity development is connected to healthy self-concept, increasing self-esteem, and resourcing to stave off the effects of discrimination.

What does this mean for our children at the intersection of race and neurodivergence? Informed by disability justice, we distinguish that individuation is a process of accessing self-power, not a process by which we reinforce individualism. More so, we make the distinction that knowing oneself is not the same as self-reliance. Our culture places a high value on self-reliance as the epitome of an actualized self. We reject this conflation and, in fact, argue that asking for support and creating the necessary care webs reflects knowing oneself well. Furthermore, we believe that this process of accessing self in the loving embrace of family and community is profoundly healing.

At the core of White supremacy, whether expressed through ableism or racism, is the premise that disabled people of color do not have selfhood. In the face of being denied personhood, what does the process of claiming oneself look like for neurodivergent children of color? Our kids are attempting to define themselves while the world actively defines them as too loud, weird, defective, and disposable. Furthermore, our children have to do this in a time of constant access to social media content that even more narrowly defines how to be in this world. All of this makes the process of coming into self even more challenging.

A significant aspect of this for our children is forming positive and healthy racial and disability identities. They deserve the chance to understand who they are in relation to their race and their neurodivergence and how those identities contribute to their overall sense of self.

Racial and Disability Identity Formation

Parenting is about helping our children develop a stronger sense of self in relation to their neurodivergent and racial identities. They move through this process at their own pace and in their own time—we cannot rush them. In developing a sense of self, it is imperative that neurodivergent children of color develop a positive racial and disability identity, especially as this is shown to support educational outcomes and build resilience. Speaking specifically to race, we know that children as young as six months notice racial differences. By the time a child is two or three, they can match people together by skin tone and have already received messages about who to trust, fear, and admire. Children of color have no choice on whether to engage: they must constantly contend with perceptions about who society expects them to be and what it tells them about their worth. On the other hand, neurodivergence, which is often not immediately visible, may lead to neurodivergent children being misunderstood and measured against neurotypical standards. As our children are trying to make sense of who they are, being told that they are not measuring up could add a layer of confusion to their self-concept as neurodivergent people.

The mirroring our children receive from us and the world around them is crucial to this process. As such, it is worth noting that the lack of representation in books, movies, music, video games, societal institutions, and who holds power and influence is a significant factor in impacting our children's identity development. Unfortunately, much of the labor falls on us parents to provide positive images and examples to counter the unrelenting and pervasive messaging from the larger society. We have to do the work of explaining racism and ableism, supporting them in responding to it when they face it, and counteracting the damage with role models and positive interactions. Many parents curate books, movies, and music to counteract the pervasiveness of Whiteness and ableism. Moreover, in many families, cultural activities, religious practices, and speaking native languages are leveraged as antidotes, a small way to disrupt.

For some of our children, their cognitive makeup may further impact the pace at which they come to understand themselves as neurodivergent in an ableist world. Awareness of differences between themselves and their peers, especially if those differences are problematized, can create a sense of otherness, which can increase feelings of anxiety and depression, stunting the positive connection to this part of their identity.

If this aspect of their development is not attended to actively, many neurodivergent children of color can fall prey to believing negative messages about themselves. Internalizing these messages leads to them seeing themselves as less than others, inevitably endangering long-term outcomes in self-concept, education, work, and relationship possibilities. Coming into acceptance of aspects of our identities is a lifelong process. Ultimately, we want our children to express themselves authentically. We want them to discover what feels good, pursue their interests, appreciate their strengths and weaknesses, use the regulatory tools that serve them best, and connect in healthy relationships that affirm their personhood.

Survival Strategies

As our children come to be in a right relationship with their identities, they might rely on some strategies to navigate dominant society. For instance, in the face of racism, children of color quickly learn to *code-switch* (the adaptation of speech, behavior, or presentation to blend in with the culture and expectations of the dominant society) in contexts where their racial identity is perceived not to be welcome. Code-switching in the US becomes a burden that White supremacist culture places on BIPOC people in order for them to feel accepted and included—to fit in. This constant pressure to navigate the world in a way that curbs their true authentic expression has an adverse impact on the health of BIPOC people—including our children of color.

Psychological masking is a term used to describe a mechanism a neurodivergent person may use to limit their authentic ways of being in social and relational situations to avoid the risk of being rejected. For example, masking can look like maintaining eye contact despite their discomfort, avoiding stimming behaviors, or limiting talking about their special interest to appear neurotypical. Kieran Rose, an autistic advocate, describes masking as an inbuilt survival mechanism in the face of lifelong developmental trauma caused by the environment. He calls attention to both unconscious and conscious aspects of masking, distinguishing it from the conscious contextual code-switching that all human beings do when we present differently according to the different roles we perform daily. Many factors affect how we perceive ourselves, and an important factor is the knowledge of how others perceive us. Masking requires an intuitive knowledge of the other for the psyche to construct and hold up the mask, which questions the popular ableist notion of mindblindness—that neurodivergent folx are incapable of understanding the perspective of another. According to Rose, masking is a survival strategy not specific to autism. Instead, it can be employed by those with any marginalized identity trying to survive within the dominant system.

For our neurodivergent youth of color, masking and code-switching support their survival under ableism, racism, settler colonialism, sexual and gender oppression, and more, depending on their marginalized identities; it is a survival response. However, to be in constant survival is damaging and can lead to burnout. For some, this may present as exhaustion and loss of engagement in special interests in others. For others, there may be increased stimming for self-regulation.

As our youth progress in their development, at whichever pace, with support and practice, they can grow in their learning of their masking and burnout patterns so that they can consciously care for their nervous system in the ways it needs to avoid or repair from burnout. Inviting them to reflect on *when* it serves them to mask or code-switch may be more helpful. Supporting them in identifying where they can be themselves is vital to their psychological development. Spaces that allow youth to be unapologetically free and authentic are essential to their mental and spiritual well-being.

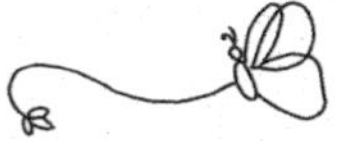

My biggest joy in raising my children is getting to revel in their joys and passions. Being able to be their home and safe space while they grow is truly a gift each day. I love watching them grow each day as the beautiful individuals that they are.

—Luisa

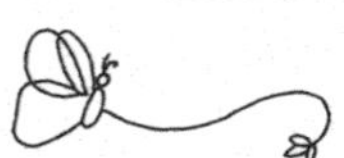

The Emotional Development Process

Children also have an emotional interior that evolves as they grow. How children's brains and bodies develop influences how they feel and express their emotions or not. Hence, it is impossible to isolate their emotional development from their physical and cognitive development. In this section, we unpack the emotional maturation of a neurodivergent child.

As with any area of our child's development, each neurodivergent child develops emotionally at a unique pace. Here also, many factors contribute to children's emotional maturation, including genetics, birth order, sex, temperament, early attachment, ongoing parent-child relationship and parenting, and a climate of emotional safety—a combination of nature and nurture.

Numerous articles and literature by neurodivergent professionals and people in the community speak about neurodivergent psychological and emotional development. Unfortunately, the conventional discourse on neurodivergence is still steeped in a narrative of deficits for neurodivergent people. True, neurodivergent people are predisposed to experience a spectrum of emotional development and regulation challenges, given the violence of this larger system. However, disability justice and the social model of disability teach us to see the strengths and inherent wisdom in our children's emotional development. It promotes seeing our neurodivergent children as wholesome individuals, developing at the right pace for each of them. Disability is not a deficit of our children but rather the deficit of society in adequately meeting the needs of our children and youth. Knowing that the environment shapes their emotional development, we wonder if the developmental trends of neurodivergent children would shift if we lived in a world free from the constant toxic stress generated by ableism and racism.

Within specific contexts, many neurodivergent children present as *younger* than their chronological age—i.e., based on social and cultural expectations, they can be seen as developing emotionally at a different pace than their neurotypical peers. When a child's emotional responses and behaviors match their chronological age according to societal expectations, they are seen to be developing appropriately. A child exhibiting a younger emotional age can present with greater emotional intensity, frequent meltdowns, more emotional rigidity, repetitive behaviors, and difficulty with self-regulation of emotions when intensity is experienced.

For our neurodivergent children, sometimes their development is slower, and sometimes it is asynchronous (i.e., a child may be emotionally younger in certain ways and emotionally more mature in other ways). This variation in development invites us to hold the perspective that while a neurotypical brain takes up to twenty-five years to develop fully, a neurodivergent brain will likely take longer.

However the developmental curve takes shape throughout childhood, it is essential to remember and trust that regardless of the level of need of our neurodivergent child, every new experience continues to shape and develop their neural networks. They are continuously moving toward growth and maturation of the whole brain, even if it is not evident to the world around them. We can see growth in the tiniest spaces if we look closely enough.

Emotional Expressions of Neurodivergent Children

Contrary to the ableist notion that neurodivergent people are devoid of emotion, neurodivergent children are deep feelers. Here, we highlight some qualities of our children's emotional expressions. While all human beings are susceptible to these expressions, neurodivergent people tend to experience any combination of them often, with greater intensity than neurotypical people. As parents and caregivers we are tasked with helping our children to learn, over time, to understand the needs that are communicated by their emotions, and collaborate with them in identifying supports. As you read this list, we invite you to ask yourself: *What is the gift within this emotional quality?* If it's hard to lean into this space now, we understand—that is a valid response. Your struggle in tending to your child's intensities matters, and you deserve support too.

- *Concrete thinking:* Concrete or black-and-white thinking is a feature of many neurodivergent brains. Gabor Maté, author of *Scattered*, identifies this as yet another byproduct of differently developed emotional circuitry. As we know, this is true for neurodivergent youth. Concrete thinking shows up in difficulty holding multiple truths at once or at understanding another's perspective, especially when flooded with their own. It also shows up when an intense feeling, say a parent's limit being perceived as unjust, precludes them from remembering that their parent still loves them.

- *Emotional hypersensitivity:* Neurodivergent individuals are exceptionally emotionally sensitive people. According to Maté, the propensity of emotional sensitivity is a hereditary trait: one is born with it. Emotional hypersensitivity refers to how neurodivergent adolescents absorb even the tiniest inputs in their emotional environment, impacting their nervous system. Many neurodivergent children are susceptible to perceiving hurt due to their concrete thinking style. However, as Maté states, emotional sensitivity also often correlates with psychosomatic experiences, where the stress of the environment affects physical health. In addition, hypersensitivity to specific sensory inputs in the environment is a correlated experience for many neurodivergent folx.

  We recognize that many neurodivergent people have been put down with the word *sensitive*, as in "Oh, stop being so sensitive!" These words can hurt anyone but hit neurodivergent people especially hard. But these words are also ableist, as they invalidate a core part of one's neurodivergence. Maté validates how emotional sensitivity has survived as a trait in the gene pool across thousands of generations because of its strengths—its ability to keep humans intuitive and, as a result, safe. Today, in the context of emotional sensitivity, we can say that neurodivergent people are natural at reading their environment for emotional safety, an innate skill doubly useful for neurodivergent folx of color who are at least doubly marginalized.
- *Meltdowns:* If we can trust that our children do their best whenever they can, we see them trying their best to regulate their frustrations when possible. However, due to our children living in an unaccepting world that feels constantly challenging to them, there comes a point, perhaps often, when the cumulative input feels too overwhelming to process within and needs to be released externally, manifesting as a meltdown. Sensory overwhelm is often an important contributor to this experience for many of our children. In addition, those who are Black, Brown, and neurodivergent have lived experiences that prime their body to experience more overwhelm, more frequently and intensely. Although it can be difficult for any parent to bear witness to an intense meltdown, it may help to see this process as a release mechanism, like a safety valve working to restore the system to equilibrium.

- *Shutdowns:* Just as the intensity can manifest in an explicit meltdown, it can also manifest internally as a shutdown. A shutdown can look like retreating to seclusion, extreme exhaustion and lethargy, falling asleep, or inability to move or communicate. There are many ways in which the human brain goes into *self-preservation* or *protect and defend* mode when perceiving a challenge to be insurmountable. Remember, the keyword here is *perceive*: what our child perceives to be a challenge may not ring true for us. When our children's experience feels confusing to us, it may help to put ourselves in their shoes and wonder about the challenge they may be perceiving.
- *Oppositionality and inflexibility:* Just as a shutdown is one response to a perceived challenge, oppositionality is another. Sometimes, when a threat or challenge is perceived by the brain/nervous system, it responds in a way to tackle, or fight, the challenge. A threat need not be a lion in the room; for our emotionally sensitive children, a threat can be a mere suggestion to pick up after themselves. That kick-starts their fight for survival. Oppositionality (the tendency to be disagreeable and to act with noncompliance) and inflexibility or rigidity (the fight to stand one's ground) are excellent examples of fighting powerlessness from within.

  Coined by developmental psychologist Gordon Neufeld, the idea of *counterwill* is the engine behind oppositionality. Describing it as "an instinctive, automatic resistance to any sense of being forced," he argues that counterwill is an essential rite of passage to holistic self-development. One's counterwill can look like verbal or passive resistance toward another individual, or even toward oneself. Counterwill is a strong component of *demand avoidance*—a term that captures the behavior of our children who tend not to be able to comply with demands that are placed on them by an authority figure. These can be specific demands that are triggering for a reason (such as brushing teeth, homework, or a specific chore), or any demand or perception of a demand at all (bringing to mind a subtype of autism called "pathological demand avoidance" or PDA, progressively reframed as "pervasive desire for autonomy"). Contrary to literature that deems oppositionality as a *won't,* Neufeld and Maté see counterwill as a *can't* and not a willful choice. When we approach our children's oppositionality this way, we can see the benefit of supporting them in nonpunitive ways, prioritizing a sense of safety and connection in relationship over the demands and expectations adults in the world hold of them. We will revisit this concept in chapter 6 to better understand the role of counterwill in our teenagers.

- *Interoceptive difficulties:* Interoception is the sense that allows us to answer the questions *How do I feel?* and *How do I know what I feel?* Many neurodivergent folx experience difficulty answering these questions. Some experience *alexithymia*, difficulty in cognitively identifying emotions experienced in the body. Difficulty in being able to attune to and identify one's internal experience can often make it hard to fully determine what our body needs for regulation and comfort.
- *Co-occurring emotional and mental health needs:* Studies have shown how two groups—neurodivergent youth and BIPOC youth—are both at high risk of experiencing mental health issues, and it is hard not to see why. When oppression does not affirm one's existence in the world, it takes a toll on them. For instance, research on autistic youth reveals that they are more likely to experience anxiety and depression. When mental distress grips our neurodivergent children, they are likely to experience their health symptoms with more intensity, where small changes in routines and environment can trigger an increase in stimming, emotional outbursts, withdrawal from preferred activities, and even self-harm. In general, typical mental health issues resulting from minority stress* can present as mood disorders, such as anxiety or depression, or as eating and compulsive behavioral disorders. In a society where our youth are oppressed and already isolated, their mental health struggles can exacerbate their isolation further, tragically resulting in attempts to die by suicide.

We invite you to take a breath here. Parenting our children with their unique combination of emotional intensities and needs round the clock can be an exhausting endeavor that demands unimaginable energy and patience from us. While some of these expressions call us to support

---

* *Minority stress* is the stress experienced by marginalized communities that results in poorer health outcomes in the long run.

our children in ways that give them the tools needed for emotional regulation, these are also some of the same ingredients that make our children who they are. We hope this section was a start to affirming your experience and your child's.

Sexual Development

Sexuality, or the way people experience and express themselves sexually, is essential to human life. It is a basic physiological need for the human species to survive and thrive. However, as individuals, we may come to identify as asexual or choose to abstain from sexual behavior. For most children, this aspect of their development drives exploration and curiosity about their body, identity, roles, emotions, and desires. It intersects with their biological, psychological, physical, social, and spiritual dimensions. All this holds for BIPOC children on the neurodivergent spectrum as well, but there are important nuances that set their trajectories apart from their White, neurotypical peers.

The process of sexual development for all human beings begins at birth. Each stage of the overall development of children includes the physical, emotional, and skill development necessary to meet the sexual health needs of the child. While young children are not conscious of their sexual needs, they are absorbing the spoken and unspoken messages about what is considered acceptable or not in the world regarding aspects of sexual health. They get messages about gender and sexual identity. They learn where it is appropriate to be naked and when touching their genitalia is OK. As they grow older, socialization also includes gaining awareness of their body parts, learning about purposeful masturbation, attraction, dating rules, and how to have relationships and safe sex. These messages all serve the purpose of preparation for their sexual maturation. Even the type of child-parent attachment developed in early childhood and thereafter holds a vital bearing on the security of the intimate partnership they can have in the future as an adult.

Sexual Development at the Intersection

Ideally, the sexual development process is the same for all children. However, race and neurodivergence affect the rate at which our children mature. Just as with some other aspects of development, sexual development for our neurodivergent children can be asynchronous. In addition, racism and ableism perpetuate negative perceptions and stereotypes of BIPOC disabled people, and they do not receive the same level of sexual health care.

Supremacy and capitalistic culture control bodies by denying people their birth rights to sexual freedom, expression, and pleasure. The sexual lives of disabled people of color have historically been a site of subjugation. They have suffered the indignities and trauma of forced sterilization and rape. They have endured negligent medical treatment.

Today, we see the continuation of this through the media. Disabled people are often used as foils for the sexual explorations of the nondisabled protagonist. People of color in the media can be negatively portrayed, such as the exoticized Asian woman, the emasculated Asian man, and the sexually dominating Black woman. Pigeonholing people into their specific identities in relation to sexuality reifies limiting narratives about what and who is acceptable. A lack of authentic and nuanced representation can leave many disabled people of color feeling disconnected from their desires and sexual selves.

Our children's vulnerabilities are also increased by systemic gaps by not being granted access to relevant, comprehensive sexual education, which leaves many of our children to piece together this integral part of their identity in isolation. A tragic outcome of having to scour the internet for sexual education can be an unfortunate entanglement with the legal system (more in chapter 10). The revoking of *Roe v. Wade* in the United States is another significant example of how the system reinforces inequities. It is disabled women of color who are most affected by this recent decision. Sadly, a lack of well-rounded sexual education and a lack of legal protections increase our children's vulnerability to being bullied, harassed, or raped, or receiving medically unsound treatment.

Raising neurodivergent children of color at this time in the United States places a heavy responsibility on us to protect our collective right to sexual and reproductive health and justice. We have to fight back with a commitment to educate and raise our upcoming generations to be sexually aware, to help them defend their right to be sexual beings, and to become sexual health advocates for themselves and others.

In addition to the societal context, we must consider the community and the more intimate family context in which our children grow up. Children receive all sorts of messages, spoken and unspoken, about sex and sexual health from the environments they grow up in, influenced by their racial, family, and religious cultures. Here are a few such messages:

- Sexuality is a normal part of life.
- Consent is important.
- Masturbation is healthy.
- It is safe to ask my parent a question about sex.
- Sex is for everybody, regardless of race or ability.

Or:

- Exploring sex and sexuality is only for grownups.
- Sex is only for procreation after marriage.
- Sex = heterosexual sex.
- Masturbation is sinful.
- Talking about sex is taboo.
- People with disabilities cannot be sexual.

In many communities of color, sex is a private matter, not to be discussed openly by anyone, especially children. In environments where sexual thoughts and discussions are stigmatized, children internalize shame for thinking and talking about sex, let alone acting on sexual impulses. Sexual development is not yet universally seen as an essential part of the overall healthy development of children, and access to sexual health information is not yet considered a universal human right. Furthermore, immigration and the stress of integrating into a new culture can complicate navigating this stage.

Given this structural, social, and cultural context, it makes sense that many BIPOC parents have not openly discussed sex and sexuality with their children. Some do not because the values they have grown up with around sex inform how they think about parenting their child. Many do not because they find an inherent conflict between the values they grew up with and the values they now hold, with little experience and skills for speaking to their newer beliefs. In addition to parental values around sex, in considering the developmental level of their neurodivergent child, parents genuinely struggle with knowing how to speak to their child about sexual health in a way they can comprehend it. Wherever you may be on this spectrum of comfort around talking to your child about sex and sexual health, we see you.

We have covered a lot of ground that may take time for you to integrate, and that is OK. Having set a foundational lens through which we view children, we invite you to return to the concepts as needed. Our neurodivergent children know and have taught us well the power of repetition.

We end this chapter by sharing one possible way of connecting in communication with our children around important topics that concern their well-being as they grow and develop.

A Map for Connected Communication

As our children develop and experience many changes in their bodies and the environment, they benefit from knowing about upcoming transitions and preparing for them, to the extent possible. We parents, being an important source of information, preparation, and emotional support for our children, are naturally tasked with communicating with them in ways that can bring them some support and confidence. Communicating big concepts to our neurodivergent kids isn't predictable, neat, or easy. You know your child the best—their developing personality, preferred communication style, and personal limits around communication. While our society often relies on and privileges verbal communication for all children, many of our neurodivergent children, even if usually verbal and speaking, may prefer to communicate in other ways around topics they may perceive as stressful. As parents, we approach our youth in ways that honor how they wish to communicate around important topics like race, disability, sex, puberty, friendships, technology, police, or school. We may start some of these topics early with some of our children, and with others we may wait longer, till the time is right. Regardless, when these topics are addressed, we take our children's lead, paying attention to their development, interests, and curiosity. We notice when they are most receptive and factor in their go-to communication/learning/thinking style. We honor their attention span and energy level for a conversation and use metaphors and special interests to meet them where they are. And we remind them that they are loved and encourage the regulatory support they need to transition into a conversation with us. Here are general guidelines to support you in curating your own template for communication with your child:

1. Check in with yourself.
   a. How do you feel about this conversation? If you are feeling any angst or doubt or hesitation, is there someone else you can process with before engaging with your child?
   b. Are you feeling regulated and ready to have this conversation? This may be a good time to check in with the body and use some of the suggested practices. Allow yourself to get active with your feelings. Squirm or stomp your way through them.
   c. Attend to your feelings on a regular basis, as self-development is an interactive process.
2. Check in with your child. Is this a time your child is regulated and ready to be in this conversation? You know your child and their cues of readiness.
3. Utilize your child's mode of communication to share what you want to. Provide a bite-size version of the topic.
   a. Break down each concept into a couple of simple sentences, developmentally and cognitively appropriate to your child.
   b. Think outside the box to consider how your child might best receive this information: Use art, play, puppets, stories, movement, and role-plays.
   c. Put yourself in your child's shoes and wonder if your child would understand and engage with your offering.
4. Listen and normalize their reaction and allow them time and space to process. Stay with their questions and their feelings. Remember that your child is processing the discussion at their own pace. So give them time and revisit.
5. Rinse and repeat.
   a. Be open and prepared for questions to emerge from your child at the least expected times and for them to repeat shared information.
   b. Normalize any anxiety that might show up in their repeated questioning.
   c. Know that it is okay to table a question if you are not ready to answer it: "That's a good question, let me think about that and get back to you." If there is no new answer to a question

from your child that is oozing with tension, just listen. Your presence and listening ear can do so much to ease their fears.

Resources for Deeper Understanding

Eugenics

National Human Genome Research Institute. "Eugenics and Scientific Racism." May 18, 2022. https://www.genome.gov/about-genomics/fact-sheets/Eugenics-and-Scientific-Racism.

IQ Tests

Conley, Nicholas. "The Messed Up Truth Behind IQ Tests." Grunge, October 31, 2020. https://www.grunge.com/198066/the-messed-up-truth-behind-iq-tests.

Dombrowski, Stefan C. "The Dark History of IQ Tests." TED-Ed, April 27, 2020. YouTube, 6:10. https://www.youtube.com/watch?v=W2bKaw2AJxs.

Whitten, Allison. "Do IQ Tests Actually Measure Intelligence?" *Discover*, July 1, 2020. https://www.discovermagazine.com/mind/do-iq-tests-actually-measure-intelligence.

PART II

OUR LIVES INSIDE THE HOME

4

BUILDING THE MODEL

Choosing to Parent Differently

I ALWAYS WANTED TO BE A MOTHER. Yet, in some ways, I feel my journey did not begin with giving birth but even earlier, as a dream, a longing. My earliest memories are living in Chennai, dressing my white porcelain doll, cutting her champagne-colored hair, cradling her in my arm, and laying her carefully made beds of towels and pillows. The smell of plastic still lingers in my mind, and the scent can now transport me instantaneously back to my childhood home, where my doll and I navigated the world.

When we moved here to the United States, in one of our first homes on the outskirts of Philadelphia, we lived next to the quintessential American family of my dreams. Even their names were so typically American. Alex and Karen were our neighbors with three kids. Karen, a nurse, reminded me of a Barbie doll. Her face, symmetrical with diminutive features, was framed by platinum blonde hair. Her limbs were lean and perpetually tan, without an ounce of fat. Alex, a physician, on the other hand, was a stout man, slightly shorter than her, with the beginnings of a beer belly and the obvious adoration of his tall, blond, beach-loving wife. I felt like I had struck gold when they entrusted me at ten years old to watch their kids, who all looked like replicas of their mom. Part of the excitement was seeing my doll come to life as three adorable blonde children with charmingly intense blue eyes. And in babysitting the kids, whose names I have long forgotten, I recall the delight I had in playing with them, feeding them, and the joy of their shrieks and coos. I wonder if it is strange that my first idea of children would be White. Or maybe it is not. Growing up in India, with skin-lightening creams and the desire for fairness at all costs, it is not unimaginable that ideas of Whiteness would invade my imagination. I am asking myself, Did I see myself in the doll and those kids of Alex and Karen? Who were the ideals here?

I had thought all mothering would be this experience—the experience of merrymaking and effortlessness. But unfortunately, I had not stayed long enough for the tantrums, the illnesses, and the calls from school that your child was in trouble.

This desire to be a mother would carry through as I grew up, explored the world, sought higher education, and came into my own. Early in my marriage, I recall the pangs of my uterus claiming a presence in discussions between my husband and me, moving us toward parenting faster than he wanted. And in our conversations, I would voice my dreams about the baby we would have. "I hope the baby has curls like you did when you were a baby, and hopefully, he has my eyes," I would offer as we lazed around on a Sunday morning in our two-bedroom condo with our dog snuggled between us.

"Or maybe we can wait a couple more years and travel the world," he would retort.

And in my dreamings of the type of parent I would be, a bit simplistic, I admit, I fashioned a relationship without valleys, only peaks. I thought I would be a parent who could endlessly play with my child, the kind of play I had with my doll and those White kids I babysat. I envisioned myself parenting with inexhaustible patience, as someone who would have dance parties with my child (this part did come true!). I thought I would only feed them organic, clothe them in pure cotton, and maybe even use a diaper service to save the environment. I pictured myself attuned and present for this child. I would offer constant emotional support. As they grew older, I visualized our profound conversations about life, politics, and existential questions. And I have gotten to do some of these things. But unfortunately, I have also gotten a lot wrong.

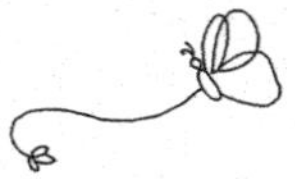

We know parents are wired for love, and children have the power to transform us. They touch our lives, even before we can touch them. They guide our thoughts and emotions. And then, when they enter our world, a parent feels a rush of love at first sight of their child.

Or perhaps not.

Many parents experience the absence of this rush of love at first sight of their child. However, maybe this postpartum love rush (which we also take to mean postadoption love rush) is a myth—a possibility that offers another kind of wisdom: that our care for our child builds the love bond, not the other way around. So, yes, we believe that parents are wired for love—perhaps slowly at times, but surely.

Parenting involves numerous diaper changes; making infinite decisions about schools, food choices, neighborhoods to live in, what TV shows are OK to watch; and having hard conversations on sex, drugs, and mental health—all within the context of an unfolding climate catastrophe and worldwide political instability. Moreover, all parenting takes place against a backdrop of school shootings and unreliable health care, and a crumbling democracy heightens our existing overwhelm and worries for our children. That we parent amid structural and ecological collapse is true for *all* parents; however, for those of us raising a child with multiple intersecting identities, societal unraveling has far-reaching implications for not only *how* we parent but also the lives of our children.

When our child is hurt, we worry about whether they will receive appropriate medical treatment as we navigate a medical system with inherent biases. When our children go to school, we are worried whether their education will be equitable, meeting their individual learning needs, and whether teachers will see their potential, not writing them off as "lazy" or "no good." When they learn to drive, we are worried not just that they are keeping their hands on their steering wheels but also that their impulsivity or different executive functioning doesn't lead them into an accident. And with our Black and Brown children, we fear that when the cops get to the scene, they might be arrested or, worse yet, gunned down.

The weight of parenting our kids is great.

Despite knowing that parenting is not for the faint of heart, especially in our current world, many of us choose to be parents. Sure, we may not anticipate that our children will be neurodivergent as we step into this role, and so we may not consider this experience in our decision. Yet, what drives us when data reveals that becoming a parent decreases happiness? In talking to parents, we learned that personal, social, emotional, ecological, physical, and cultural factors informed the motivation to become a parent. How we come into parenting is the starting point. What happens after our child enters our world is wildly different because of these intersections. But regardless of how we come into parenting, raising children offers us the opportunity to parent the way we need to be parented. It reveals a portal through which we can travel backward to heal and repair what has been unaddressed in our families and cultures, to correct our children's experiences today.

Parenting Differently

Becoming a parent attunes you to differences. We learn very quickly, even in the conversations around pregnancy, that there are differences to be celebrated and those to be concerned about or hidden. Noticing that your child is not meeting milestones, that there is something perceivably different than what you were expecting, naturally surfaces uncomfortable emotions, even when we recognize the same qualities in ourselves. Why do these differences in our children unsettle us?

Maybe because, as adults, we have had plenty of practice finding our way through this world that does not always celebrate our race, culture, neurodivergence, sexuality, and other lived experiences. We have found strategic ways to shine and thrive despite living under oppressive systems. Faced with the possibility that our child will have to navigate a similar trajectory is heartbreaking and scary. We were already prepared to support them to be Black or Brown children in this country. We can see that a difference in thinking, learning, communicating, and relating will add another dimension to our child's experience in the world that will pose challenges and struggles.

Growing up, living in a White supremacist culture, we have had to learn that straying from the perceived norm is costly. Our differences are seen as foreign or as criminal. Words like *dirty*, *lazy*, *geek*, *thug*, and *terrorist* are routinely used to describe our various communities. Additionally, our culture of origin and our families reinforce the messages about not standing out too boldly. So many of us were raised with the following messages as ways to remain pleasing, especially amid the White gaze:

- "Don't be too loud."
- "Don't be too angry."

- "Don't show your sadness."
- "Don't show off."
- "Don't rock the boat, go with the flow."

Our upbringing in an ableist society has taught us that people who are disabled in any way are less desired and not as worthy. That the world can see our child in this way crushes us as parents. And maybe because of our internalized ableism, we can reinforce these messages through our parenting when we struggle with our child's differences. They provoke an intergenerational fear: differences can oust you from the group, label and place you in confining boxes, mean an unshakeable target on your back, and kill you.

Predictably, because capitalism props up White supremacy, these intergenerational fears are then hijacked and fed through a machine that churns out products and services that promise to alleviate our concerns. Capitalism leverages parental fear about belonging and safety and sells us the notion that consuming the "right" products, experiences, and services will protect our kids from being seen as different. And parenting during a time of hyperconnectivity and social media, we are inundated with information about what good parenting looks like.

So to provide the best for our children, we may surrender to the pressure to enlist our children in the right classes and buy them the most relevant products. And when our income does not allow for it, we are made to feel bad. But ultimately, because capitalism can only commodify our worry about how our children will be treated, buying something does not relieve our anxieties either.

Our parent community shares the messages they received about what it means to be different. Kim says, "I grew up as a child with perceivable differences. As a Korean American in a Jewish family, I certainly drew attention. My adoptive mother also has a physical disability. In my family, we ignored those differences. They were seen as nonlimiters but also not special or unique either. I received a message of conformity, assimilation, and 'color blindness.'" Sanvi also talks about blending in. "In our South Asian family, we did not air dirty laundry, kept everything close to us, and worried about what the community would think."

Luisa experienced trying to break free from intergenerational messages about differences. "Coming from a Hispanic culture or Latino culture, there's a beauty in the collectiveness of the family. There's so much strength and interconnectedness that comes from there. And yet, at the same time, that interconnectedness can be challenging when you're trying to find your individuality and break intergenerational cycles. I think every generation is going through cycles that they're kind of breaking through. Both my grandmother and mom broke through certain things. Coming from a family that has gone through immigration and had challenging government situations in their countries, we have a lot of fear: *I can't stand out, I can't be different.* It's dangerous to stand out, especially when you've had this displacement from your country. I think that that just adds a different layer. And so for me to come out and identify that we're different and talk about it out loud and embrace it, does scare me. Speaking about it creates discord in the family, and it gets sticky."

Joy's experience as a Black woman speaks to how differences are seen inside compared to outside of the family. "Differences of others were not a bad thing in our household, but at the same time, we were given this standard that we were required to uphold. We were not to be an embarrassment to our family or to do things that they found bothersome. So we were very accepting of others but not so much of ourselves. Raising my child with autism has been somewhat of a challenge for my internalized ableism, especially when my son was younger, with more challenging outbursts and the social and mental pressures of being a new mom. But it's not so bad now."

Elizabeth says, "I was different as a child [she is half Black], and my mom, who is White, didn't shy away from talking about how I looked different from my family and my peers. Being raised in a 'liberal' environment, there was very little overt animosity about my differences, but there were microaggressions galore."

Fortunately, not all of us were taught that differences are bad. In families like Mumbi's, differences are to be celebrated. She says that in her East African home, she grew up with this message: "Black is beautiful, and you can do anything you put your mind to. Rainbow families are special bridge builders. Ignore the haters and believe in yourself as someone who can make the world better. Leave this world better than you found it."

The fact that many of us do not consider that our child could be neurodivergent reveals how we are conditioned to see disabilities as distant, not part of our imaginal landscape. Julie is a Taiwanese American with a daughter with ADHD, apraxia, and an intellectual disability.

As Julie says, "It never dawned on me that my kiddo could have a developmental and intellectual disability—it was such a non-possibility. I didn't grow up with siblings or cousins with a disability, and there is a privilege to not consider this a possibility."

Some parents do consider disability a very real possibility, especially if they have adopted a child or if there are other family members who are neurodivergent. Rupa tells us that during the adoption process, they had to fill out a form that asked what medical conditions, including neurodivergence, they and their partner would be OK with. Identifying that ableism is built into the adoption process, Rupa names, "If you can't handle differences, then maybe don't be a parent. No one gets to choose how their kid will be. It gives a false sense of control."

Valento speaks to that feeling of realizing there is no control. Two of his kids are neurodivergent. So when he and his partner accidentally got pregnant with their third, he says he knew it was a real possibility. He talks about how his understanding of neurodivergence shapes how he sees his new daughter. "With my three-month-old child, I am finding that I am not enjoying being with her enough—I feel like I'm seeing signs everywhere that probably don't even exist."

Learning to Parent

Deciding to parent means facing the question of *how* to parent. That question is especially salient in raising our children with multiple intersecting identities. The standard strategies and tips normed against White and neurotypical kids do not work for us.

We can thank the influence of the media for perpetuating narrow ideals about what a good parent looks like. For instance, we often see White, straight, class-privileged parents who always have time to repair with their kids. And even if we do see BIPOC parent representation, they are often presented as caricatures and stereotypes, and they are hardly ever shown dealing with how to parent within the various systems of supremacy. Often these portrayals can leave us unsatisfied, feeling like we are not good enough and even more isolated. When we turn to experts, the books are often written by cis, White, neurotypical, heterosexual experts and often do not consider the experiences of neurodivergence, disability, sexuality, and race.

So how do we learn to parent? Who do we look to for answers? Many of us who are Black and Brown use our immediate family and cultures as reference points. We must navigate what is being portrayed as the "norm" with what we see at home. Some of the parents reflected this reliance on family as a model. Joy offers, "My role models were my parents. They love each other, display affection and commitment, and set aside family time as a priority (family meetings, dinner at the table, game nights, vacations, etc.). I also loved that they encouraged us to do our best and advocated for us fiercely." Sanvi tells us that her parenting is shaped by the fierce love and loyalty her mother and aunts offered her: "I know that these women will show up for me and fight to the end. If something was ever to happen to my husband and me, these women would without a doubt show up for my kids and provide a village for them." Josefina says, "My mother has taught me to be strong and determined, as she raised a daughter with cerebral palsy too. She has taught me to be patient, understanding, and loving in parenting my son."

While our parents may offer stellar modeling, sometimes trying to emulate them can create more pressure than we need. Meena, a mom of two neurodivergent children, shares, "I place a lot of *should*s on myself, though no one's here in my home checking on me. But I always feel like I am falling short of my expectations. I want to do right by my child, and I do it, but I'm exhausted. And then I'm just mad. A lot of those expectations are hardwired somewhere. It's how my mom raised me, and I always compare myself to her. I feel like she was always there for me, and I worry I'm not always there for my child. It is weird, because I don't think my son feels that way. While we struggle a lot and he and I argue and yell at each other, we are still close, and he shares everything with me."

When parents and other family members are not the people we look to for how to parent, others in our community can provide the modeling. One parent we spoke to told us that she did not want to parent like her Asian mom, whom she experienced as critical and demanding. So she turned to her former mentors and therapists to provide a template for healthy attachment. Elizabeth states that growing up in a divorced family with stepparents, she did not have immediate models of good parenting. She reflects on how the types of models she saw on television did not match what she saw at home. When we asked Jasmine, a Black single mother who is raising a child with ADHD and anxiety, she responded, "I had no one, so I had to teach myself to be the best mom for my son."

Min, a first-generation Chinese Guamanian mother, says, "I don't have any role models in my family that I can look to, so I read a lot of parenting books, I listen to podcasts, and I know how I don't want to parent based on the way that I was raised. I did learn a lot from a woman who was our neighbor. She entrusted me with responsibilities at a young age and taught me how to drive. Her confidence in me allowed me to grow into an independent person. This is what I try to do for my kids—foster independence in my children. I want to allow them to make mistakes and not be a helicopter parent."

Our Inheritance

If our parents, grandparents, aunts, and uncles have been our reference points for how to parent, it is worth considering what they have taught us. Some have taught us what unconditionality looks like. Others have shown us the depths of their generosity. They have demonstrated what unwavering support looks like. Some of our parents, with deep wounding, have shown us how unprocessed trauma can disrupt the connection between us.

Many of our family members have implicitly and explicitly communicated that the world is scary and unsafe. When our people witness or directly experience harm due to living under oppressive conditions, fear gets encoded into their memories, the ways their families get organized, and even their DNA (see chapter 8 for more of a discussion on this). We do not resent our grandparents and parents, who leveraged fear to survive. On the contrary, we honor them for finding their way. We understand that they had to learn to assess a situation quickly and keep their bodies and behavior in check. Over time, this way of orienting in the world conditions one to be afraid, cautious, and not trusting. Embodying this stance of fear inevitably seeps into how many of us were parented. When we have been parented with fear, it is not surprising that fear may show up in the ways we parent. Parental love animated by fear is constricting and disconnecting.

It's important to note, however, that this fear is not without basis, even today. From genocide to enslavement, internment, exclusion, propaganda, detainment, incarceration, and institutionalization, the world has been and continues to be unsafe for Black, Latinx, Indigenous, and Brown people. The feeling of fear is justified. We hold this with much love.

Yet, like any other feeling, fear can be translated into action. Let's look at the many costumes fear wears.

Rigidity

Fear can present as excessive restrictions on what the child can and can't do, implying not only that the world is frightening but also that the child is incapable of handling it. Ultimately, when parents restrict, they want their children to avoid the pain and agony they endured. Speaking to this, Malika tells us about her parents coming to this country with ambition in their bones, hope in their hearts, very little money in their pockets, and two young girls in tow. She recognizes that they gave up their successes in India and started over by scraping together what they could to make a home. With humility and confidence, they relentlessly worked for a better future for their daughters. "And in this piecing together of a new life, making meaning out of situations so foreign to them, my parents had to organize around fear as an anchoring force to survive. Fear of sleepovers, fear of school dances, fear of driving on the highway, fear of sending their daughters to the mall, fear of phone calls from boys, fear of drugs, etc. This fear has been part of my inheritance in my parenting," she says.

Shaming

Another way fear can manifest is through shaming. As therapists, we know firsthand that the best way to combat shame is to shine a light on it, because it breeds in the dark. So let's talk about it. When we as parents feel desperate, afraid, and unable to connect effectively with our children, we can shame. Whether we do it knowingly or not, shaming can look like:

- Comparing our children to others.
- Deriding them for their behaviors directly and publicly.
- Speaking about them in negative, critical ways to others.
- Name-calling.

Shaming our kids may be rooted in wanting to keep them safe from the White gaze. As parents of color, we are scrutinized. For instance, we are likely to get side-eyes at a restaurant when our children are acting up, whereas if a White child is throwing a tantrum publicly, it will be chalked up to a bad day for the kid or, at worst, a judgment the parents are ineffective. For parents of color, this grace is not afforded. Our children's behavior is a reflection not only of us but also of our whole communities. And in addition to that, with our neurodivergent children, when the behaviors that manifest poke at acceptable social norms, we are doubly penalized. So it is understandable on some level why we may resort to shame.

Shame can also be an indication of the exhaustion and overwhelm that we are experiencing at the moment. Shaming our kids may be the first indication that we, as parents, need more support. When we shame in front of others, we engage in the age-old tactic, stemming from supremacy culture, of putting down someone with lesser power to gain some sense of control. Feeling power over our children like this is a way adultism presents. Furthermore, this does not result in an internal sense of well-being. There is no thundering applause from other parents if we diminish our little people. It does not serve the purpose we want it to. Instead, it reinforces the voice in our children's heads that says they are broken. We are ashamed because we have been shamed by our parents, our families, and society at large. Shame is like a hot potato we keep passing around.

In this fast-paced world we live in, there is little time for slowing down and attending to our feelings to examine the ways we as parents have been shamed. As a result, there is little opportunity to shed the shame so it doesn't get passed down to our children. Findings from brain science confirm what we have intuitively known for a long time: when stressed or triggered, we cannot think well or make sound decisions about ourselves and the people we love.

As a small antidote, and in the spirit of wanting to show up fully for our children, we find that setting up time to connect with a friend, another parent, a sibling, or a therapist can be a safe way to process our stored hurts and fears, so we can emerge feeling less burdened with them. We want to honor both the goodness in our child and the validity of our feelings, because there usually is no one objective truth in parenting, in relationships, or in life.

Physical Discipline

Fear can manifest through physical discipline, for example, spanking. Talking about physical discipline is an uncomfortable topic, and there are not many spaces in our culture where we can openly unpack this without fear of being shamed for being a bad parent, or, worse, reported to child protection services. To be clear, we are not condoning physical discipline. But we value unpacking the context in which a parent might hit their child. Parents can become harsh when we have no way to channel and metabolize the oppressions we experience. The reality is that when a parent hits and a child receives this punishment, it is profoundly painful for both. In talking about it plainly, we desire to reveal the humanity in all of us during these challenging moments.

We ask that you consider the conditions parents may be going through. We are not saying that these conditions automatically lead to physical discipline. We are saying that sometimes there is a lot behind the moment when a parent engages in physical punishment, and we want to give space for all the factors contributing to a parent behaving harmfully. Simplified explanations that rely on good and bad binaries only perpetuate more harm. Imagine for a moment the following scenarios.

Imagine a Black parent facing the real fear that the police could murder her child. To keep her child alive, she may resort to physical discipline at home to ensure that her child understands the implications of his behavior in the outside world. A slap, then, stems not only from the suffocating fear she is experiencing but also from her immeasurable love for her child.

Imagine an immigrant single father, for whom the legacy of colonialism and being a perpetual foreigner in a land that is not his home inform his interactions with his daughter. Her attempts for freedom provoke a generational fear of the unforgiving White gaze. Hitting her in moments of disagreement is about the parts of him that are so frightened that they cannot envision another world where his humanity, his wholeness, is intact. Hitting then appears to offer a release of the layers of generationally held stuck energy.

Imagine a Latinx parent who is overworked and exhausted. She comes home to an unclean kitchen. She finds her kids are struggling to shift their attention away from video games to complete their schoolwork. Over the day, she has dealt with microaggressions at work, unrelenting traffic, and a headache that won't succumb to Tylenol. The accumulation of stress, with nowhere to go, and the weight of navigating the demands, can erupt in a moment and take the form of physical discipline.

Body Check

Notice what is happening in your body. What does your body want to do? Collapse, look away, tremble? Permit yourself to lean into these sensations. There is wisdom there. What feelings come up? Guilt, sadness, rage, compassion? All of them? We encourage you to hold these feelings with gentleness. Do they provoke memories of the ways you were parented? What information do these memories keep? Slow down, be with what is arising, and take care of yourself.

For most parents, hitting a child does not feel good. There is often regret and shame, and sometimes a distancing from one's child to protect them. We also know that as a child growing up in a family where physical discipline is employed, it is frightening and confusing that those who love us the most will hurt us. To be hit by those we look up to is humiliating. It is unimaginably confusing to be hit and then to find our parents pulling away.

While repair after an incident is protective for both parent and child, the consistent use of physical discipline has longer-term impacts on attachment patterns and sense of self. We would argue that this is true for the child and the parent as well, with the understanding that how we show up with our kids interrupts or reinforces our attachment histories. Our relationships with primary caregivers provide a template of what future relationships can look like. And growing up where physical discipline is normalized can distort the sending and receiving of signals about safety.

Naming abuse is essential, not because we parents deserve to be shamed for it, but because we deserve compassion and permission to face it, deconstruct it, and heal from it. Our parenting ethical code states firmly and lovingly that we are responsible for committing to returning to our sound judgment and thinking about how to love our children well during hard times. Because we parents *always* want to love our children well. We just get lost in the *how* sometimes.

An example of interrupting the intergenerational inheritance of fear-based spanking, Janne and Valento offer their experiences from growing up in Black families. Janne tells us that when she was bringing her son up, her mom would tell her to beat him to get him in line. In that, she recognized how her mom parented her. "The last time my mother hit me, when I was eleven, she accused me of something, and she had her hands around my neck and said, 'I should kill you.' She finally let go of me when I told her my real mother would not do that. Instead, she asked my dad to hit me, and when my dad came up and saw me standing in a boxer's stance, he decided we should talk instead. I think he saw himself in me and how his parents disciplined him." She tells us that this is not how parenting is supposed to be. She gives an example of how she broke the cycle with her autistic son when he was having a meltdown by hugging him tightly. "As he gradually calmed down, the light would come back into his eyes," she says.

Valento's story also speaks to his choice to do something different from his family. "My immediate family understands our kids, but my extended family wants me to yell and spank them to discipline them. As a Black family, it all comes back to discipline. I don't like going to places anymore unless there is emotional safety and acceptance for my children there."

Regardless of how fear shows up, it is a constricting emotion. Our bodies tighten, our focus narrows, and our world gets smaller. To move toward a type of parenting that is free and liberatory for our BIPOC neurodivergent children means examining how fear shows up in the day-to-day with our kids. It means holding ourselves with compassion and forgiveness: we don't choose to be fearful. It means looking at the function of fear in our lives. It is inquiring into how it impacts our relationships with our most beloved children. We invite you at this moment to pause and reflect on how fear shows up in your life and in your parenting.

Body Check

Try focusing on one part of your body. Maybe it is your feet, back, or stomach. And as you zoom into this part of the body, notice the temperature of your skin in that area. Is it warm, cold, or sweaty? Is there another part of your body where it feels the opposite? What is it like to shift your attention between the two?

Setting Limits, Showing Warmth

Parenting is in the delicate balance between setting the right limits and being warm and responsive to our children's reactions to these limits. The *circle of security* model is a framework that helps us to understand this relationship between limits and warmth. Our children want to know that they can explore the world around them with explicitly stated limits. They need to feel confident that they will be met with comfort when they return from their exploration. This gives children the security they need to move through this world. This approach positions parents to be supportive and interested in their children while allowing them to make mistakes. Parents help prepare their children for the road ahead rather than paving it for them. As a result, children grow up self-assured and well adjusted.

Limits, also known as boundaries, are intended to lovingly protect and guide. The limits we set cue our children as to what is OK, what is safe, and what we are able to tolerate. They can also support our children in regulating their feelings and eventually learning to set limits for themselves. An excellent way to distinguish between a *limit* and a *punishment* is that the former is intended to support the child and the latter is intended to give parents some temporary relief and a sense of control, often unintentionally leaving a child feeling hurt, confused, and less in control. Joshua and Minnie state, "We set limits on the sugar they eat, as we have seen it impacts their neurodivergent brains . . . but we question whether the limit we set is for our convenience or about meeting them where they are."

Once we set a limit, it also allows us the space to delight in our kids' exploration, get curious about their experiences, and encourage them to take healthy risks. You can think of limits like a fence around a playground. The fence defines where it is OK to play and where it is not. Imagine taking your child to a play area without a marked boundary. Notice the stress and anxiety it can provoke in you. In a playground with clear markings of where the space begins and ends, we can feel more confident in allowing our children to follow their curiosity, which is a crucial component to play. In the same way, a thoughtfully expressed parental limit can be helpful to both parent and child. For the parent, it supports us in being more attuned to our child. For the child, it offers a sense of security and contained freedom, which allows them to be less stressed.

Setting limits can be especially important for neurodivergent children, for whom change can be a source of anxiety. Limits offer stability and ease transitions, which our neurodivergent kids can find challenging. And the limits we set may be different than those for neurotypical kids. For instance, it may be important that a limit is stated explicitly and repeatedly. For an autistic child, implied limits are often not helpful; it is essential to state outright what is safe. One parent shared that for her children with ADHD, she often reviewed expectations with her children before events and activities to help them remember. But the limits we set for our neurodivergent children don't always need to be stricter. For example, recognizing that the world around them already places a lot of constraints and demands, we may relax the limits we set around technology or food at home to mitigate the effects of constantly being limited elsewhere.

As parents of children of color, however, we may resort to stricter limits out of a subconscious or conscious fear around how the world will treat our child or how the world will judge us if we don't set firmer limits—that is when we are often more likely to be punished and shamed for how we parent, for not keeping our child in line. Therefore, limits, sometimes more than needed, are a big way we ensure the safety of our children under the White gaze, both emotionally and physically.

Our children have unique needs. Knowing them most intimately, we parent the child that we have, considering their distinctive personality with their strengths and challenges, to meet their needs and to protect them. Julie tells us, "With my kid with intellectual disabilities, I know she ruminates, and she says things because she is anxious and does not understand the rules of engagement. I am more direct and firmer, and I know she needs guidance. I know if she sees she can get a reaction, she will keep doing it to engage. It is my job to know that her brain works differently, and I can't use the same tactics I do with my older daughter. I want to make sure she is not bringing more negative attention. It comes from a place of wanting to help, not control. I have to set more explicit limits because she does not have the language or ability to tell me why she is angry. Whereas, with my other daughter, if she wants to do something, I will inquire and figure out what is behind the desire and then spend time talking about it and thinking it through with her."

The other side of limits is warmth: limits and warmth in tandem provide the security our children need to thrive. Warmth is a visceral and unquantifiable relationship experience that confirms presence, attunement, and care.

Warmth is how we show our children *I am here with you* in a way that feels safe to them. Filtered through the prism of the family's origin, culture, gender identities, neurotypicality, and socialization, warmth can present itself in various ways. It may also be impacted by our own traumas. Those who grew up in homes where care was shown through service may have internalized that being warm with our kids is caring for them through active gestures, such as making lunches for school, driving them to music lessons to support their interests, and having clothes washed for the week. For those of us who grew up in cultures where emotions are not to be shown, we may be less emotive with our kids. Some of us from these same cultures may long for affection to be more visible and offer our kids more of that emotional experience. We may take more opportunities to say, "I love you" and "I am proud of you."

Our gender socialization can also affect how open and responsive we are. It is worth inquiring into how we impose our understanding of gender onto how we show up with our kids. For instance, are we more likely to use words of emotions when attending to a girl child, and are we more likely to use achievement-oriented language with our boys?

Similarly, our own neurodivergence may also define how we offer warmth. Neurotypical metrics can portray neurodivergent parents as not being affectionate or responsive enough. In our suggestions here, we are cautious of using standards that do not reflect the lived experiences of neurodivergent parents. Warmth has many shades and shows up in different ways—in our body, through our tone of voice, through our actions. We are inviting you to get curious, set judgment aside, lean into understanding how you feel, and offer warmth most authentically.

Even though we parents aspire to approach our children with our warmth as much as possible, it can be difficult. Our ability to show our children *I am here with you* depends on how emotionally regulated we are. Essentially, we want to be emotionally regulated enough to reach for our children and have their responses not flood or overwhelm us, because when we are overwhelmed, it makes it hard to attune and stay grounded with them. More so, living under the tyranny of oppressive systems like supremacy and capitalism makes it harder for parents to find their center consistently, so it is natural that we lose it. We want to normalize that if we can't access regulation at any moment, sometimes the warmest thing we can do for our child is to step away. We do our best, and in those moments that we can't, we offer healing to our children and ourselves through repair.

When we show up with warmth, it is natural to expect it to be reciprocated in similar ways. But in reality, our differently wired children often reciprocate love in the least-expected ways. They may not be able to return your rapt, loving gaze on them, babble to you as another baby would, or give you a loving hug when you enter the home after a long workday. But the absence of such (neurotypical) responses is not equivalent to a lack of love within your child. While it is hard not to take such moments personally, we hope it helps to know that:

- Your child loves you no less.
- Your child needs you no less.
- Your child needs your love no less.
- You count no less.
- You are the exact parent your child needs to thrive in this world.

We understand that these tiny differences in parenting neurodivergence hold much emotional weight. When our child does not reciprocate in expected ways, it is normal to wrestle with grief for our loss and the guilt for judging how our child is showing up in the world. These emotional experiences are here to stay. And you are not a bad parent for them—only a smart one, to allow yourself to notice the dissonance. Taking care of yourself will help you to come back to your child with confidence in yourself and them and to see the beauty that was earlier clouded by fear.

We know that when there are high levels of parental warmth in the form of presence and attunement, it can support the positive development of youth mental health. However, before we can be responsive, accepting, and present to our children, we must understand our capacity in any given situation. For example, in the circle of security model, if we are the hands that hold our children, who supports us? What support are we getting that allows us to process fear, grief, and stress so that we may be present for our children?

There are countless moments of joy, like when he shows interest in learning something new, when he proudly comes to show me a drawing or writing, when he plays lovingly, gently with his sister, when he holds hands and walks with his sister, when he gives heartfelt hugs to his grandmother, when he lovingly calls me a baby mum mum, when he spontaneously gives me hugs/kisses, and many more.

—Anamika

Parenting and Other Relationships

Some days it can feel like it is just you and your kid. However, our laser focus on our neurodivergent children can impact other aspects of our life, especially the relationships with our partners and other children.

Relationships with Partners

One of the biggest challenges many parents face is the impact on their partnerships with significant others. Battles over chores and whose work is more important, managing finances, finding time to sleep, and finding time to be intimate can all place stress on a relationship. And these stressors are exacerbated in families with children whose needs require more attention.

Such drastic changes in the composition and constitution of family life will inevitably bring our attachment needs, longings, and desires into sharp relief. Unsurprisingly, partners can become critical, blaming, and defensive, often resulting in a relationship dynamic that is neither helpful nor connecting. Part of navigating these difficulties means discovering how to process the unexpected, making intentional time to slow down and connect, and remembering you are on the same team.

Valento shares that "the relationship between my wife and me was hard at the beginning. We were grouchy and short with each other." Raising two neurodivergent kids made it hard to prioritize their relationship. However, he offers us a valuable reminder to make time and to have honest conversations with our partners. "Once we, as a couple, sat down and talked about our kids and how our life was too short being upset with each other, we could begin to shift. We have learned to take a breather and be there for each other. Our motto is 'We are in it to win it.' We have been together for twenty years, we have been through a lot, and we can handle this." Valento and his wife recently had their third child.

Similarly, Leela speaks to the genuine struggle of finding time for each other as well as the implications of being the one who is primarily involved in the children's care. She is a South Asian immigrant married to a White man and is raising two kids, one of whom is autistic. She says, "I am the primary caregiver for the kids. I do most of the therapies with them, thereby taking in the input from doctors. By five o'clock, I get to a point where I do not want to share what I have learned and then get frustrated that he can't mind read. This is probably the worst period, and we are not in each other's lives. At the most, we get an hour together in a week, and most conversations are about the kids."

Sometimes in our relationships we can forget to be a team, and we channel the helplessness, frustrations, and exhaustion onto our partner, resulting in the feeling that you are not aligned. Meena speaks to forgetting that she and her spouse want the same for their child. Her story reminds us to orient to the shared goals, even in moments of disagreement: "For us, it's been hard to get on the same page. We initially fought so much on our way of parenting, thinking our ways were the best for our child. But, over the years, we can now communicate without arguing or fighting; we can disagree and navigate and return to what is best for our child. My husband's biggest strength is he doesn't have as many triggers as I do from his childhood or anything else. So when there is a situation with our child, he's much more balanced, he's not as reactive, and he can take space and learn to process emotion. One of my biggest strengths is not being afraid to ask for help. I'm not afraid to reach out and say I'm feeling isolated. I need to talk to somebody. We are in a place now where we can see that the differences in our approaches stem from our love for him. Remembering that is helpful."

Sanvi speaks about the differences in the approach to parenting she and her husband take in parenting their neurodivergent child. She says, "I tend to be more concerned about the grades, the IEP (individual education plan), and about her thriving in the world as an adult. Because he is also neurodivergent, he tends to worry less and says, 'Our kid will be fine.' I do wish he worried more, and I am sure he wishes I worried less. I think I worry that I am seen as the mean or tough parent while he is the easygoing one. He gets to be a hero. Luckily, for many things we parent similarly."

However, not all partnerships can endure the stresses, and sometimes the best decision is to part ways and support our children in the ways we know best. Dontea shares that the father of her son was unable to be involved in the day-to-day raising of their son. They decided it would be best to split, and while she does most of the child-rearing, she celebrates how her ex shows up for their son. Her graciousness and acceptance of what each is capable of is something to strive for.

Relationships with Other Children

Other relationships that are impacted are the ones with our other children, especially those who are not neurodivergent. As parents, we can unknowingly see them as not needing as much attention or support. As a result, we begin to depend on them not to add more stress and worry to our plate. The psychological impact of being perceived as a "well enough" child in a family system should not be downplayed.

Malika recollects this from her family. "My husband and I are sitting in our living room, animatedly debating, arguing about how to parent our older child. In the middle of us is a cherubic and delicious one-and-half-year-old performing the most stunning acts of cuteness. Our oldest child was not even home. This scene is emblematic of our almost unreasonable obsession with our older son and his well-being. I remember looking down at our little one and passionately arguing my sadness for this child whose life we are missing out on. As I reflect on this moment, my heart breaks open for all of us. We were floundering and trying to find a balance on how to parent our child with ADHD. It is hard to tell what the unfolding impact is on our children, but I can guess that it is the impact of being caught between being overly seen and not. Future therapists will become holders of this part of the story, which we may or may not come to learn."

Sanvi shares, "I sometimes worry that our younger child can see that he does not get a lot of attention and that we focus more on our older child. I am concerned he feels unheard sometimes." Hana has noticed that she relies on her older child to be more self-sufficient and that she does not get a lot of attention. She says, "I feel bad that I am not there for her as much, because I am hyperfocused on my son." Julie also talks about the psychological impact on her other daughter. "I do not want my other daughter to be burdened with the care for her sibling when we die. We are actively working on setting up a trust and an executor for that trust, so she does not have to be responsible. We want her to have her own life too."

Relationships between neurodivergent and neurotypical siblings are a common source of strife in many families. It is natural for us to worry about the weight that our neurotypical children unintentionally take on as we get too focused on the needs of our neurodivergent kids. Driven by our desire to fix everything, we often struggle to find the fine line between intervention and going hands off during sibling moments. We forget that quiet support and listening are an option. Leela tells us how she would step in when her youngest, who is autistic, would physically hit his older brother. In conversations with her older son, she learned he longed for space to figure it out with his sibling and wished Mom would not step in.

Mary talks about how having two neurodivergent siblings can impact the family dynamics: "The kids are opposites in their strengths, weaknesses, personalities, and sensitivities. Because they are neurodivergent, the idea of the older sibling being the more mature one does not always apply to them. Because of their differences, we have to run two different systems in the house to suit their individual needs (which is almost impossible), and they do compare and complain about why the rules are different among them. Because of their differences, we don't achieve a lot when we do anything together as a family (going out for dinner, traveling, or even playing a board game, etc.). There's always a kid melting down at different stages of the journey, and everyone has to slow down and wait. Because of their differences, they often get irritated at each other."

Connecting to Self, Relating to Your Child

When we are allowed to heal our inherited wounding, develop more space within ourselves, and release the supremacist and colonial legacy of fear and shame, we can connect with our children in generous and loving ways. We recognize that it is a privilege to attend to our worries and fears and reflect on our childhood and how it shapes our parenting today. So much is asked of us as we raise racialized neurodivergent children. As our best versions of ourselves, we want to believe in them and their capacity to love, grow, and develop amid our grief and fears. We want to believe in our capacity to provide our children with what they need during this phase. We want to be able to create a healthy degree of separation and not take it personally when they hurl a giant hurt at us.

Parents deserve to be supported in finding the time and space to reflect. Furthermore, our children deserve parents who can show up with spaciousness and curiosity. The tangible ways in which we show up with our children, connect with them, and honor them can be the difference that matters in their lives. Accessing this lens allows us to see them as good and whole and supports a loving and healing connection with our children. We can embody a parenting love ethic, proposed in the beginning of this book, through these interactions rooted in self-awareness and unconditional positive regard.

What are the practices that support you in returning to this place?

Reflection Questions

- Who were your first models of parenting, and what did you learn? What about those parenting models was appealing to you?
- What messages about how to be a good parent did you receive from the people and systems around you?
- How did you come to decide you wanted to parent? Was there a singular moment, or has it been something you have always thought about?
- How do you define "good enough" parenting?
- What are your hopes for yourself as you continue on this parenting journey?

Resources for Deeper Understanding

Parenting and Mental Health

Cohrdes, Caroline, and Kristin Göbel. "A Lot of Warmth and a Bit of Control? How Parenting Mediates the Relationship Between Parental Personality and Their Children's Mental Health Problems." *Journal of Child and Family Studies* 31 (January 4, 2022): 2661–2675. https://doi.org/10.1007/s10826-021-02210-z.

Ebrahimi, Loghman, Mohsen Amiri, Maryam Mohamadlou, and Roya Rezapur. "Attachment Styles, Parenting Styles, and Depression." *International Journal of Mental Health and Addiction* 15 (June 9, 2017): 1064–1068. https://doi.org/10.1007/S11469-017-9770-Y.

Parenting Developmental Stages

Quinlan, Deidre, presenter. "Why COSP: A Path to Good Enough." Circle of Security International, 9:16. https://www.circleofsecurityinternational.com/resources-for-parents.

Smetana, Judith G. *Adolescents, Families, and Social Development: How Teens Construct Their Worlds*. New York: Wiley-Blackwell, 2010.

Anti-oppressive Parenting

Chen, Iris. *Untigering: Peaceful Parenting for the Deconstructing Tiger Parent*. N.p.: Untigering, 2021.

Wipfler, Patty, and Tosha Schore. *Listen: Five Simple Tools to Meet Your Everyday Parenting Challenges*. San Francisco: Hand in Hand Parenting, 2016.

5

UNCOVERING VIBRANT PLAYGROUNDS

Embracing a Diversity of Play

Oh, the privilege of being able to get a 3D ultrasound during my pregnancy! A luxury, ten weeks prior to my due date. Would I be able to meet my son before he was even born? Would I be able to see his facial features? Would I be able to catch him snoozing? The butterflies in my stomach were just uncontainable. The visit proved most remarkable, for my child's father and I caught him in a story. A story of a little boy playing with his umbilical cord. He grabbed on it and attempted to put it in his mouth, but alas, the cord slipped away. It put a visible frown on his beautiful face, with golf-ball cheeks, showing utmost disappointment at not bringing his plan to fruition. My baby had made his introduction to me through play.

As my child started growing, we would notice differences in him that made us do a double take. I remember him standing in a diaper at the age of one and a half in front of the kitchen wall in our old condo, discovering his shadow. Unlike other memories, this one is verifiable, as I had the foresight to videotape his dance with his shadow. He moves in and out of the room, mesmerized by this curious sidekick that appears and disappears. Instead of being afraid or ignoring it, he gets curious. His awe is my awe. This moment sticks with me because it is one of the first times I notice that the way my child engages with his external and internal world is distinctive. I am transported into his world, where he is genuinely curious by this odd figure who does whatever he does.

Play Diversity

Play is a child's primary language. Yes, even for a neurodivergent child.

Neurotypical literature tells us that a child is in play in their earliest moments, from their kick in utero to the rapture in their eyes as they gaze into their adult's eyes, to their first smile and first babble. As much as there is truth to that for neurotypical children, many parents of neurodivergent children experience a different reality. More often than not, they have yearned for that gaze or that reciprocal coo to their playful bids. More often than not, their child's entry into the world was accompanied by a series of checkboxes that determined whether they played as typically expected or not. More often than not, parents are told that their neurodivergent child's primary language is lacking.

Informed by the lens of neurodiversity, we recognize that our neurodivergent children are not lacking but *different*. If we embrace this idea that all brains are capable and worthy, it follows that all kinds of play orchestrated by these capable minds and hearts are worthy, even if we can't see or comprehend them. Embedded within this framework is the fundamental trust that our neurodivergent children have the wisdom to play, that they know to play just as well as a plant knows to grow and bloom.

Taking this conversation further, what if we advocated for *play diversity*, as we do for neurodiversity? Seen through this lens, there is no right way to play. We parents become curious cheerleaders for our children and may be able to discover our child's play in their tiny grunts, in their hyperfocus on a shadow, in their repetitive stimming movements, or lovable monologues about dragons.

In play diversity, we can see and embrace our child's play with strengths, not deficits. When our child's play does not make sense to us, we lean in with curiosity, enter their world, and try to understand it through their eyes. When we struggle to be curious and see their strengths in play, because we are human too, we gently forgive ourselves. We notice our perceptions and assumptions of them and reconnect with our trust in them and the richness within their neurodivergent minds that we are unable to see.

We ask ourselves:

- What is play to my child?

- In what ways does my child seek joy?
- Is it possible that my perception of my child's play is different from theirs?
- How can I connect with my trust in my child's invisible wisdom and richness in play?
- How can I join them in their joy?
- How do I defend my child's birthright to play?

We expand our lens and definition of play so our children can expand theirs.

So how does one define play? Author Dr. Stuart Brown defines play as a seemingly purposeless activity that is enjoyable, suspends a sense of time and self-consciousness, and cultivates a desire to continue. Each attribute of this definition points toward the subjective experience of playing.

When we think of a child in play, we think of toys, imaginative play, physical play, playing with friends, sports, and board games. Play for adults conjures up images of gadgets, art, music, games, fitness, and social events. But what if play was not necessarily an activity we engage in but a foundational lens through which we see the world? Play in its truest nature is not dependent on rules or goals. Instead, it is an innate spark that allows us to return to our true self, in any context, at home or work. This expanded definition will enable us to recognize even our own excitement and creativity and hold the notion that play is always in us and around us—a particularly helpful notion to hold for our neurodivergent children who play differently.

Luisa noticed that her daughter clued them in on an important internal experience through her play behavior. "My daughter has always had a strong creative inclination since she was little and absolutely loves art. It got sticky when she started formal preschool and kindergarten when her artistic passion fell to the wayside. I think the school's academic pressure and rigorous expectations of such young children really got to her and she didn't feel safe. When she lost that joy in creating art, that was a big alarm bell for us. It clued us into how she was experiencing school, and we eventually decided that wasn't the right environment for her and switched to homeschooling. It was validating and relieving for us to see her play shift back as she reclaimed her happy place in the art upon this transition."

With the advancements in research, we know that play originates in us as early as the development of our brain stem. This is the area of the brain responsible for survival functions such as respiration and sleep, making play a primal need. Perhaps it is not as essential to the body as food or respiration, but it is a very close sister, akin to sleep. We can probably go without it for a few days, but if continually restrained, our physical body and mind are impacted by its deficit. Life starts to feel heavy, our spirit feels constrained, and we find it difficult to think clearly. Examples in nature show us how a state of play deficit can diminish an animal's brain development and how an active state of play promotes rapid neural growth.

Dr. Brown highlights the sea squirt as one such proof that not only does life create play but play creates life. He shares that as long as a juvenile sea squirt moves and plays, it grows, but once it attaches itself to a rock in adulthood for a sedentary life, its growth diminishes, ending in its demise.

Since play creates life, why does life make it so hard to play? Structural oppression makes it difficult for all of us to play.

- Capitalism tells us there is no time to play.
- Sexism and cis-heteronormativity tell us we should only play in certain ways.
- Ableism tells us some are just not able to play or that their play doesn't look right.
- Racism tells us we could be gunned down if we play.

These messages trickle down into our children's sanctuaries at home and school, where they get scrutinized, micromanaged, and disciplined for playing or not playing in certain ways, according to the pressures of White supremacy. Schools decrease play times for children to make way for more work. Parents absorb and succumb to the capitalistic narrative of success and are pressured to overschedule a child's calendar with activities and services with the best intention to help them succeed, leaving little to no time for them to play at home as well. If we parents don't have enough play in our life, it can be hard to play with our children. Employment sectors pressure us to work more and play less. We are also then left with little time to nurture our child's desire for play.

Dolores knows these pressures well. "I find it difficult to play as a parent, especially when you are busy taking care of two children, a household, and a business. I don't remember the last time I played. I think when I get time to sleep or do nothing is when I can play and do my self-care. *Of course* this has impacted my life in a negative way. I need to play so I can feel refreshed." Malika agrees: "When I have a million and one things to do, I find it hard to tune into my child's request to play. But I'm learning that my children's call to play is also the call from the universe. They are saying, *Slow down, Mamma, breathe, notice the joy*. The to-do list will wait."

While, as Malika says, sometimes it is possible to intentionally remind ourselves of our child's bid to play and repattern our tendency to not take our child's bid, Dolores shares how, with an infant in tow, she has found it useful to accept the reality of the hardship. "I think play most of the time happens accidentally, and we just let it be and have fun when this happens. For example, when I am busy doing household chores and I ask my son to be with his baby sister, he would play with her. And when I am done with my chores, seeing them play, I am eager to join in."

But our ability to be playful is also largely dependent on how well exercised our play muscles are. If we were not allowed to play freely or if we were not played with much when we were children, it can be hard to know how to be playful with our own children. Our experiences with racism and other structural forces can hinder how we play too. Deepti remembers how difficult it was for her to play with her daughter after they collectively experienced overt racism. "When my daughter and I were repeatedly called racist slurs by a White man in a public place I dragged her and stormed out, leaving my then five-year-old so confused and angry at me. For weeks a massive pile-up of my own fear and powerlessness, along with my daughter's, engulfed my ability to play. Leaning on my support system helped me shed my fears and recover my inner power and motivation to play, which my daughter desperately needed so I could support her in healing through her own experience."

Other adults in our child's life may also have difficulty leaning into their play. The professionals that our child interacts with—teachers, doctors, psychologists, applied behavioral therapists, and even mental health therapists—all have their own agendas and cannot afford to play. One parent shared with us how a vision therapist that her child worked with could not see how her child's persistence in sharing his jokes was his playful way of connecting with the therapist. "The therapist, who was supposedly trained to work with kids, could not hold attention for my child and gave him a warning, with a mild threat that he may not receive a sticker at the end if he persisted further upon distracting from the session. I never went back there with my son again." Even our well-meaning family members may find it hard to play with our child. They may feel threatened by their play or bored, activating our protective instinct to swoop our child into conforming to socially acceptable play and playful connection.

So, what are some specific ways in which our rigidity or stuckness around play shows up?

- We may value play in our children's younger years and de-emphasize its significance as they come of school age.
- We may try sitting with our children in play but just not be able to focus and attune.
- We may not be able to tolerate their messes.
- We may be startled when our child brings a vicious dinosaur toward us.
- We may be scared when our child wrestles us with more force than anticipated.
- We may set too many limits when our child's play triggers us, or no limits at all when play feels enjoyable or easier for us.
- We may be tempted to go hard on our children in play, to prepare them for the tough world outside.
- We may not accept our child in certain kinds of play so as to not encourage such play in public.
- We may be just too exhausted.

It is no surprise that we are experiencing a national social play crisis today at school and home, in which children's play times have been reduced drastically. The UN High Commissioner for Human Rights has recognized play as a fundamental human right of every child. Collectively they urge us to defend our children's right to play by advocating for the changes necessary in their environments to increase their opportunities for play.

Body Check

What is your favorite song? Can you make space now to sing out even a couple of lines? Don't worry about how you sound or whether you are in perfect pitch. Your voice and your song matter regardless.

Play as Resistance

For our children, in the context of the many *no*'s they get from adults and the system, their wisdom to play despite and within it speaks to play as a fundamental form of resistance. Play allows a child to connect with their deepest self, affirm their existence, and rekindle a flame that gets continuously dimmed by the forces around it. The flame signifies resilience and helps us appreciate a brilliant human design. In essence, our children play because they must.

Oppression is going to be here for a while. So we listen to our children's intuition and our own to rise above it. We remind ourselves that for centuries our oppressed ancestors played to resist, heal, empower themselves, survive, and carve a path for us to exist here today. Indigenous peoples engaged in storytelling as a way to pass on and restore language, culture, and traditions in the face of colonial oppression and erasure. Music was central to the resistance of Black people in the United States, giving rise to the blues and all it influenced. Enslaved African peoples in Brazil created the capoeira martial art form as an organized tool of empowerment and resistance. Author adrienne maree brown reminds us that to feel and reclaim our right to pleasure is an act of resistance. If play is pleasure, play is resistance.

Knowing this as parents, perhaps in our child's wisdom to play we can see them channeling the wisdom of our ancestors and paying (*playing)* it forward. Our role in regards to play, then, without question, is to protect a legacy of liberation.

Play as Physical and Mental Development

From developing both gross and fine motor skills to building strength, flexibility, and stamina, physical play of any kind nurtures physical health benefits. Cognitively, play provides a platform for intellectual curiosity. Children can set up problems to solve and compare solutions. Play is how they learn to attune to and communicate with their caregiver, learn about and make sense of their environment, and confirm their existence in relation to their caregivers and the world. Play keeps us all growing by creating new neural pathways in our brains, promoting intellectual growth and curiosity, and building empathy for others and emotional flexibility within. Play literally builds a child's brain.

Play as Emotional Well-Being

Play also contributes to children's social and emotional well-being. It is how they relieve stress, build confidence, and create joy. Through it, they come to feel safe and learn to express their hurts and heal from them and feel powerful. It is why play is utilized in many therapy modalities for children. Occupational therapists, speech therapists, and mental health therapists, especially play therapists, all utilize play in various ways to help children learn, grow, and heal. In addition, many parenting experts recommend using play to strengthen the parent-child bond.

Deepti shares how play has been a critical component of her daughter's emotional and mental well-being. "During a phase when she was showing resistance to school, morning routines were proving to be hard, and we were perpetually late to school. I intentionally made time to start our mornings with a few minutes of play. My daughter loved it and looked forward to it, and needless to say, it made such a big difference to our mornings. There was more excitement and laughter and less tension in the air around all of us. And we started getting to school more on time."

There are four therapeutic powers inherent in play that act as change mechanisms for emotional expression and healing. These four powers emphasize how play in itself can be considered the main change agent, not the moderator or the medium, though the latter powers are often important in creating the conditions necessary for a child to play.

Play:

- Facilitates communication.
- Fosters emotional wellness.
- Enhances social relationships.
- Increases personal strengths.

When a child plays, it is an organic, spontaneous process, not a premeditated event. A child is present in the here and now, and they play however their psyche directs them. In the presence of a safe adult, children are naturally drawn to processing their unresolved hurts, curiosities, and desires with them. Play becomes a way for children to express and understand their inner world, their thoughts and feelings; and integrate their life experiences. Science confirms that the more we allow children to play, the more they make meaning of themselves and their place in the world and the more emotionally resilient and well adjusted they will be. All children deserve this, our neurodivergent children of color included.

Furthermore, when they encounter racist and ableist microaggressions every day, as well as explicit teasing, bullying, or shaming by peers or adults, it increases the load of toxic stress on their systems. It is therefore critical for our children to have a regular, safe outlet to discharge their stress on a consistent basis. What better way to do that than play?

Play as Safety and Security

Play also has the power to inoculate a child against future stress and fear by cultivating a sense of safety. We parents can bring this power into our relationship with our children by helping to restore the feeling that all is well in their little world. This is what Luisa did in her anecdote earlier, when she leaned into safety to attend to her daughter's stuckness in play.

Safety for a child is not absolute and objective. It is a subjective perception. Children (and adults) *feel* safety before they *know* safety. A child's perception of what is safe can be very different from a parent's. They may perceive a threat when encountering:

- A stern look or a tight voice.
- An inability to feel their parent or caregiver's closeness for a short period of time.
- A constantly changing environment or an environment where expectations of them are unpredictable.
- The perception of being laughed at instead of laughed with.
- Environmental toxic stress, such as the pandemic.

Even as well-meaning, loving parents, we hold the potential to cause these safety disruptions in our children. But we also hold the potential to recreate safety, and one important way is through play.

"I can see this so much in my children's play," says Louisa. "For them, their art is play, and I can see them finding their connection to self when they go into their creative process. It's a space they know that feels comfortable and familiar and they can be free to explore new ideas and possibilities. When the world around them may get too overwhelming or unpredictable, their art and play is a welcome place that centers them and brings them back to themselves." In essence, play is a way to regulate amid unpredictability.

As we discussed in chapter 3, children are wired to depend on their caregiver to "rock the baby" to a state of *emotional regulation*. When we as parents are regulated in our own system, we are able to access our own confidence first, which our children can then absorb. When parents are anxious themselves and have not yet accessed their own regulation, whether or not they try to mask it, children absorb that anxiety on a physiological level. Child psychologist Dr. Larry Cohen calls this the "second chicken" effect. He noticed, observing chickens, that a chicken is more willing to venture out and take risks when they have a second brave chicken for a model by their side that struts about confidently.

It is also not easy to find the second chicken within ourselves. But with time and knowledge, we have been able to feel less anxious and more able to play, laugh, be creative, enjoy beauty in all forms, and give life to the second chicken. When our children see the second chicken in us, they follow suit by giving themselves permission to play, laugh, and take risks. They can feel, despite all the chaos around us, *In my little bubble with my parents, I am OK, I am safe.* Offering such a sense of safety amid environmental turmoil is not disingenuous. Rather, it is a commitment that parents make to children, to temper the impacts of stress on them, especially as their developing brains are not fully prepared to understand and temper their fears.

How Our Children Play

Having considered the significance of play in child development, let us explore the nuances of play for our neurodivergent children of color. Reconnecting with the framework of play diversity, we remind ourselves that there is no one right way to play, and that play belongs to every child. It is that felt, embodied sense that is experienced by a child playing hide-and-seek or being forever enthralled by little drains or trash cans on the street, or when hyperfocused on a *Minecraft* game and nothing else. We parents may have completely valid feelings about it, but it still doesn't take away from the fact that the play centers of our child's brain light up when they engage in these means. Your neurodivergent child knows to play.

Play diversity also recognizes that children know to play regardless of racial, gender, or sexual identities. It's necessary for us to recognize how race plays into (no pun intended) this topic because it affects how our children are *allowed* to play in a world dominated by White supremacy, not how they *know* to play. Your child of color knows to play.

So what are the many ways in which our neurodivergent children play? The spectrum of neurodivergent play is as wide as the term *neurodivergence*. It may range anywhere from lots of repetitive play (such as always arranging objects in a line) to sensory-seeking (crashing into the pillows) or sensory-avoidant play (avoiding the touch of sand, let alone playing in it). Not all neurodivergent play looks the same. Their play is not good or bad. It just is.

For many parents, their children's play was their first sign of knowing that there was something different about their children. Parents noticed a tendency for their neurodivergent children to play in particular ways that were different from what they had seen in neurotypical children. Min shares, "Once at Petco my son discovered a broom and a dustpan to sweep up loose feathers and bird seeds. That's it. No trip was complete without a thirty-minute sweeping session. The only way I could get him to leave the building was to have the manager come and thank him for his sweeping and ask for the broom back." Kim also shares the joy that her son's particular interest repeatedly brought him. "I remember we took him to the zoo and all he did the entire time was look for trash cans." And Joy says, "I often found my son inspecting objects instead of manipulating them, and stacking cars as opposed to rolling them or pretending to drive them."

These anecdotes remind us that with their expansive attitude to play, our children have the innate power to find play anywhere and everywhere. While this can bring them much joy, it can also be a path to disappointment. Min remembers a trip to the zoo with her son. "There was an exhibit where a broom and brush were cemented into the display and could not be moved. My son, being obsessed with brushes, cried and cried and cried because he wanted to pull the brush off the wall and was insistent on taking it home."

Another type of play that often brings neurodivergent children much joy is solitary play. Some neurodivergent kids rarely if ever involve others in their play. Valento said of his daughter, "If you don't make her, she is totally fine playing by herself. When she gets home, she has her 'office' (her closet), where she brings snacks and her tablet and has a ball by herself—you can hear her laughing." Anamika shares how her son's preferences in solitary play have shifted over the years and recalls how in his younger days he was fascinated with spinning objects. "He could watch things spin for hours. He would even play trucks upside down just to get the wheels to spin." His excitement was palpable. Kim observed a lot of preference for individual play in her son, in the form of lining up cars, playing with his trash truck, and building with Duplos and blocks. Another parent identified their son's solitary fascinations with spinners and buttons on a metal loop. Sophia shares how, no matter what they play with and how, her children appear content in solitary play. "My daughter loves her animals and takes them around."

Sometimes, however, our children's solitary play may look less than vibrant, making it hard for surrounding adults to understand if it is serving them. Solitary play makes parents wonder: Do you leave a child alone when they wish to be in their own space? Or do you try to insert yourself to make them engage? Which is the child-centered way?

Deepti shares how she discerns when her daughter's solitary play serves her and when it doesn't: "There are times when I notice how content she is when hyperfocusing on a challenge in a game—it is intense but she is in her element. At other times she displays signs of frustration that slowly build up in her body as she is engaged with her game alone, and I know she could use my support, so I step in—sometimes a suggestion for a break works, but sometimes all I can do is sit by her, breathe, and validate her feelings, and I see that it does help."

Deepti's experience reminds us of the importance of flexible thinking around our children's needs and engaging with questions like *Is my child feeling content and connected to their inner self in play? If not, how can I respectfully step in to support them?* Perhaps it is not the specific solutions she arrived at but the process of arrival that makes her efforts child centered.

We love our kid, we talk all the time about how blessed we are to have him. He is a complete joy and delight—everyone just falls in love with him! So he brings us tremendous joy. We like to laugh, play video games, watch movies, and eat great food. Sometimes it's hard to center joy when there is always so much work to do.

—Joy

While it may be beneficial for our neurodivergent children to expand their play skills, let us not forget that our lens of play diversity presupposes that our children are well *as they are.* In fact, solitary play has its benefits for all human beings. Think about your own solitary explorations—hiking solo in the woods, curling up with a book, building Legos or a jigsaw puzzle, creating music, or enjoying a quiet sit by the river—and how fun and satisfying they can be when it is a choice to engage in solitary play.

The joy of interacting with an object on their own terms, at their own pace, can be incredibly satisfying to a child, as long as they are feeling well connected to their caregiver. If they are feeling disconnected from their caregiver instead, their state of dis-ease may result in anxiety-infused solitary play, making it not a constructive, integrative experience. But when they have internalized a felt sense of safety and connection and are able to co-regulate with their caregiver, they are free to explore their solitary path and, in the process, explore their attachment to themselves.

Within solitary play, Anamika's child, like many neurodivergent children, can also play in a repetitive way, enacting the exact same sequence of tasks repeatedly, never failing to be enamored. Joy notices this in her child too: "Repetitive play was the only way he played, and even now he plays that way very often." Kim shares, "My son could spend hours dumping and refilling his toy trash cans." Luisa, mother of two neurodivergent children, says, "My daughter loved her art materials, but my son was just not interested in them. Every time I gave him something to play with, his thing was to take it apart. He loved his Matchbox cars and Transformers but only loved lining them up. I had an aha moment when I realized that, gosh, he's playing a little bit differently. His play was repetitive." She adds how she notices her children delight in repetitive play. "There is so much safety, processing, and joy in it!"

On the other hand, Anamika shares how her observation of her son's play led her to her intuition that in addition to his favorite kinds of repetitive play, he could benefit from expanding his play palate and building new skills. She chose to introduce new kinds of play with him, while open to the possibilities that he might or might not take to the new ways shared. These contrasting stories highlight that a parent's well-placed intuition is instrumental in determining the support that is sought for a child—there is more than one right way.

Symbolic play (the idea that one object can be a symbolic representation of another) is another category of play that children engage in. According to conventional developmental frameworks, symbolic play looks different at different developmental stages: for example, it starts off as functional play, where play food stands for real food in play, and later moves into pretend/imaginary play, where a block may stand for a car and an empty hand may hold up a "phone," and that may eventually develop into a dramatic role-play of "cops and robbers" with a peer. Neurotypical children may begin functional play in toddlerhood and engage in imaginary play until four to six years of age. Neurodivergent children, however, often vary in their play in this regard.

For many neurodivergent children who are concrete thinkers, symbolism may be challenging to access, and thus we may not see them engage in pretend/imaginary play much, or at all. Among other neurodivergent children who do engage in symbolic play, how and when in their life they access functional and pretend play can raise concerns from well-meaning adults. For example, when a toy car truly feels like a dinosaur to our neurodivergent tween, how do we respond? Do we jump in with worry to correct them or do we approach them with curiosity? Perhaps, when our children's play does not measure up to the metric of normality, it is an opportunity to seek the wisdom inherent in them. If we listen closely, we can hear their sweet inner rebel asking the world, *Who says I should play the way you think I should?* As Dr. Akómoláfé encourages us in his poetic foreword, let's take a breath, even if for a moment, and notice the magic in their play.

Movement in play can take many forms for our neurodivergent children. For instance, often they may engage in repetitive body movements to regulate their nervous system, a process known as *stimming*, which brilliantly utilizes repetitive body moments to regulate anxiety, boredom, or sensory overwhelm. But our children also may wish to move for sensory exploration; they may be curious about their body in space or simply enjoy their body in movement. Regardless of our perception, it is important to stay curious about and allow for a child's need to move.

Rupa shares how their son moves to play: "When we're outside, he loves running back and forth against a wall and looking at it out of the side of his eye, feeling the wall, licking the wall (which *we* do not love), or running up and down ramps—he loves movement." Kim supports her son's high energy level, as he enjoyed physical movement through wrestling, pushing, pulling, running, jumping: "For his physicality, we put up obstacle courses, made room for a lot of outside time, and were mindful of his physical input." Malika tells us that her younger child plays through sports, biking, and climbing. "He does not just like to bike, he needs to do stunts, go down ramps, and go really fast. When he was younger, he would climb everything he could get nearby. Once he climbed into our dryer!"

Sometimes our children's movement may not always be easy to support. Min's son was a constant mover, and she shares, "He was definitely a sensory seeker; he did so many little kid 'adrenaline junkie' things that scared me out of my wits sometimes. He loved to jump from play equipment and keep me on my toes."

Rupa's anecdote about their son's love of movement also illustrates the power of sensory stimulation in play. For many children, a neurodivergent diagnosis like ADHD or autism coexists with strong sensory preferences or aversions. Many of us know children who are absolutely delighted to throw themselves into cushions on the couch. Deepti remembers how her daughter loved to make up physical games that provided her body with just the kind of pressure that she needed: "She loved running and crashing onto her bed, and wrestling with me still continues to be her happy place." Kim recollects being creative in play after becoming aware of her son's sensory needs: "We utilized sensory sacks, pillows, weighted blankets, heavy jugs of water, and other items that would give him deep input into his muscles." Hana speaks about her son's attraction to visual stimuli and how video gaming has been a hit with him.

Luisa shares how sensory play is a favorite in their household: "In our home, we have really embraced our sensory experiences and continue to explore sensory tools and toys that help us find joy and regulation. Exploring sensory materials has become a playful experience for my kids and myself, and we discover fun ways to move our bodies that also help us feel grounded and connected to ourselves. We have trampolines, swings, crash mats, spinning chairs, and obstacle courses that are woven into playful games and experiences while also providing the sensory input needed for regulation. Stimming can also be a playful experience. We have fun discovering, playing with, and using fidgets to support the kids' sensory needs and regulation."

While some children seek sensory experiences in play, other children may have sensory aversions. Joy shares how her son used to "hate anything wet, dirty, or slimy feeling on his hands, but he is more tolerant now." Other kids dislike loud noises and crowds. Malika speaks to this: "My older son will not go to loud places like malls or concerts without earplugs, because these environments can be too much for him. As a teenager, my son's play right now looks like hanging out with his friends at the mall or going to concerts. Even though loud environments bother him, he has learned to make adjustments like wearing earplugs so that he can have fun, be social, and also attend to his needs."

Play is also often shaped by auditory preferences. Rupa speaks about their son's love of music. They tell us that their son "absolutely loves changing the music constantly, picking a song, making up a dance to that song, making up things we're supposed to do—he's nonspeaking, so we have to guess what he wants us to do!" Anamika also recounts how her son was very musical at the age of two—"he recited poems and big, long traditional cultural songs"—but "something shifted, and at this present stage he is music averse, to the point that he asks his dad and me to switch any music off." Sensory preferences and aversions sometimes ebb and flow over time, and kids shift their play accordingly.

In addition, neurodivergent children are often strong in constructive and organized play. Janne recalls how her now adult son absolutely loved his Legos and could be immersed in solitary constructive Lego play forever. Luisa too shares how her son created Lego structures with such organized symmetry: "My son could build a Transformer with the most perfect color symmetry on each side. In it I saw art and creativity and appreciated how he sees the world around him." Hana's and Luisa's sons also took their love of construction online, where they could unleash their creativity through games such as *Minecraft*. Organized construction for Valento's son showed up from a very young age, when he would organize objects by color. Everything had to be a certain way, lined up exactly straight; any crookedness would upset him. Anamika also experiences patterned play with her son, where his dinosaurs are arranged in a particular way and any disruption in the pattern would be upsetting.

For the neurodivergent child, when the internal world of emotions and behaviors feels uncontrollable and their relationship to the external world feels unpredictable, perhaps there is a sense of safety to be found in predictable, organized play on repeat mode.

Another aspect of neurodivergence that impacts how children play relates to the quality of attention they hold and demonstrate throughout their development. It is very common for neurodivergent children to not be able to sustain their focus on one type of play for long. Malika shares how her teenager "shifts his interest from one activity to another and gets focused on that for a while. For instance, he will go deep into learning about Bitcoin and then a couple of weeks later shift to learning about fonts. It took us a while to realize that this is how he plays."

But when the level of interest or challenge is just right, they may also hyperfocus on the play task to the extent that they tune out the rest of the world. Dontea shares how her son "remained focused on one activity for long periods of time." Previous anecdotes shared by Anamika and Valento highlight this hyper-attentiveness in their children too, a quality that is a part of the neurodivergent makeup for many. Janne remembers how her son was really focused on subjects like dinosaurs, sea creatures, and airplanes in his early years. Valento shares how his son is going through a phase where he "doesn't want to do or talk about anything but *Minecraft* right now. So if his friends knock on the door, he might play with them, but he is either talking about *Minecraft*, thinking about *Minecraft*, or rushing home to play *Minecraft*."

Many parents have shared how technology has influenced their children's play. Sophia shares that her children love their tablets. "It has opened up a whole new world to them," she says, "that was not available to me growing up." She is proud of how her daughter learns Spanish and her son is teaching himself Korean on the tablet. "At the same time, I try to balance their tech time with other playful opportunities." Rupa speaks to how they used technology to lean into their son's musical interests. "I made a music station for him with an iPhone and turned on guided access so he would *just* be able to use Spotify." Rupa also grapples with the challenges of technology. "We wonder if we should give him more time with the tablet since he's learning so much language—but we also know those game developers are not a neutral third party and they deliberately design things to be addictive." Many parents struggle with this dilemma, which is why we have dedicated chapter 7 to the considerations around technology in the lives of our neurodivergent children.

As parenting goes, there are many ways to support our children to learn and grow, and perhaps there is no one right answer for all parents and children, as long as we are treating our children with respect and listening to their desires throughout the process. While we acknowledge our desire to intervene in our child's play from time to time, we speak later in this chapter about the importance of protecting child-directed play for our children and the numerous benefits that it brings to them and our relationship with them.

Aggression in Play

Having considered various themes of play unique to neurodivergent children, we look at play that is not special to this population but can be particularly triggering for parents to witness and support, especially given the layers of oppression and fear that families are under. While our notion of play diversity invites you to have an open mind and meet your child where they are at with curiosity, this is so much easier said than done. It is easy to be curious when our child's play is accepted under the gaze of other adults and society at large. Heavy play themes such as anger, aggression, and gun play toward self, and others can be one of the hardest things to meet and join in on.

Anger and aggression show up in children's play often, and for most adults, it is the hardest and most feared theme of play to see in their children. At a basic level, we know that anger is an emotion just like sadness or anxiety. All of us have felt angry in our life. Most of us have had aggressive thoughts in our life, have felt the aggression rush through our veins. Many of us have even acted with aggression toward either ourselves or others. If you are shaking your head in disagreement, think passionate cuss words, bangs on the table, door slams, deathly grunts, or the urge to punch someone. Aggression is a means through which humans express underlying emotions: sadness, anger, or, most often, fear. Aggression is expressed through words and actions but also through play, especially for children. Aggression in play might look like two mean-looking guy dolls fighting, but it can also look like stomping on egg cartons, intense penciling on paper until the paper tears, or just making a plain old mess: it is this *intensity* that defines aggression.

If we could wish away systemic oppression for a minute, we can possibly pause to reorient ourselves with the word *aggression* itself and see it for what it is: a behavioral response to inner turmoil that a person is experiencing, external information about how someone is feeling internally. Often the connotation that accompanies this word is negative, and we are acculturated to see aggression, and therefore the person experiencing aggression, as bad.

If we could step back for a minute, we could attempt to perceive aggression with more neutrality and remind ourselves that our child has a valid *why* for the pent-up feelings driving the aggression. We can then ask ourselves, *How can I stay regulated while my child plays in ways that are uncomfortable to me?* And *How can I meet my child's aggressive needs safely?*, instead of *How can I stop my child's aggressive behavior?*

The latter question is not meeting our child's needs, because:

- Aggression is a cover for deeper feelings or motivations. Stopping a child's aggressive play can prevent them from making sense of their experience and addressing their own root needs.
- In aggressive play, your child is showing you: "Look! Here is how I'm feeling inside." Stopping their play is akin to rejecting their bid to connect.
- Stopping your child's aggressive play without allowing space to express their inner turmoil may likely result in your child's underlying need being met in other undesired ways.

Our children may explore a theme of aggression in play because they have experienced or been a witness to aggression. Maybe they saw their friend treated aggressively or heard about a police shooting on the news. Or maybe it is the slow cumulative effects of racial microaggressions and the need to constantly mask themselves in public. Aggression in play, then, is a way to make sense of the aggression in the external world. Our human psyches can only tolerate so much, and for our young people, that is especially true. When our children exceed their capacity to hold the oppressive impacts of our society, they need to let out some steam, just like we do. Aggression is the cost of oppression.

There are many viewpoints on whether children should be allowed to show aggression. We believe, as do many neuroscience experts, that it is healthy for children to express and work through their aggression *in the presence of a caring, nonjudgmental adult*, who is not fazed by the child's aggression and is still able to show the child their love and confidence in them.

It is also important to note that aggression can be expressed differently between boys and girls. Since aggression is so heavily linked to male culture in our society, neurodivergent girls, who are more prone to masking their neurodivergent traits, may not readily express aggression in play. But cultivating a culture of listening through play can support any child in surfacing their true needs, be it aggression or something else, and help them learn that it is OK to channel this intensity through play. For many parents, this may be a very tall ask, and we see you and understand why. In this chapter we attend to a variety of choices parents may make regarding aggressive play when parenting children at the intersection of race and neurodivergence.

Constructive Play and Destructive Play

When play is used to channel aggression, it can be done either constructively or destructively. *Constructive aggressive play* is when a child expresses their aggression in play with a trusted adult as a way to better understand themselves: they show this through their intensity of play or by manipulating toys (dolls or puppets) in ways that express their aggression in the third person. This kind of externalized play creates a safe emotional distance for expressing aggressive impulses. If a neurodivergent child finds pretend or symbolic play difficult, they may welcome rough-and-tumble play with a safe adult to support their intensity. Many experts have studied the numerous benefits of rough-and-tumble play for mammals. Humans are no different, and children particularly reap wonderful benefits of physical strength, emotional strength (confidence), closeness with their playmates, and understanding of their limits and themselves in relationship with another—just through rough-and-tumble play.

Of course, it is imperative with any kind of play that we approach our children with sensitivity toward their needs. Your neurodivergent children may require a gentler entry into rough-and-tumble play. They may have particular sensory sensitivities to certain kinds of touch and play positions in space. They may not welcome sudden surprises and may value a heads-up about a change in the direction of play before it occurs. Being attuned to your children's needs at each moment in play can help them to release the pent-up intensity they are holding within.

Destructive aggression, on the other hand, can manifest when, sometimes out of sheer tension and despair, children whack us, throw a toy at us, or hurt themselves or the toy. They may take a joke too far, or intentionally harm people or property. When children or adults feel threatened to the extent that their recourse is to assert power over others, that is not play; that is violence. Here, oppression becomes the cost of aggression. In an ideal world, constructive aggression is permitted—invited, even, in our steady presence—and destructive aggression is stopped, and the underlying emotions and psychological needs are attended to.

While most of us see destructive aggression as violence, many of us worry about allowing constructive aggressive play for the fear that it could more likely slip into destructive aggression. Research in the field of play therapy has shown that supporting constructive aggressive play in the presence of a nonjudgmental, caring adult actually decreases overall aggression outside the relationship.

Gun Play and Death Play

Pretend-gun play is another form of play that can be hard for many parents to witness or reciprocate. It may not necessarily stem from anger; it can occur simply out of curiosity: to process all the real gun stories around us, to make sense of the senseless power that guns hold and the real people behind them. This is especially true for children in urban settings where guns are simply a part of their lives. But adults can often mistakenly associate gun play with aggression and become uncomfortable with it.

Play therapists have differing opinions as to whether a child's therapeutic playroom should include a toy gun. Some argue that children need to have the opportunity to play with toy guns if their subconscious drives them there. By asserting their power over the toy in the presence of a safe, reflective adult, they are given the opportunity to channel their impulse in a constructive way. And children can engage in pretend-gun play regardless of the presence of a tangible toy gun to play with, simply by using their imagination. A pair of hands or a stick found on the ground can just as easily become a pretend gun, so in reality, there is little we can do to completely prevent this type of play.

As parents raising neurodivergent children of color, however, there are many good reasons why gun play triggers in us our deepest fears. Elizabeth shares how her son was really drawn to dark things and wanted to be the "bad guy." He is fascinated with violence, which she attributes to traumatic experiences he underwent prior to adoption. Noticing that his play manifested as aggressive behaviors at school, she and her wife had to set boundaries on their son's use of toy guns and the types of video games he plays. They have found that this helps. It is true in parenting that when we are scared, we tend to set more limits. Valento, too, has been clear in his limits around gun play. "I absolutely forbid my child from playing with toy guys." He shares an incident that happened at a public playground: "Some kid on a playground left a big toy gun. My son picked it up, and for a second. it looked like he had a real gun. I went into a panic yelling for him to drop it and walk away. My son was confused about it. I had to explain the hard consequences of it, that someone might get killed and go to jail. It's scary. I don't think he understood it completely, but we will be continuing to talk."

Many families of color share Valento and Elizabeth's sentiments. It is a painful question to ask, to consider leaning into gun play with curiosity, because racism and ableism do not award us time for curiosity. With the potential cost of curiosity being death, the stakes are just too high. For all parents reading: your various play choices and limits are valid, regardless of what cutting-edge research says.

Death play, like gun play, is often expected to correlate with aggression. But this form of play, which looks like someone being "killed" or someone being asked to "kill" them, can have its own constructive purpose—as ironic as it might sound! It may be helpful for us to not presume death play is about aggression but consider its symbolism and the meaning that children derive from how their safe adults show up in death play with them. Perhaps death play could be an opportunity for a child to make meaning of loss, to explore the state of helplessness, or it could be a metaphor for a metamorphosis. Within the creation of death lies abundant hope and the possibility of new birth—and, more practically, a solution to something a child may be internally grappling with. When an adult survives the highs and the lows in the death play that is created by the child, the child internalizes a piece of that, learning that they too can possibly survive the highs and lows of life.

When parenting children with many marginalized identities, our definitions of play can be limited. Ultimately, with all play, especially the kind that tests their adults, a child is asking this underlying question: *Will you still love me if I show up in this way?* We have the power to decide how we want to answer that question.

Body Check

Sit or stand. Notice the length and weight of your body. Begin to gently sway from side to side, shifting your weight. Check in with your breath as you do this. What does it feel like to find your center while moving?

How Parents Play with Their Kids

How do these common themes of neurodivergent play intersect with parenting? How do parents feel about their child's play, and how does it impact their response to them? These are critical questions that can help validate how parents play with their neurodivergent children.

As with all aspects of neurodivergence, play is an area that is rife with expectations—expectations to connect and bond, laugh, and have fun with your child. Expectations to bridge your interests with theirs. Expectations for your child to develop in play a certain way. When parents of neurodivergent children notice their expectations differing from the reality of how they play with their children, they experience a loss.

Anamika speaks of the moment of coming to terms with her son's neurodivergent play. She expected that play would be a natural skill for him, but "he needed me to facilitate or guide his play." For Sophia, the moments that brought out differences were peer play situations. "Their play was very regular to my eyes. I could see more differences when my kids were social with other kids." Elizabeth, too, names her loss in the dynamic of peer play—or lack thereof. Her son's friends "didn't understand why he wanted to play the way that he did—because he doesn't pick up on social cues, he doesn't have a lot of friends. That's really hard to watch, and we try and coach him when we can, but it is definitely isolating for him and us." Hana also speaks to her child's social struggles as being difficult to witness: "He gets finicky when things don't go as he wants. I'm trying to teach him it's a give and take. It is difficult." No matter how much parents love their children and see their strengths, losses come in packages big and small. They are real and deserve to be grieved.

For many parents, there are times when witnessing and supporting their child's neurodivergent play is challenging and confusing. Many spoke about having to readjust their own expectations as they learned more about their child's neurotype. One parent, Rupa, found that play meant a lot of guesswork with her nonspeaking autistic child. Joy speaks to the hardship of understanding how to cultivate her son's interest in toys. "His play needs were a little tricky at first, because we were buying toys he didn't take any interest in. We decided to stop that unless he showed interest." Leela spoke about how her toddler appeared to hurt himself a lot in play. "He would start shoving his chin into hard places on my body," something that prompted her to seek an evaluation to understand and support his needs better. Deepti speaks of a prolonged phase in her child's life where play was hard. "My daughter was hyperfocused on competitive games but could not stand to lose. Almost every time we played, we ended up in big meltdowns and aggression. I was darned if I won, I was darned if I gave in and let her win. I eventually figured out that she just needed me to understand the depth of her frustrations. Still, it made playtime confusing, and I felt really discouraged."

Despite wading through uncharted territories with their neurodivergent child, many parents spoke to their intuition to lean into their child's play with curiosity. For some, that meant meeting their children where they are and curiously following their interests. Rupa simply says, "When we're playing with him, we just play with him! We talk about what he's doing, we follow him, we find ways to make more ramps!"

Valento shares how he tries to place himself in his child's shoes so he can appreciate his children's needs better: "I don't know how their minds fully work, so I never want to put them in a situation that might be stressful and trigger some sort of anxiety for them. So if my daughter wants to go down to the closet, I go down to the closet and sit with her. I even bring her some snacks, and then leave her alone." Josefina shares how she believed in her teenage son with profound disability and limited mobility to play: "My son really likes toys with lights and music, like pianos and toy cars that are for two-year-olds. I have always tried introducing other types of toys, but he always comes back to the same ones, so in a way, it is a little easier for me to stick with them."

These parents feel strongly about defending their children's right to play in ways that bring them joy, placing less emphasis on conforming to the world. But how did they get there? Luisa speaks to her discomfort with the forceful agenda that she was asked to bring to her child during his creative and joyful pursuit of play. "I received well-meaning advice from a psychologist to get in there and disrupt my son's repetitive play to help his play expand. I even tried it out, but it didn't feel right to me, and I didn't pursue it further. I fell back on my intuition that my son's play will shift if and when he is ready." Valento shares that his conviction took time to form. "In the beginning, it was hard to play with them how they wanted to play, but it didn't take me that long to get used to it. Kids have to grow up so, so fast in today's modern society, and if they want to play, however they want to play, I am for letting them do their own thing. I let the kids be themselves. That's all they can be."

Seeing our children's strengths in the way they play in the here and now reaps important benefits. We learn how our child thinks and expresses their emotions, we notice how they persevere or give up, what draws them in, we appreciate how much patience and focus they have around play that draws them in and not. When we lean in in this way, we start to ask ourselves, *What is my child trying to learn/figure out in their play?*

Rupa recalls how staying in the present moment helped them learn that their son was so determined that he taught himself a skill. They share with excitement that, after many repeated attempts, "today he did his first somersault on his own—which he taught himself how to do! There aren't many adults doing somersaults in front of him." Kim shares how she and her partner just met their son where he was. "We went down the rabbit hole of the *Titanic*, or trash cans, or the immune system with him." Their collective curiosities merged. Luisa, too, shares, "When I just sat and allowed myself to watch how my son plays, I witnessed his creativity in taking things apart. I could see him enjoying the process of taking things apart. And it started to become okay."

But curiosity in play, for some parents, also means supporting their child in expanding their potential. While Luisa and Valento share a trust in their children's ability to develop and expand their potential in play at their own pace, Anamika shares how she connected to her intuition that in addition to his favorite kinds of repetitive play, her son could benefit from her support in expanding his play palate and building new skills. She chose to introduce new kinds of play with him, while remaining open to the possibilities that he might or might not take to the new ways shared. Even in the field of play therapy, many approaches exist that support both Luisa and Anamika's thinking around the development of play in children. This variety of thinking highlights how a parent's (or a professional's) well-placed intuition is instrumental in determining how they support their child today and tomorrow—there is more than one right way.

How we choose to support our children's play largely depends on how we feel about it. Approaching our children's play with spaciousness helps to affirm their strengths and build their self-esteem. In practice, this looks like us becoming conscious of our *why* around how we support our children's play. *Are we wanting to expose our child to new ways of play largely out of love or fear?* The answer matters, for it is within this answer that lies our capacity to center our child. When our process is clouded with fear, we struggle to think well about what our child truly needs. Thus, invoking the throughline of the book once again, we invite you into a space of compassionate self-inquiry around your fears, and we remind you, you are not alone in them. The fears we hold are the work of the systems around us.

- Sit with your challenging emotions around your child's play and allow yourself to express them. What comes up for you?
- Imagine your child's challenging play. What do you notice in your body? What support does it need?
- Share with a trusted friend, or journal: *Is this fear familiar? Have I felt it in my life before—earlier in my parenting journey or in*

my own childhood? What is the worst thing that can happen if my child played in this (challenging) manner for a while?

Create a Culture of Play in Your Home

With all that we consciously recognize as barriers to play, it is up to us as parents to defend our child's right, and our family's right, to play. How do we do this?

The Power of Child-Directed Play

In a world where our children experience constant direction, redirection, and limits from towering adults around them, *even in play*, having a protected time that offers them an antidote to this powerlessness is essential. Rooted in neuroscience, a particular type of playful antidote has the power to help children fill up their emotional cups and feel powerful: *child-directed play*. This philosophy has been adopted by many parenting and play-therapy models, including Hand in Hand Parenting's Special Time, DIR (Developmental, Individual-differences, and Relationship-based model) Floortime, filial play therapy or "special playtime," and AutPlay's Follow Me Approach.

One example of child-directed play, emerging from the Hand in Hand Parenting model called Special Time, looks like a timed amount of protected one-on-one playtime with a safe, resourced adult. The child is in charge of what and how to play; the adult oversees overall safety and follows the child's lead with as few limits as possible. This results in a dynamic in which the child feels powerful, with the adult delighting in their every move or being a keen listener to all feelings that may emerge during play. Such play can be offered by parents either proactively or in response to any emerging show of distress.

In addition to building power and connection, child-directed play naturally creates a dose of emotional safety, because a caring, trusted adult is attending to a child. It makes sense that Patty Wipfler, founder of Hand in Hand Parenting, calls special time "attention vitamins" for children's emotional nourishment—something that we offer them regularly without fail to keep them emotionally healthy, just like vitamins for physical health, and something we prioritize especially when our child is struggling emotionally or behaviorally.

Child-directed play is a significant tool for our neurodivergent children of color, with numerous benefits:

- It brings parents and children closer together and makes a big love deposit in our child's emotional bank.
- Practiced regularly, it lightens the burdens experienced by both adults and children.
- Even though they may not show it immediately, it helps our children feel capable, confident, powerful, flexible, and more willing to take risks over time.
- In a world where they can't be their true selves and need to mask, child-directed play gives them a safe bubble where they can unmask.
- When we show up for them no matter how they are—happy, excited, whiny, sad, mad, disengaged, distracted—they will receive the message that they are loved unconditionally. This is a powerful message for our neurodivergent children of color to feel and internalize.
- Our children are the boss during this time. How often do they get to be in other spaces? They get to squeal with laughter, change up the rules halfway, whine about being a sore loser, throw a tantrum, or boss their adult around. No matter the level of awareness or engagement of your child in this format, they get to show up however they need to with your delight and compassionate listening. That is the level of emotional safety you offer—something that children do not get any place else.

Malika shares how she leans into child-directed play with her son: "My child loves arcade games. So one day we went to the arcades, and he led me around, showing me his favorite games, and he proposed the order in which we would play the games. Having my son lead me was unexpectedly freeing. I had to be the adult and make sure that everything we were doing was safe and that we stayed within a budget. But beyond that, I had to just show up with my curiosity. And when I put my agenda aside, I could be present to this emerging person, brimming with ideas and opinions. I was open to catching his enthusiasm and for a brief time could release the worries that plague my days."

Luisa also shares her experience with child-directed play with her children: "We have both formal and informal child-led play experiences.

We do have times that we set aside for interactive child-led play so the kids know it's a time to play a specific game they have wanted to share with us; it's been *Minecraft* and video gaming time lately. And, we also have child-led play interactions that happen spontaneously and informally throughout the day. As I have grown as a parent, I have seen the intrinsic value of honoring our children's autonomy in their life choices, and this extends to their play as well. Child-led play opens space to embrace a child's autonomy in and through play. It strengthens our relationship each time we honor their autonomy and their right to play in a way that brings them joy. When we show them that we share in their joy of their play, I can see them light up and show confidence in our connection."

The Power of Laughter

Laughter (that does not stem from nervousness or ridicule) is healing and promotes numerous health benefits. As adults, we seek a good laugh as we attend a comedy show, watch TV sitcoms, or engage in improv acting classes. We gravitate toward relationships and friendships that match our kind of humor. Laughter brings people closer. It creates lightness and helps us feel less stressed. It helps shed fears and build confidence. Laughter increases our longevity (the premise of laughter yoga), as it renews our batteries and our zest for life.

Laughter is an important ingredient in play. Creating opportunities for laughter, whether spontaneous (when a child laughs at something you do, so you do more of it) or strategic (when you offer your struggling child a bid to play), can be a great way to build closeness and internal power.* Deepti shares the power of following her child's laughter. "One favorite game in my household is the 'sock game': I try to pull off my daughter's (stinky) sock, bundle it up, and try to throw it at her, and vice versa. It is an absolute guarantee that this game makes our home erupt into squeals of laughter as we run around the house trying to get each other. Of course, I ensure that my child has the upper hand in the game so that she 'wins,' and that makes her feel proud and powerful. Entering such a bubble of giggles on a stressful day has

* One such tool that recognizes the power of laughter and internal power is playlistening, from Hand in Hand Parenting.

been so therapeutic for us both. It has been our way of coming closer together to restore connection during distress and dare I say, to disrupt capitalism, by making time to laugh and play."

Often our sweet neurodivergent children have a unique sense of humor. This can make it challenging for adults to connect with them in ways that elicit laughter. If this is you, fret not! The rule of laughter is to try and experiment (without tickling, as tickling induces forced laughter in children, on the brink of fear), do more of what works, and when something doesn't work, don't take it personally—try something different! If your child lets a smile slip when you try something new, make a note of this discovery. Maybe you know your child has a favorite cartoon or video game character or song that they crack up at, or maybe they love the way a fabric feels on their skin and it throws them into a giggle fit.

Sometimes laughter can backfire though. There is a fine line between humor and mockery, and parents must tread that line carefully. Children are not always in the mood for humor, and it's OK to abort the process and listen to their frustrations if your attempt at humor falls flat.

The Power of Playful Rituals

Given the diversity of our neurodivergent children's play, it may help to see play not as an event within your day but as a quality that is sprinkled throughout your daily moments. If one of the goals of play is to experience joy, why put that on hold till six at night? Just by being an observer in your own home, you may discover how play is already infused into your day.

Valento talks about a culture of play that has organically emerged in his household. When the children aren't full-on playing, play is integrated into his family's daily rituals. "Instead of greeting her grandpa with a hug, my daughter headbutts him—that's how she greets him, and he finds it funny. My mother-in-law loves to pick her up and swing her, and she expects that as a ritual now." Valento speaks to how he has learned to find play in these small moments. Rupa shares how they told a friend that their nonspeaking son is into the phrase 'You found me!' "And when [my son] ran into the living room, my friend spontaneously shouted out, 'You found me!' He was so thrilled and wanted to play it over and over again." Deepti shares how there is always a playful spirit in the home with her daughter's humor. "She is always telling me her latest favorite jokes, trying to pull a prank on me, or giggling while reading her comics by herself!"

Consider how play is sprinkled throughout your day, or how you would like it to be. *What brings your child joy? What brings you joy? What is a simple playful act of love you can infuse into transition points during the day?*

Expanding Parents' Internal Playground

When we practice a parenting love ethic, we commit to leaning into ourselves so we can lean into our children. One way to honor this commitment is to reclaim our own right to play and expand our own internal playground.

When our children play or don't play in certain ways, we can feel triggered. We may get annoyed, scared, sad, or bored, and as a result, get rigid in our ways of playing with them, play in an inauthentic, half-hearted way, or graciously volunteer another family member to play with our child. This results in us not supporting our children in play in the ways that they need. It is thus imperative that we listen to our own feelings and needs so that we can consciously work on our rigidities and show up how our children need us to: with lightheartedness in our choices and our limits around play.

When we think about the practice of healing work, we honor that there are numerous ways about this. Some are cognitive and cerebral; some are spiritual and heart centered. Some are typical therapeutic approaches, and others are more culturally informed methods of healing. Some ways allow us to express our feelings and thoughts and elicit introspection, and some channel our raw emotions directly through our body and help us connect with our true inner playful spirit.

Luisa shares how she plays: "My play is in setting up learning and playful environments for my own kids and the students I work with. I find so much joy in planning and collecting toys and art materials to set up play spaces for kids. I also play through my kid's, nieces' and nephews', and students' play. I find so much joy in seeing them play and being invited into their play and imaginative worlds. I love coloring with my kids, and I also love a good book! Reading for me is play, because I can escape into my imagination, and you can often find me reading a book from my ever-growing pile of favorite books."

Here are more ways in which parents we have interviewed have supported their internal growth process:

Journaling	Meditation
Art	Prayer
Music	Exercise
Talking to a therapist	Hiking
Parent support groups	Martial arts
Talking to friends	Stand-up
Yoga	Open mic
Tai chi	Poetry

We don't always have to seek these processes in isolation. Enlisting a partner, a friend, or even our child in our personal play project is a way we can remind ourselves that we don't have to do this alone, and we can multiply the joy and pleasure.

When we lean into ourselves, we lean into our children. Play becomes a portal to embody the parenting love ethic. Specifically, play offers us a way to lovingly and gently investigate our inner longings and fears, increasing our self-awareness. Focusing on our own needs in play has numerous benefits. We can

- Reparent ourselves, nurture our old wounds, and heal them.
- Restore our sense of confidence in ourselves and our parenting.
- Take greater risks in parenting.
- Approach our children's play with lightness.
- Build greater empathy for ourselves and our children.

Often, our hesitation to play can reflect some of the messages we have received and the judgments we may have about ourselves—how we don't feel like a playful parent, how we would rather outsource playtime to our partner, how grown-up play is overrated, how we don't do XYZ kind of play, etc. It may be helpful, then, to reflect on our own stories around play that may inform our perceptions today—not because we need them to change but because bringing awareness to us can help us lean into our children more.

Reflection Questions

- What were your favorite childhood memories of play?
- How did your safe adults (parents/teachers) lean into your play, or not?
- How does rigidity show up for you in play? For example, is messy play hard to engage with?
- What makes you shy away from your child's play? For example, are you afraid you'll get hurt?
- Have you experienced this rigidity in a different context, perhaps earlier in your life, even in childhood?
- What is one small step you can take to counter your rigidity? For example, if constructive aggression is hard for you to engage in, try stomping on egg cartons when no one is looking. *Shh, we won't tell.*
- What is a regular body or mind practice you engage in or would like to try to reconnect with your playful spirit?

In summary, play diversity puts your heart at ease. Your Black and Brown neurodivergent child knows how to play. Our society, governed by systems steeped in White supremacy and capitalism, actively discourages play, every day, everywhere. The onus to defend our children's right to play falls on us parents, and we owe our children and ourselves the gift of healing by reconnecting with our playful spirit.

Resources for Deeper Understanding

Research on Play Therapy

Peabody, Mary Anne, and Charles E. Schaefer, "The Therapeutic Powers of Play: The Heart and Soul of Play Therapy," *Play Therapy* (September 2019). https://cdn.ymaws.com/www.a4pt.org/resource/.esmgr/magazine_articles/2019-20/Peabody_&_Schaefer.pdf.

Parenting and Play Therapy Models

AutPlay Therapy. "About." https://autplaytherapy.com/about-autplay-therapy.

Cohen, Lawrence J., Ph.D. *Playful Parenting: A Bold New Way to Nurture Close Connections, Solve Behavior Problems, and Encourage Children's Confidence*. New York: Ballantine, 2001.

Cornett, Dr. Nick. "Filial Play Therapy: 'Special Playtime' in Child Parent Relationship Therapy (CPRT)." February 22, 2016. YouTube, 4:21. https://www.youtube.com/watch?v=i2GBoxA2JI8.

Greenspan Floortime Approach. "For Parents/Caregivers." https://stanleygreenspan.com/floortime-parents.

Synergetic Play Therapy Institute. "Synergetic Parenting—Short Videos." Accessed August 3, 2023. https://synergeticplaytherapy.com/synergetic-parenting-short-videos/.

Wipfler, Patty, and Tosha Schore. *Listen: Five Simple Tools to Meet Your Everyday Parenting Challenges*. San Francisco: Hand in Hand Parenting, 2016.

6

STANDING IN THE DOORWAY OF ADULTHOOD

Parenting Our Adolescents

Dear God,
Why do you make some people less lucky than others?

Appa says we all have the same brains. It all depends on how we use it. I don't believe so. That's all crap. Then how come Einstein was a genius, and I am not?

You see, Swami has a plan, as I always like to think. Everyone is his child. Every child is gifted in one way or another. But some children are more gifted than others, and there ain't nothing you can do about it. You just have to accept it. Sad, but true. Now, if you may allow me to drown myself in my tears, I will be thankful. My only source of relief.

These are words that sit heavy in my childhood journal. My narratives of self-worth and ability, nature and nurture, possibility and fate, hopelessness and faith were formulated early in my childhood, solidified throughout it, and eventually sat frozen in my psyche. Moment after moment, year after year, my narrative became more true, more validated, as it etched deeper into a comfortable, cozy crevice, further and further away from any warmth that could touch it, let alone thaw it.

In my entry, I tug on my faith, desperately seeking goodness and strength and meaning. At least in God I would be good and whole. And

I would belong. Yet any tinge of hope was dimmed by overpowering messages I had collected and internalized. I was rooted in my belief that my unrecognized neurodivergence was an undesirable trait, that it was inconvenient, embarrassing, shameful. Or a plain excuse for being lazy. No, actually, the belief was that I *(not my neurodivergence) was inconvenient, embarrassing, shameful, and lazy. When I hadn't known to name my difference, all of me became deviant, and un-enough. This slippery turn that causes one to internalize shame to such depth has a name:* toxic shame.

It is a sadly amazing thing, to reflect on the wisdom of my young psyche as it constructed an understanding of its intelligence, because to construct anything at all at the brink of confusion is an act of survival. There was comfort in having an answer for my difference to default to when hopelessness struck. Any answer was the right one for my survival.

I have acknowledged, processed, and forgiven many times, and yet there are many layers to peel and many iterations of processing and forgiveness to go through. Every time I think about the profound impact that a system can have on any child's impressionable self-esteem—the way it had on me—I notice my temperature rising again. I start to feel my rage again. How did my world serve to manufacture and perpetuate my belief around "intelligence"? How did it stand by and watch me diminish myself and my worth over a slow-simmering decade?

Exploring these questions and feeling and channeling my rage in my adulthood have served me well in my parenting of my own child today.

As the saying goes, the days are long, but the years are short. Before we know it, our tiny children that we could once pick up and swirl in the air are a little bulky for us. Within a blink of an eye, our children morph into mini adults: they look different, sound different, smell different, and just *feel* different. They tower over us yet depend on us, needing us and yet not showing it. One moment they act like an adult, and the next they behave like a toddler. Just when we have figured out what they need from us and how to show up for them, they may have moved on, requiring us to catch up to the next challenge. The transition from childhood to adolescence is monumental, and the transition to a neurodivergent adolescence as a child of color is even more so.*

Having parented our children with relentless love, energy, and caution over the first decade, having shouldered many of the burdens and advocacy needs that come hand in hand with parenting children, it is natural to yearn for the moment that your children need you just a *little bit* less. Given the considerable variation in our children's development and needs during the adolescent phase, some of us may be able to experience breaks in our parenting, and others not so much. As we navigate this phase, it is not uncommon for us to wish to escape the challenges of adolescence just for a moment.

But when we allow ourselves to stay and attune to our authentic feelings, we realize that most of us enter the phase of neurodivergent adolescent parenting with a list of valid fears:

- How will my child adjust to puberty?
- How will they make friends? Will they be bullied?
- How will they navigate dating and relationships?
- Can they make good decisions? Will they be able to be independent one day?
- Will they find their passion and career interest?
- Will they stay out of trouble and be safe?

In a way, these worries have always been there in us since we became parents, but the combination of our own adolescent stories and the unknown of our children's adolescent trajectory resurface our fears. There is no escaping them now. We toggle between feeling confused and connected, discouraged and hopeful, helpless and confident. We learn that change is the only constant.

It may be helpful to realize that these feelings are not just our own, but they mirror our child's too. As hard as it may feel for us parents,

* We use the terms *youth, adolescent,* and *teenager* interchangeably in this chapter. For many parents of color, the term *teenager* feels more relatable, giving us the semblance of surety, defined by concrete numbers on each end. The teenage phase is often just considered a chronological marking in communities of color: a stage to pass through when children grow into adults. But the term *adolescent* transcends the chronological markers, providing more room for the fluid nature of development and occurs at a pace unique to each child. It also captures the holistic nature of development that teenagers go through across physical, cognitive, psychological, emotional, and social domains.

we invite you to remember that it is not easy being a teenager in this world today, especially a teenager who is different in more ways than one from many peers. When we take the time to see the world through our child's eyes, it makes sense that this phase of parenting our children can be such an emotional roller coaster.

Getting to know your child, not for who you want them to be but for who they are, is protective for them.
—Jasmine

The Uniqueness of BIPOC Neurodivergent Adolescence

Adolescence as a distinct phase is a privilege often only awarded to White, neurotypical, nondisabled children from higher socioeconomic brackets. Though communities of color worldwide have historically had rituals recognizing and celebrating the construct of children's coming of age, many communities have unfortunately lost their ritualistic acknowledgments of adolescence due to impositions of capitalism and colonization.

As Black and Brown young people grow taller and bigger (some way faster than others) *and* look, need, and act differently, society no longer just sees them as different and unworthy but also sees them as adults and unjustly judges them by adult standards. This is known as the *adultification bias*, which causes adults to perceive children of color, especially Black children, as older than they are. Black girls are considered older, more responsible, and undeserving of protection and emotional support. Stereotypes like *aggressive*, *deviant*, *hypersexual*, and *angry*, which are used to describe Black adults, are transferred to Black youth. All of this leads to Black kids growing up faster than they need to. One study found that girls as young as eleven or twelve are presumed to be sexually active and, due to this bias, are sexualized well before they know about adult concepts and introduced to them well before White counterparts. We will see in the education and legal chapters how the adultification bias can have tragic consequences for our children, pushing them through the *preschool-to-prison pipeline.**

A neurodivergent adolescent also stands out more prominently due to their *asynchronicity*—the idea that different aspects of their development may blossom at different paces. Our child may develop physically as typically expected but play and relate in ways that are still emotionally younger. Our teen may be an encyclopedia of knowledge about intersectional feminism but may not be interested in making new friends or may still wish to co-sleep with you. The demands of a neurotypical world, with its emphasis on social relationships and increased scrutiny and judgment, make our children more vulnerable during this phase.

Jasmine illustrates this dynamic. "My son looks like a typical thirteen-year-old, but he requires a lot of reinforcement even at home: I have to still go behind him and make sure he brushes his teeth and washes his face. I make sure he eats and drinks. I make sure he takes his baths and his clothes are put on properly. People don't even know these daily struggles. If you don't spend that amount of time with him, you wouldn't know. If you knew, you would judge and wonder *Well, why is he not doing this?*"

We ask a lot of our adolescents. In our quest to help them come home safe at the end of the day, we encourage them to comply with what our society sees as acceptable. We seek to empower our children with information and awareness about their world to survive racism and ableism. But truthfully, our children's neurodivergent minds may not be cognitively or emotionally ready to engage in this conversation. Our efforts often feel futile as we grapple with how to navigate this tumultuous phase, mainly when notions of success are also dictated by Whiteness. In parenting our children in this phase, we get another opportunity to evaluate our ideas and expectations about success.

When our teenage children are not able to meet these expectations, the world around them gets more easily frustrated—at school, at the library, at the grocery store, at the mall, on the streets, and at home. Glares and judgments are abundant in public spaces, directed both at our youth and at us for our parenting. It is rare for us parents to receive

---

* A disturbing trend of channeling children from preschools into prisons. We talk more about this in chapter 10.

kindness and empathy from those around us when our teenager is pacing up and down to the sweet sound of their echolalia or falling to the floor with a meltdown. But in this phase, as with all phases of raising children, children and parents experience many strengths and joys as well. Having raised our kids thus far, we can take confidence in knowing that we have created a secure enough base for them during this transition. If nothing else, we can trust in the connection we have built this far to serve as an important anchor for the turbulence that they may experience during this phase of life.

"It brings me joy to witness my teen's goodness," says Malika. "I love how he is so compassionate and always there for his friends. I love his curiosity for everything under the sun, his out-of-the-box thinking and quirky humor!" Josefina shares that her "greatest joy is to see that my son is happy in his own world, he does not worry of how others see him or what they might say about him, he will always turn to see you with a big smile."

Luisa finds that in this stage, her daughter "is so caring and gentle with those around her. She is bright, curious, and often trying to figure out the *why* behind things. She has this ability to pay attention to and really see all the little details of the world around her. Her attention to detail in her environment coupled with her creativity has led her to create some beautiful home designs that we wish we could actually live in and some impressive characters that we wish we could meet!" In addition, she shares, "My son's strengths are his loyalty and commitment to those he cares about. He is unabashedly himself and models to others how to be true to themselves. His imagination is so big, and the joy he finds in his imaginative play is palpable and contagious. His art is a peek into his imaginative world. He also has quite the gift of building symmetry in his play and creativity."

For Jasmine, her son's adolescence has shown her that "even with all the hard things he's going through, my son is funny. He has a natural sense of humor. He is so talented. He'll start storytelling to just random people and he will have them laughing. And then he's very good with his hands; he can build anything out of paper. He loves art; he's into photography, and he's gotten into making video content. He's very creative. He's very genuine, very loving to be around, very giving."

Earlier we presented a way to think about children's development across race and neurodivergence. We now focus on the impact of the adolescent phase on our parenting, specifically how we respond and adapt to their changing bodies, emotions, and developing identities. Zion, a Black mother of eleven, beams at the thought of adolescence: "I love this phase. It is fun because parents become guides—it is not about control but about partnership. I tell them what I expect, not how they should do it."

Parenting During Puberty

A hallmark transition during this period is puberty, and in many cultures, this transition is welcomed and celebrated.* Some celebrations are social and public, while others are more intimate and religious or spiritual, but all recognize this critical transition for children in a meaningful way.

Puberty is not a single event—it is a long, drawn-out phase over a nebulous timeline. Each child has their own biological clock and order according to which bodily changes occur, and it is difficult to lay out a set plan tailored for our children on a calendar. Many aspects of puberty make it particularly difficult and daunting for neurodivergent children.

For our BIPOC neurodivergent children, puberty may be a time of confusion and powerlessness, and parents can absorb this sense of powerlessness too. When we are in this place, we find it hard to know how to support them best. The roots of our powerlessness can often be connected to our coming-of-age stories. If the cultures we grew up in did not support open conversations about puberty and sexuality, or if our parents did not tend to these changes in us in a way that prepared us better, we might not have a natural template to fall back on. Meena shares that she struggled to talk about puberty, because she grew up in a cultural context with rules that did not support that kind of discussion. She expressed gratitude that her husband could talk about this with more ease. "We talked about the changes to death, which was so new for me from Indian culture."

For many neurodivergent youth, the onset of puberty is closely preceded by heightened emotional sensitivity that can strain family and

* When speaking to puberty experiences across biological sexes, these authors will be using the term *female* or *girl* to mean female bodied and *male* or *boy* to mean male bodied while holding the intersex identity implicitly across both sexes and acknowledging the fact that these terms may not align with the gender of the child.

social relationships, inviting increased isolation into our child's experience. Puberty is also particularly challenging for neurodivergent children due to many experiencing various sensory challenges.* As these children age into puberty, the transitional process offers many new sensory experiences that can cause children much distress, such as the sight of blood, the texture of a menstrual pad, the sensation of body hair, the scent of sweat, the sound of a changing voice, or the growth of breasts. Add to that the hormonal and emotional roller coaster and the internal body sensations, ranging from the pain of menstrual cramps to the pleasure of masturbation. Each of these new body experiences creates new obstacles to overcome, heightening the adjustment process for our children.

Adjusting to changes, no matter how small, is effortful for our children, and easier adjustment to transitions is a lifetime goal for many, making puberty an even more consequential phase. At times, their adolescence may remind them of toddlerhood again, with an uptick in meltdowns, anxiety, or even aggression. Meena says about her son, "As the body went through changes, he was nervous about every new thing that happened and that did not happen according to plan. He had a question about everything. He is getting angrier, getting stuck with black-and-white thoughts. He coped with it by constant questioning. I think this helped him feel more control, and he needed to be in control during an ever-changing time." Min also speaks to the rigidity that she experiences from both of her neurodivergent teenagers. "My kids are inflexible about time. Both get very angry if I am late to drop them off or pick them up from their activities." Meena's and Min's experiences reveal that our neurodivergent children depend heavily on predictability and that the unannounced changes brought about by puberty, and the anticipation of the next shift, can cause tremendous emotional distress, making puberty a more arduous journey for them for these reasons alone.

Race is also an important dimension in thinking about puberty. The reality is that girls of color, especially Black girls, tend to reach puberty faster than White girls. To consider this trend as something intrinsic to these racial groups is problematic. The acceleration of puberty cannot

---

* Whether or not a child meets the criteria for a diagnosis of sensory processing disorder, the existence of sensory preferences and aversions may bear a significant impact on a child's life. The smallest activities that many adults often take for granted can be a big ordeal for some children (and adults). Aversions to certain sights, textures, and smells can feel like the greatest threat to the nervous system, making any task much more arduous.

be separated from the conditions created by toxic stress, which pushes the body to start the process of reproduction.

Unfortunately, the long-term costs of early-onset puberty, also known as *precocious puberty*, further aggravate the experience of being a child of color in this world. As a result, they can experience mental health conditions such as depression and eating disorders. Reaching puberty earlier means being seen as older, which increases the likelihood of bullying, sexual harassment, and discrimination. All of this further exacerbates the levels of toxic stress. As we think about the impacts of toxic stress already endured by our children, in addition to the hypervigilance they carry from the anticipation of the next racist or ableist experience, the best antidote to raising our children in a world filled with unknowns is to make known as many of these unknowns as possible through our parenting.

Because some of our children have an increased likelihood of entering puberty early, and because we know that our children learn differently and may take time to absorb new information, it makes sense for us to broach the topic of puberty sooner with them, and in ways that they can understand. See "A Map for Connected Communication" in chapter 3 (p. 51) for basic guidelines on starting the conversation, and consider the following real-life examples.

Sophia shares, "My kids are young and at the normal stage of exploring their bodies or/and asking where babies come from. So far, I have been honest and welcoming. I try to explain things in a way they can understand."

Carmen, whose twin children are closer to puberty than Sophia's, shares a fear: "I'm actually dreading the conversation, because he has just started to grow body hair, so I've already had that scare. And I'm just like, oh my god, like, when do I have to talk? Yeah, I think I'm just gonna wait until he gets closer. Because with my son, if you tell him something too early, it's just gonna, like, go in one ear and come out the other. I find that when teaching something hard, it is better in the moment; if not, I'm wasting my time."

Malika shares how her experience growing up influenced her parenting intuition regarding puberty talk. "We started talking about body changes and puberty early on with our kids. My husband and I come from immigrant families that did not openly discuss things like body parts, sex, and emotions. With our kids, we wanted to change that, because we remembered our confusion about not knowing and not being able to go to our parents. So from an early age, we always used proper terms for body parts and plainly and openly answered emerging questions as their bodies changed. Having children with ADHD, we recognized the value of having bite-sized conversations instead of one big conversation that could be overwhelming. Often I will check in on them while walking or driving by asking if there are any questions they have. We will often use the media they are watching as an entry point into conversations around topics like consent, sex, dating, etc."

Deepti shares how regular talk has traditionally backfired in her household, with her daughter checking out of them quickly. She shares how it was important for them to find the right time and medium for helping her child adjust to signs of puberty and a new hygiene routine: "Humor and play have been critical in our 'conversations' around puberty. We have read humorous books about puberty and played games around the issue of hygiene and body odor (which seems to be no problem for kids like mine to live with). For example, we have a fun (a.k.a. gross) game we play before bedtime that goes something like this:

> Me: "Mmm. I know for sure my dear child's armpits are soo fragrant. I can't wait to smell my favorite armpits!"
>
> My Child: *Giggles* "Oh yea, of course, wanna smell? I just showered and put on some deodorant!" *[Note to Reader: NOPE.]*
>
> Me: *So excited* "Bring it on! I need a lovely scent!"
>
> My Child: *Bringing her stinky armpits to me*
>
> Me: *Exaggeratedly shocked; one sniff knocks me off my bed!*
>
> My Child: *Giggles* "Okay Amma, I promise my other armpit smells of roses!"
>
> Me: *I fearfully muster up the courage to trust her word*
>
> My Child: *Tricks me again; giggles abound*

"The game sees a few iterations, throws us into a fit of laughter, and I realize, *Wow, we're so connected right now*. I nudge her playfully to start her hygiene routine, and because of the connection we have, she is ready to start her hygiene routine willingly and comes in proud with her truly fragrant armpits."

"It was hard," says Zion about her daughter entering puberty. "She was eight years old when [she] started her cycle. It was hard. She was treated like she was older, but I had to constantly remind her to take the care needed, though I trusted that experience will teach her. I would send extra clothes to school. At times, the whole school knew that she had a period. It was embarrassing to me, confusing to her. But I built her a bubble. Given how hard this time is for any kid, I gave all my kids gift baskets when they started their cycles. Parents need to understand that this is a partnership."

Angela shares how interactions around puberty with her nonspeaking autistic daughter looked like social stories,* picture-based sequencing, and persistent action. "My daughter had a hard time adjusting to wearing sanitary napkins. She would just pull them out randomly. I persisted in teaching her through experience and found other alternatives like period-proof underwear that worked better. She is now well trained as a young adult, but it took us sweet persistence to get here."

There are myriad experiences around puberty and myriad ways to parent our children through them; as we have throughout this book, we trust that you will choose to parent in a way that best fits your family. We continue to offer insights and opportunities for parents to stretch their thinking, reflect on their values, and be critical thinkers for their children because they deserve that from their parents. So take what feels relevant to you, allow yourself to extend your thinking, question what feels far-fetched and why, and integrate what feels important from your learning.

Body Check

Let's pause. As you read, we invite you to check in with your breath. Is it deep or shallow? As you breathe, where do you notice it most? In your nostrils? On the in or out breath? Or maybe in your chest or in your abdomen?

Supporting Our Kids' Sexual Exploration

As children hit puberty, it is natural and expected that our youth will begin to develop romantic and sexual attraction and may consider dating. For neurodivergent children, as with other aspects of their development, there is a full spectrum of variation here. Systemic forces, cultural

* Social stories are those that help children with navigating social situations, specifically born out of supporting autistic children.

narratives, and our children's vulnerability makes parenting in this phase more challenging. It not only surfaces our fear and transports us back to our own awkward teenage years but also requires fortitude and resolve to move through with spaciousness, love, and compassion for both our child and us.

Ableism has conditioned society at large to see people with disabilities as sexually less than, not worthy of reproductive rights, and incapable of being parents. Kim Sauder, a disabled author, discusses how "disabled people have been culturally desexualized." Angela recalls that when her now adult daughter attained puberty years ago, a doctor once offered her the option to remove her daughter's uterus to make dealing with menstruations easier for her. Appalled, Angela refused, in defense of her daughter's reproductive rights. Sadly, this doctor's suggestion is not an isolated story but a horrifying viewpoint that is rampant across society, especially when it comes to people with disabilities that require more care. Angela's daughter, being autistic and nonspeaking, was immediately deemed unworthy of her rights to her body and incapable of decision-making.

We can attribute an absence of sex education catering to the needs of neurodivergent children of color to the structural forces of ableism. With more neurodivergent kids today identifying as gender expansive, their sexual explorations deserve to be met with comprehensive sexual education.

Racism and sexism further taint the perception of the intersection where our children reside—through, for instance, the hypersexualization of minoritized girls and Black boys and the emasculation of Asian boys.

We may find it hard to support our children within this context, because in addition to holding the impacts of these forces at bay, we must also navigate the messages we have received from our own racial and ethnic upbringings. For instance, in many immigrant communities of color, dating in adolescence is not a culturally accepted or comfortable phenomenon. Adolescence is often a phase when children are expected to figure out their careers and how they will provide for future families, an intergenerational response that connects back to survival as a marginalized community under colonization. For many parents raising children in a different social context from their childhoods, where dating is accepted for instance, we might feel the tug between our pasts and our future.

While wrestling with our cultural inheritances, parents need to be sensitively responsive to the questions, worries, and rapid changes that occur in a pronounced way during our children's sexual development. Our children may struggle to read social cues and experience interoceptive difficulties that make it difficult for them to assess for a romantic spark within them or others. Our children's *sensory profile* (combination of sensory triggers and preferences) has many implications for their romantic explorations. Sensitivities to certain touches may impact our children's ways of providing and receiving intimate affection. Sensitivities to sounds, lighting, and ambience may make going on dates extremely stressful. They may also experience confusion around their sexuality, questioning if they are attractive to others or if they are asexual. While some may be, others may jump to this conclusion because of information and opportunities not afforded to them.

However our children's sensitivities show up, it is important to recognize them as differences alone and not as a reflection of their ability to love or be in a romantic partnership. If our children are unable to explore and know themselves fully in this context, it may contribute to a sense of low self-worth or futility at the possibility of ever finding a romantic connection. As parents we can be a supportive ear, create a safe space, and be there to hold their worries and questions. Meena shares her experience of holding space for her son's fears about being in a romantic relationship in the future. She empathizes with his struggle around something that is still so intangible. "He thinks a lot about girls and worries whether he will fall in love and if someone would love him back with his autism," she says. Janne, too, shares how it was hard to see her autistic son struggling to manage romantic relationships: "He tends to idolize his situations"—putting the possibility of romantic connections on a pedestal without considering the many nuances—"owing to his black-and-white thinking style." Julie shares how her daughter went through a period of being obsessed about boys and how she "pursued it in very childish ways." She worries if her daughter will have romantic relationships: "It feels hard enough to have friends."

It is painful to see our children struggle, and our pain deserves holding too, for when we are held, we can hold them confidently. Showing up more confidently for our children may allow them to be more accepting of our support in helping them notice their sexual/romantic feelings and needs, set and respect boundaries, and understand the importance of consent and showing affection in appropriate ways. Supporting them to express their romantic interest in ways that are welcome to others is crucial so that they are not mistaken for willful perpetrators of sexual harassment.

On the other side of this conversation is the fact that our children can also be susceptible to sexual victimization. Angela, whose daughter has high needs, says, "I have constantly been afraid of my daughter's vulnerability to sexual assault, as she will not be able to defend herself and advocate for herself." Julie shares this fear for her profoundly autistic child too. "I worry that my child's intellectual disabilities will make her more susceptible to unwanted sexual advances." Disabled children are indeed at an increased risk of being sexually victimized (up to 3.4 times more likely) due to their social vulnerabilities. Experiencing sexual victimization as a neurodivergent child of color can have tremendous immediate and long-term impacts on their physical and psychological health. It compounds the effects of toxic stress that our children experience, further exacerbating their sense of safety, stability, and inner power in a world already imposing oppression. Without a support system to turn to, our children may naturally retreat.

As parents, we want to support our children through their sexual development, but sometimes they are not ready to have conversations with us about sex and sexuality. Other times, our own discomfort can make broaching the subject difficult. So it makes perfect sense that embracing a sex-positive outlook can be a long journey. Know that any effort you're able to make, regardless of your comfort and skill level, will matter to your relationship with your child. Even if you aren't ready to have these conversations now—or ever—your efforts to foster a close, loving home base can support your child's good thinking around sexuality and sexual choices.

Janne recalls how, during her son's adolescence, he always avoided talking to her about sex. "But after his suicide attempt, he had an excellent therapist with whom he had a strong connection, who handled the sex questions, which was helpful." Knowing her son's hesitance in speaking with her about sex, Janne ensured there was another safe adult in his life that he could turn to for understanding and exploring his sexuality.

The Emotional World of Neurodivergent Adolescents of Color

A hallmark behavior during adolescence is *counterwill*—the quality that makes children seem feisty and rebellious (see p. 46). While it is often seen as a natural part of individuation in adolescence, we believe that at its root, counterwill is the natural push-against-all-demands response to feeling powerless in our adultist, ableist, racist, oppressive society. For many neurotypical and White children, counterwill is afforded grace and written off as typical teen behavior. To be oppositional as a child of color carries far greater consequences, especially in school, where defying or contradicting an adult or standing up for their own rights is rarely validated as a bid for empowerment. It more often leads to suspensions, expulsions, or falling into the clutches of the juvenile justice system.

Physically speaking, adolescence is a time when hormonal production and rapid neural development heighten emotionality. Because our neurodivergent adolescents are highly attuned and sensitive, they are more likely to absorb the impacts of systemic oppression, their social environment, and the changes within them. Unsupported, these emotional intensities can make our children more vulnerable to feelings of isolation and can result in mental health issues such as depression, anxiety, and eating disorders—even epilepsy, especially for autistic children. In a sociocultural context in which emotional sensitivity is coded as weak amid the pressure for peer acceptance, many of our youth may struggle with this aspect of themselves. Parenting them through the ups and downs requires patience and perspective. Meena shares her insight into her son's intensity: "There's a lot of anger now. I think he's feeling his fears and his insecurities, and it is coming from helplessness and frustration. Then, he'll burst into tears."

Sensitivity can also worsen the experiences of feeling rejected, whether real or perceived. Janne shares how her son got offended as a youth, thinking he was being called a dog when his peers asked him, "What's up, dawg?"

Even in adolescence, our children may express their intense feelings by screaming, crying, running away, or falling to the floor and covering their ears—all behaviors that communicate something important and valid. In response, however, they're often inundated with social expectations about "reasonable" and "rational" communication. Our children who develop asynchronously are asked to conform to neurotypical communication styles like making eye contact, verbalizing needs, and controlling their emotions.

Despite knowing about our children's unique challenges and needs intimately, we parents may also resort to demands like "Use your words" or "Look at me," with the best of intentions, forgetting that language, verbal communication, and eye contact may not be accessible to all our children by design. We expect it because it was expected of us. Sadly for us parents mired in the demands of society, work, and family, it is hard to hear what our children are truly saying. All we can see at that moment is a behavior that does not fit our expectations.

Mary shares how her teenager's minimal verbal communication style was hard on her: "My son has always been quiet and does not like to talk much. This is probably because he does not understand his emotions or know how to express himself very well either. This is also the time that teachers are transitioning away from communicating with parents, and that makes it hard for me to know what's happening unless we talk to him. The vicious cycle usually begins with me asking him a question, not understanding his response, and asking more questions for clarification. But this puts him at an even more uncomfortable spot. I then need to decide if I will press on the questions more or just let it go."

When the unforgiving world does not see our youth's behaviors as developmentally appropriate, parenting becomes hard. An area that gets especially confusing is limit setting. What does it mean to set limits on our adolescents within a world that is already so limiting? And conventional parenting advice may not land for many of our neurodivergent teens.

On the one hand, our neurodivergent youth may still be more concrete and inflexible in their thinking. Thus, strategies like withholding their privileges or demanding their cooperation in order to receive something they want do not get to the root of their behavior and do not help them learn. Instead, it worsens their powerlessness as they lose screen time or dessert or are sent to their room for a time-out, leaving them more confused and frustrated. Min speaks to how her son grappled for power during adolescence: "My son, for the past two years, has been very oppositional. He refuses to do things I ask on my timeline; he wants to do things on his timeline. For example, he does his own laundry but leaves all the clean items on the floor of his room and *slowly* cleans it up on his own schedule."

On the other hand, many challenges arise even when we do make an effort to understand what is bothering our young people or what is behind their behavior by talking to them:

- Many of our youth's interoceptive difficulties can make this sort of communication challenging and frustrating for parents. But we can gain some needed perspective by reminding ourselves that this inability to label and give shape to one's internal world must be equally if not more frustrating for our children.
- Many of our children of color, especially boys and those presenting as such, have been conditioned to learn that emotions are not to be shared. They can be seen as whiny and weak when they do dare to share.
- For children who have grown up in immigrant homes, parents may find it more difficult to model by sharing feelings. We know that the trauma of living under oppressive systems can promote the numbing of one's emotional experience as a way to survive, and weeding through the numbing is not easy.

Body Check

Make room for any memories of your adolescence that are making themselves known. What is happening in this memory—who is there, how old are you? If this memory could speak, what would it say? What does it want you to know?

Identity Development During Adolescence

Neurotypical literature tells us that when children enter adolescence, the fundamental psychological task of this stage is to answer the question *Who am I?* At the crux of this question is "how much one is similar to, or different from, others who occupy the same collective, or social identities" such as race, neurodivergence, gender, sexual orientation, socioeconomic class, nationality, immigrant status, caste, career, and religion. We are told that navigating this question is a necessary conduit to adulthood.

However, when we think of our doubly marginalized children, we wonder if the allocation of the question *Who am I?* to the adolescence phase is a luxury awarded only to White and/or nondisabled children.

For BIPOC and disabled youth, the world decides for them who they are long before they have an opportunity to define themselves. Systems sort our children (and us) into desirable and less desirable boxes, with little space and opportunity to step out of them. In the crevices of difference and otherization, answering *Who am I?* is a suffocating experience, and our children are forced to confront these differences in themselves earlier than they would otherwise.

Just as racial development for our children begins when they're as young as six months old—when babies start to attune to differences in skin color—children with disabilities are also primed to perceive their differences early in childhood. Given the early attunement to one's own racial and neurodivergent differences, our children's process of identity construction starts early. And yet, given the amount of variation within neurodivergence, it serves our youth well if we approach their identity construction process through the lens of asynchronicity, especially since the invisibility of our youth's neurodivergence has implications for how they see themselves and how they are treated by others (knowingly and unknowingly). In adopting this lens we can hold any and every path with strength amidst the challenges: some of our adolescents may be more attuned and have an advanced perspective on race, disability, and other identities; others may be limited by their disability from engaging in a nuanced understanding of who they are; many do engage and yet unfortunately the complexity of their meaning-making may be largely invisible to their loved ones; many others will take their sweet time navigating the question, perhaps arriving at answers much later in adulthood.

How Our Children Find Themselves

At the heart of our youth's exploration of their identity is the desire to belong. There are many factors that contribute to their understanding of who they are, including aspects of their neurodivergence and racial and ethnic/cultural identities. While we are often led to believe that identity development is primarily a cognitive process, it is also an emotional process whereby we *feel* who we are as individuals and in connection to others. This helps us understand that even if and when our youth may struggle with cognitive challenges, they hold important wisdom that supports their identity development.

Many models exist to provide insight into the racial identity development of children. These models communicate that the search for where our children belong racially is especially vital when our children are already flagged as different. Depending on our family composition, we may or may not reflect our child's race. Regardless, opportunities for our child to build relationships with and spend time with other children and adults of their race is critical to shaping their experience and creating a sense of belonging. As our child grows up, their experiences of racism spur confusion and help them confront the value placed on their race in a White-dominant society. Having important attachment relationships by their side to validate, listen, and empower our children is paramount to their sense of self and racial development process. Some of our children may become curious about their racial history, seek out role models, explore via experimentation, or question the cultural rituals we raised them with, the languages they speak, the cultural food they eat, the clothes they wear, and the cultural values we try to parent them by. These all become a part of our children's narratives. They begin to discern which aspects still fit them. They begin to embrace these elements of their racial and ethnic roots and celebrate them.

We believe that a similar process is true with respect to neurodivergence and neurodivergent identity development, where our youth develop into greater conscious understanding over time about what it means for them to be neurodivergent in the world. They begin to learn about their strengths and challenges based on the feedback they receive from the world. They begin to learn about their behaviors and coping strategies under stress and the ways in which they try to mask or fit in. They may begin to explore the effects of masking on their psyche and question the ableist messages they have received about how to be in the world. They meet others like them who have found their place in the world, providing new confidence. They begin to advocate for themselves. They see themselves as whole, not broken.

As our children continue to develop, their sense of self may strengthen or weaken as they absorb messages of otherization or of empowerment. We can appreciate, then, that as our youth accumulate more experiences in life, they will develop in their identity construction further. This is thus not a linear process but a cyclical one, as a sense of empowerment and security both builds from and leads to exploration of a new aspect of their identity.

As our kids begin to experiment in tangible and intangible ways with roles, clothes, speech patterns, interests, ethnic heritage, cultural stories, and family values, it is hard for us parents to not notice. Meena's son "tried on new things—he started rapping a few years ago, experimenting with languages, trying on different costumes, seeking how to be cool and special." Malika says that her child explored by dyeing their hair, and learning languages like Turkish. "Initially I was confused about the desire to learn Turkish, but I came to understand that not only was this about trying things on, but it was also about satisfying his insatiable curiosity." Min shares, "My daughter is now very interested in piercings. She took a needle and pierced a second earring hole in her earlobe. She has exhibited an interest in getting more ear piercings and tattoos too." Jasmine reflects on how she has been able to support her son's identity development. "It has been important for me to create a safe boundary within which my child can be messy and wild and free to explore their identities."

Another important way our children can find themselves is through activism.* For many, their strong emotional sensitivity can lead them to care about social injustices that relate to them and the world. Encouraging them in their discovery of this path is a huge step in their own self-discovery and meaning-making. Resisting their own oppression and the oppression of the world is an important means through which our youth find their voice and power over systems of dominance. Kristin Henning, author of *The Rage of Innocence*, speaks poignantly to the transformation that youth activism can create within our children at such a critically powerless time of their life. Some benefits of activism for our youth include:

- Connection with many others with shared values and interests. It brings marginalized youth like them together, often breaking the deep isolation experienced by them through their life.
- The impulses to resist, to question, to exercise counterwill through meaningful opposition, and to build strength and resiliency.
- An invaluable avenue for youth to channel their rage at the world that rages at them.

* Activism is really any act that promotes liberation from systems of oppression.

- Many psychological benefits for our youth, by providing them a sense of direction, increasing their internal sense of power and confidence, and perhaps for the first time, creating hope of an alternate world for youth like them, thereby increasing their resiliency to overcome the continuing adversities in life.

Malika notices that the conversations they have had at the dinner table about privilege and oppression and attending protest marches against illegal detention and police brutality have made an impact on both of her kids. "My younger child's teacher shared with us how he contributes to class discussions by bringing up what he has learned about racism and why it's wrong. Listening to the teacher, I could recognize that speaking up was an important part of my son's sense of self." She also tells us that her older child, who is in high school, recognized that some of his White peers were taking up space when talking about racism and identified that he needed to check his own privilege when the conversation turned to sexism. "Whether my kids explicitly identify as activists, I can see that being attuned to these societal undercurrents is important to their development and confidence."

Finding Self Through Peer Relationships

It is appropriate that adolescents peel away from parents and seek increased peer connections. But neurodivergent youth may not do this at the expected time and may also experience relational differences that can make navigating this transition challenging, especially since many of our youth are not comfortable with neurotypical expectations of social behavior, including eye contact or sitting and having a reciprocal conversation. And when not feeling resourced or ready, even sustaining a connection with an old friend can feel like too much. More so, adolescence becomes a time when the expectations to be more social in neurotypical ways are increased due to the design of schools, family and cultural expectations, and media portrayal.

In response, it may be natural for parents to turn to social-skills classes as a way to support their children. What we do not realize is that most of these classes are designed to get our children to conform to neurotypical standards without affirming our children's inherent strengths and wisdom. However, many parents may choose to utilize these classes as a way to find support, which is completely understandable given the structural pressures and isolation of our existence.

In talking to the parents who contributed to this book, we learned that our children's passionate interests are portals through which our youth can find peer connection, without classes that try to change them. Malika shares how she noticed her son gravitated toward social experiences that connected to his special interests: "When I could step away from the neurotypical social pressures, I could see him making choices to connect with others in the ways that felt good to him." Luisa also shares how online games assisted her children in connecting with their peers: "I love watching my kids play with their friends online. There is so much opportunity for conversation and collaboration through games, especially when they are so passionate about it." Deepti shares how her daughter's love of sports has been an important conduit for her social experiences. "My daughter eats, sleeps, and dreams of soccer. Relating with peers who know or play the sport lights her up. When we need to enter new social spaces, it is important to her to think through the interests she may share with other kids she meets, as a way to make the unknown known and soothe her nervous system before social encounters."

Even with special interests as a way for our kids to connect, sometimes they may need social support in ways we didn't anticipate. Serena speaks about having to remind her daughter to set social engagements: "It made sense doing it in elementary school, but now that she is a teenager, I am surprised that I am still nudging her to call friends and set up times to hang out." Malika echoes this: "We have been talking to our children about trying to nurture connections with people they like to hang out with. We do this because we want them to have friends, but we also recognize that it is our agenda and maybe our children are OK the way they connect."

Sadly, the cost of not adhering to the neurotypical gold standard of relational skills is high. Other teens may ridicule our children for being "weird" in social situations. It comes in the form of social judgments, peer exclusion, lack of meaningful friendships, bullying, and victimization. Peer rejection has a strong correlation with anxiety, depression, low self-esteem, substance use, and even suicide ideations and attempts. This is the tragic story of Janne's son, who attempted to escape an environment of unchecked ridicule and bullying through a suicide attempt. Such stories are real, rooted in society's idealization of normal.

As parents, we can feel helpless and powerless as we watch our children find their way. But maybe, if we don't go chasing the neurotypical ideal, we may be able to notice how our youth both desire and experience social connection. They have capacity for relationships, but in a way that meets the unique needs of their particular nervous system. Angela shares how during her nonspeaking daughter's teenage years, despite her social and relational challenges, "she was and still is so happy to see familiar people. The way she smiles when she sees her caregiver in the morning, the way her face lights up when she sees her dad, the way she hugs her brother when she sees him, were and are precious signs to indicate that she loves being with people and enjoys their company—just on her own terms and timing." Angela reminds us that perhaps the questions to ask ourselves are:

- How, where, and when is my child most social and relational?
- How can I tell when they are comfortable?
- What do they need in places where they are not feeling social and relational?
- How do I honor their wisdom and agency in deciding when to pause and when to take social risks?

Meena shares how she and her husband have approached her son's preferences around social and professional relationships: "As hard as it is sometimes, I listen to him and let him take the lead. For example, we asked him what therapist he felt comfortable with, and there were a couple he didn't feel a connection with, so we took his lead and said 'OK, let's try someone else.' It was worth it, because once he trusts someone, they become his best friend." Similarly, she shared how it was important for her to learn to step back and not push when her son was clear that he did not desire any social interactions at any one point.

Malika notices how so many of the typical bonding activities, like football games, dances, and pep rallies, can be unfriendly places for children with sensory sensitivities. "Our son decided to not go to a dance because of concerns around sounds and the number of people. While we wanted him to socialize and connect with other kids, we had to honor our child's inner wisdom and confidence in knowing that certain spaces would not be supportive. As an immigrant who did not get to partake in these ways that are glorified by popular culture, I wanted him to have these experiences. But the more I sat with it, I could see that I was wanting something for my child that did not fit him."

Providing our children with some agency over their life and decisions may be one of the hardest things to do in parenting them, especially when our instinct is so strong to scoop them up and protect them from the harsh perceptions of society. Giving them agency helps to validate their ability to tune into the needs of their nervous system, paving the path to emotional regulation and perhaps further down that path, to feeling ready to take a risk, such as saying hello to an acquaintance, on their own terms.

Min shares how she holds agency and protection for her children: "I support what they want to do unless it harms them. Of course I want to protect them. I believe their friend relationships are safe and healthy at this time. I know their friends and parents too. I want to protect them from nicotine, drugs, and emotional and mental distress. I want to protect her from herself." Malika offers, "I find myself stepping into decisions my kid needs to make on his own, even if it is necessarily not a sound one. I give too much power to ADHD, worrying that because of executive function or impulsivity, my kid needs more intervention. But what I am learning is to see and celebrate his full humanity means to allow him also to make mistakes. Overly coddling him can be also a disservice, so I am trying to balance figuring out when to back off, when to step in. But more often than not, if I listen, my kid is telling me where that line is."

Ultimately, the familial, social, political, and community environments can have a vital impact on our youth's construction of self. Imagine if we lived in a world where neurotypical people could learn to be in relationships with neurodivergent people in a manner that is driven by curiosity, nonjudgment, patience, and listening. Maybe then, our youth could continue to develop a better understanding of their own self in relation to others at a pace that is right for them. It is thus critical for all adults who come in contact with neurodivergent children to internalize that we have a significant role and privilege in impacting our children in ways that only we can, especially when the world fails. So when the world holds up a broken mirror to our child, you may not be able to fix it, but you can stand in front of it and hold up your own—to reflect, truly and authentically, the beauty and potential that is your child.

Whether unspoken or explicitly named, the expectation of adolescence is that it will come to an end at some point. But what does this mean for our emotionally younger children who may not be ready to transition into the neurotypical responsibilities of adulthood at eighteen, twenty-five, or even forty-five? In the next section we will look at how we parents think about our children's transition into adulthood and all that that may bring. As we step into that discussion, we offer some prompts for your reflection. Reflecting on our adolescent stories can help us validate our own fears, appreciate our child's fears and challenges, and motivate us to lean in more, knowing that their journey will be unique and likely different from ours.

Reflection Questions

- What kind of preparation and support did you receive from your caregivers around puberty?
- What messages did you absorb from the world around you about puberty and the value of sex and sexuality?
- What are your strengths and areas of discomfort around preparing your child for puberty?
- Identify and talk about any embarrassment that you carry from the coming-of-age stories, either for yourself or for your preteen/teen.
- What were your questions about sex growing up? How did you get them answered?
- How do you feel about talking to your child about sex? How may your feelings be connected to your earlier experiences?
- How did you explore your identities? How were you limited?
- How can you lean into your child's identity explorations? What would feel difficult for you?

Parenting Our Adolescents into Adulthood

Childhood. Adolescence. Adulthood. While these are distinct developmental stages in a human being's life, these transitions are also social constructs to a large extent. Thus, we acknowledge that eighteen is an arbitrary number for the advent of adulthood, especially when neuroscience today shows us that the neurotypical adult brain is only fully formed at around twenty-five. When we factor in neurodivergence, we can expect that it may take even longer, and that is OK.

If this transition is a social construct, so too are the expectations of *empty nesting* the family home at eighteen. In fact, in many cultures around the world, youth continue to live with their parents until they feel the need to move. In collectivist cultures, youth contribute to the joint household with greater responsibilities as they establish their careers, and they build and grow their own families in an extended-family context. Though this may not be everyone's ideal arrangement, such a community-oriented family structure holds many cultural, intergenerational, and child-rearing benefits. Unfortunately, with modernization and migration, families have become smaller, and familial support systems for parents have diminished. This has been a huge loss for society, especially for families raising children who need a higher level of care.

When we think about our neurodivergent youth of color growing out of their teenage years within a society dominated by White supremacy, myriad feelings hit us. We are afraid. We rightfully worry if our children will be ready for it. We grieve the future we had imagined for our child before we had them in our life. We grieve the future we had imagined for ourselves. We are so exhausted by the here and now that it feels hard or too scary to even imagine this next phase. Let us then explore what launching our children into adulthood means through the voices of our parents.

Launching Means Confronting the Idea of Independence

Meena holds the idea of an independent future for her son with fear and caution. "I am so scared about what is ahead for him. I really want him to go to college and live on his own, but I worry if he is going to be completely independent." She also shares her worries about her son's happiness in the future: "What if his grandiose dreams don't come true? I'm worried he might be disappointed."

Valento reflects on how the question of independence really depends on the individual child and their needs and how he holds two separate truths for his children. "I have become a little relaxed with my son, since he really wants to have friends and be part of a group. So when the neighborhood kids come over and ask for him to come out and play, I let him go play in the area with them. But my daughter sadly needs constant supervision: she is a wanderer, and the last time I let her go to a birthday party without me being present, she managed to run away from the party. While I feel like my son would be able to function without constant guidance, I do worry about whether my daughter can ever be independent."

Janne shares that she did her best for her adult son to foster his independence and believed in him. "The natural progression is for the fledgling to leave the nest. We have always encouraged his independence, but it may never be enough to get him to full independence. My advice to parents: Do the best you can!"

Launching Means Grieving a Future—Theirs, Yours, Your Family's

Julie shares her vision for her daughter's future. "When I think about the future, I think about having the right peers and teachers who can help her quality of life. I think about making sure someone will always be there to look after her. How will she have the quality of relationships and life she deserves? I worry that the support she gets will depend on what is available in our environment."

Valento speaks to the stuckness he experiences in imagining his children's adulthoods as being "the scary part for me, because I have had a lot of plans for things I would like to have done by now, but raising two neurodivergent children has pretty much taken all my time. So really, I don't like making plans, because I often will get depressed when I can't even attempt it."

Dolores says, "My fear is always that my son will find it difficult to assimilate socially as he grows older without the help of medication and therapy. He is very scattered and slow to respond to social cues."

Launching Means Needing Community Support

Janne shares how they have had to come to terms with a future they had not imagined: "Because of our son's needs, my husband has continued working (after having retired two or three times), so we can support him financially." But she acknowledges her biggest fear and speaks for many parents when she asks, "What happens when his parents are no longer alive?"

Angela couldn't agree more and worries about what will happen to her daughter after her time. As a first-generation immigrant, she migrated to the United States primarily motivated by the level of awareness and support for autistic children with higher levels of need in this country over her home country. However, now that her daughter is an adult, her fear drives her to seek a solution back in her home country, out of valid mistrust of the long-term care facilities in the US system.

Launching Means Questioning Western Models

Given the vast spectrum of development for neurodivergent youth, we recognize that the launching phase looks very different for youth on opposite ends of the neurodivergent development spectrum. While some parents can entertain the thought of cautiously launching their child into the world, others have needed to be practical and come to terms with the real possibility that their children may never be ready for full-on independence. Perhaps this challenge then becomes an opportunity for us to disrupt the systems above us, in big ways and small. Here are how some parents have made sense of this phase.

Zion shares her bold philosophy around launching in the face of capitalism and White supremacy. She says, "Society lies to us: a support system doesn't stop at eighteen. I parent by the mother eagle theory. I don't launch any of my kids. I'm there as long as they need me to be. The nest may get pricklier, but I'm never going to allow my kids to fall through it." On raising her neurodivergent teen, she says, "They never stop needing guidance. They just need it differently as they grow up."

Min agrees, as she centers her children's agency in this process: "I don't know what [launching] means, because eighteen is 'usually' when kids graduate from high school. Sometimes kids want to move out on their own with friends, sometimes they want to stay home and go to a local college, sometimes they want to leave home and experience some independence and different life in a different location. I think it's up to a child to know when they want to launch and go out on their own and to what degree."

Dolores sees the concept of empty nesting as something foreign to her upbringing as a first-generation Chinese Indonesian. "It is a revolving door for our cultures (me and my husband's). Family is first. So we would be available for him whenever he needs us through his adulthood without creating a dependency."

Malika says, "I am also releasing the idea that my children need to be done growing at eighteen, that somehow parenting is complete then. For kids whose executive functioning matures at a different pace, I realize we are on a different timeline and that is OK."

Angela shares a similar path she created for her adult daughter, centered on maximizing her learning potential. "I plan not to rush her into getting a job and living an independent life. She still has so much to learn and is excited to learn. Instead, I want to help her focus on her academics, to help her take her interest and skill in adaptive communication to her highest potential so she can read and write better. If she goes to vocational school, she will be placated at a skill and job level that matches her current ability and won't be challenged further."

Launching Means Channeling Our Fears to Prepare for Their Future

Some parents share how they channel their fears of the adulthood phase into concrete undertakings. Meena speaks of becoming aware of her fears as a first step to channeling them: "I know I must stop letting my fears dictate so much of my actions. There is only so much I can do to protect him. I am working on when to push, when not, and when to let him rest."

Sophia, a single mother of two young neurodivergent children, shares that because adulthood for her children is out in the distant future, it's hard to imagine, yet it shapes her present life. "I'm working on creating a career as a screenwriter, so that allows me to make life choices that benefit us all regardless of the level of care my children need from me." Similarly, Sophia's ongoing parenting project includes looking out for her children's "strengths and talents that might help them establish an identity and a career for their future."

Angela concurs. While she made a conscious choice to live with her adult daughter, she has always prioritized opportunities and experiences to help her daughter gain and master independent skills through her childhood. "I am doing everything I can to help her increase her sense of independence in multiple ways: she can sleep by herself, take care of toilet needs by herself, and she has a strong bond with her caregiver, where she can successfully do sleepovers away from me. That is huge." Angela is also looking at longer-term care for her daughter so that she has a care plan beyond Angela's time. Similarly, Carmen shares her thoughts about her son's future: "There are many things he is good at, but if [he] is unable to be independent in adulthood, I am going into a career where I can take him with me on my travel job."

Looking into the Horizon

Parenting at the doorway of our children's adulthood is an emotionally demanding process. And alongside our emotional preparation, we must contend with the logistics of this transition.

Logistically, for some youth moving into adulthood, a minimal amount of accommodations and support is needed; for others, it is so much more. For neurodivergent youth who experience moderate to higher levels of care, there is a plethora of resources that parents can tap into as they prepare for the continuation of their care into the future, from applying for Supplementary Security Income (SSI) state funding through a Department of State Health Services (DSHS) Regional Service Center to accessing respite care. If your child has an IEP (individual education plan) through a public-school district, there are also many options available when it comes to education and career choices, depending on your child's level of need, readiness, and interest. These options provide us parents an invitation to keep an open mind for the future path that our children are able and may wish to take. There are also many local organizations or programs in each state that can support your child in pursuing their interests as they near adulthood.

Despite the programs available, many barriers prevent parents from knowing or accessing care for their youth through these channels. One of the main barriers is simply the awareness of resources, but other barriers include exhausting paperwork, a lack of comfort navigating the system, and the relentless energy needed to jump through the hoops the system creates for us. Angela calls this energy "sweet persistence," attributing the sweetness to the gentle tact which she has needed to learn to successfully advocate for her daughter's needs within all systems. Angela also speaks to how parents must shoulder the burden of acquiring information and advocating for services: "Parents like me must prove in court that their child deserves continued funding for a supportive service. Despite all my effort, energy, and preparation, I lost the case to continue state funding for my daughter's facilitated communication support, simply because they don't believe in it." Sadly, Angela is not alone in such an unjust position, where advocacy for our children becomes a never-ending endeavor against systems that are designed to infringe on our children's right to a well-supported and dignified life.

Navigating the maze of supportive services for our young adults can be harder in the context of our own feelings about the possibility that parenting will continue relentlessly into our children's adulthood; grief, anxiety, helplessness, and guilt can all show up at our doors once again. Reconnecting with yourself in nourishing ways and strengthening your own village is still just as important, since parenting our children at this intersection may never end, even as they transition into adulthood.

Resources for Deeper Understanding

Education Advocacy

Davis-Pierre, Maria. "Protecting and Preparing Back to School Edition with Cheryl Poe." August 19, 2022. *Autism in Black Podcast*. https://www.autisminblack.org/AIB036.

Identity Development

Damour, Lisa. *The Emotional Lives of Teenagers: Raising Connected, Capable, and Compassionate Adolescents*. New York: Ballantine, 2023.

Helms, Janet E., ed. *Black and White Racial Identity: Theory, Research, and Practice*. Westport, CT: Greenwood Press, 1990.

Henning, Kristin. *The Rage of Innocence: How America Criminalizes Black Youth*. New York: Pantheon, 2021.

Nieto, Leticia. *Beyond Inclusion, Beyond Empowerment: A Developmental Strategy to Liberate Everyone*. Cuetzpalin, 2010.

Orenstein, Gabriel A., and Lindsay Lewis. "Erikson's Stages of Psychosocial Development." StatPearls, November 7, 2022. https://www.ncbi.nlm.nih.gov/books/NBK556096/.

ScienceDirect. "Identity in Childhood and Adolescence." https://www.sciencedirect.com/topics/psychology/identity-development.

Sex Education

Cazalis, Fabienne, Elisabeth Reyes, Séverine Leduc, and David Gourion. "Evidence That Nine Autistic Women Out of Ten Have Been Victims of Sexual Violence." *Frontiers in Behavioral Neruoscience* 16 (April 26, 2022): https://www.frontiersin.org/articles/10.3389/fnbeh.2022.852203/full.

Dame. "Tips for Neurodiverse Dating." July 21, 2022. https://dame.com/tips-for-neurodiverse-dating/.

Loftus, Yolande. "Sexuality in Neurodivergent Individuals." *Autism Parenting Magazine*, May 25, 2022. https://www.autismparentingmagazine.com/autism-sexuality/.

National LGBT Health Education Center. "Neurodiversity and Gender-Diverse Youth: An Affirming Approach to Care." 2020. https://www.lgbtqiahealtheducation.org/wp-content/uploads/2020/08/Neurodiversity-and-Gender-Diverse-Youth_An-Affirming-Approach-to-Care_2020.pdf.

Planned Parenthood. "Sexuality Education for Youth on the Autism Spectrum." https://www.plannedparenthood.org/planned-parenthood-massachusetts/local-training-education/parent-buzz-newsletter/parent-buzz-e-newsletters/sexuality-education-youth-autism-spectrum.

7

PARENTING AT THE EDGE OF UNDERSTANDING

Setting Boundaries with Tech

As someone who grew up playing outside with friends from the neighborhood and reading books, it has been a rude shock to see how much of my kids' lives revolve around technology, including using laptops in school. The lines between play and work are blurred. This discrepancy between our childhoods, the global shifts in our lives, and the ubiquitousness of technology make it challenging to parent. Unfortunately, it also makes it challenging to be a child.

Some of the biggest arguments in our home have been about the use of technology. My children want more time on their devices, and I want them to have less. In conversations with my spouse, trusted friends, and therapist, I wrangle with why I want them to have less. Much of it concerns the stories I tell myself when I see my children at the screen. There are times when practicality and reasonableness inform the metrics I use to determine how much screen time is too much. For instance, I want my kids to contribute to the family, finish schoolwork, and get outside for some fresh air. Screen time that gets in the way of this irks me. There are also times when I spin out and imagine that excessive screen time will inevitably lead to my kids giving up on showers, sustaining themselves on Cheetos, and not moving out of our proverbial basement. Beneath this unhelpful and catastrophic picture of their future is a fear animated by simplistic descriptions of productivity and performance. To not spin out is my work.

If I globalize screen time without unpacking how and what they are doing, I can quickly slip into a rigid stance. One of my children loves to watch old soccer games to improve his game. Another is on the screen to make music. Screen use for learning and creating cannot be equated with the mindless watching of YouTube videos of someone else playing a video game. In our household, we have created different buckets to think about their usage. The buckets include creation, connection, consumption for learning, and consumption for entertainment. We encourage the first three. We do not discourage the last one but think of it like dessert: we want them to be more mindful of the ratios.

While we have never aimed to be perfect, we do want to be consistent. My husband and I want our children to build a healthy relationship with the various technologies by allowing them to learn to self-regulate. We know that we are (hopefully) not moving in with our kids if they go to college or leave home for other adventures. We will not always be there to turn the internet off. They have to learn.

Then there are times we do not feel so reasonable. We find ourselves wanting to set firmer limits and be a guard of their precious attention and time. Part of the reason is that our children struggle to regulate and channel their attention due to ADHD. I sometimes worry that these sites and devices are designed to manipulate their attention; handing a tablet over with unfettered access is setting our kids up unfairly.

Raising two Brown children, we think long and hard about the racism they may encounter in the sites they visit and the games they play. I know I can't shield our kids from all the bad in the world and that they will experience racism. When it is offline on a playground, in a conversation, or on a course assignment, it feels like we can pause, process, and respond appropriately. However, when it happens online, we as parents do not always know it has happened, and our children may not know who is behind a handle, making it more challenging to follow up and process.

I am also concerned that these platforms normalize a narrow definition of acceptability, worth, and beauty. This is one more place in their world where they can be told that they are not enough. Finding a steady stance has been challenging.

The Waters We Swim In

Today, anywhere we look, we can see someone looking at a screen—a smartphone, an iPad, a gaming console, or a laptop. We find screens in schools, where children use iPads as a learning tool. When we check in for appointments, we find a tablet in doctors' offices. We see screens on our appliances—a fridge that can connect you to recipe lists and order groceries. They are even in the most private spaces, like bathrooms. So screens are not just something we seek out and use; they are a part of our environmental landscape.

Our children are called *digital natives*, born into the world of cell phones and tablets. Many have only known a world where broadband internet is readily accessible and may treat it the way we as parents treat utility companies. Some of us parents, meanwhile, are still tourists in this world of digital platforms, consuming the highlights of what it offers with maybe a hope that we might go back to the world as we knew it. On the other hand, most of us have settled in, getting accustomed to the ways of this world and adopting many of its offerings. Regardless of where we are on this spectrum of integration, we know that we are parenting in a time when this technology is omnipresent. This inevitably affects how we parent our BIPOC neurodivergent children.

When our children know nothing but this way of life, it becomes impossible to shield them fully from accessing smartphones, the internet, and video games—and should we even do that? One of the fundamental tasks of childhood, especially in later years, is pulling away from parents to find out more about oneself. For parents, this means letting go and allowing our children more freedom. But, unfortunately, the technology available to our children now speeds up the dance of pulling away and letting go. More so, it adds doubt to how we parent. For instance, we might not consider reading our children's diaries. But should we check their texts and social media? Where is the line between freedom and safety?

Our worries for our children's safety are not random; they are a rightful response to the strategic and disingenuous ways in which technology serves capitalism. Interestingly, the top ten social media technology companies today have products that are free to use yet are raking in combined annual revenue of upwards of $100 billion. How can that be? It may not be an exaggeration to state that they have honed their platforms to monetize our collective attention by understanding our preferences and interests and then selling those to advertisers—*we* are the product they provide to advertisers. In a landscape that is vast, fragmented, and diverse, these companies have concluded that human attention is the gold to be mined. They have created what economist Herbert Simon conceptualized the *attention economy*, with the goal to capture, retain, and exploit it as far as they can. More eyes, more money. Their unprecedented success has been the result of tapping into research on how the human mind works.

And so as business meets and marries psychology to uphold capitalism, we parents are left to figure out the hard parts: What does it mean to give our kids more freedom in digital spaces that are rapidly evolving? When do we give our children these tools? What will our limits look like, and how do we connect with them around these platforms? This is the water they swim in. We as parents need to act as their lifeguards: swim with them, support them in finding safe swim holes and learning how to get out from unpredictable rip currents.

In this chapter, we evaluate the challenges this technology presents and, at the same time, explore the many benefits that same technology has to offer to our children. As therapists, we find evaluating anything through a single lens is limiting and polarizing. We also know multiple factors are at play when parenting in relationship to technology and exploring them all to make informed parenting choices is a luxury most of us do not have.

Parents are doing their best to weigh the pros and the cons for their children, and there are many valid parenting choices around technology. We welcome you to take what resonates and question what doesn't. We get that parenting is hard enough without having to be reprimanded for our choices. As always, this is a no-shame zone.

A Snapchat to Sonic the Hedgehog

He is sitting in his usual spot in the living room, at the edge of our worn-down leather couch, his back straight. His face reveals a scowl. I know instinctively he is playing his favorite game, and I also know that he is not doing as well as he would like. With his rapt attention on the screen, he does not hear my question about food. Taking a deep breath, I repeat myself, louder and a tad bit annoyed. In these moments, I am struggling to not take it personally, that my towering teen is more interested in a screen—I miss my kid. I also swallow my worry that he has been playing for two hours straight. But this is how my autistic son gets to talk to his friend and experience connection. I breathe again and tell him I am setting a timer to wind down for dinner. The timer is a practiced tool that helps transition.

No conversation about parenting is complete without a discussion of video games. From the quaint favorites of yesteryear such as *Pong* and *Pac-Man*, to the Hollywood-quality affairs of today such as *Call of Duty*, they have evolved to become vastly more sophisticated in graphics and storytelling. Yet today's video games are not a monolith. There are arcade games, role-playing games, racing games, simulation games, platformer games, first-person shooters, massively multiplayer online role-playing games, word games, adventure games, real-time strategy games, and many more. They can be played on TVs, game consoles, desktop computers, and smartphones. They can provide entertainment, community building, artistic experiences, and education. And last but not the least, they are played by people for a variety of reasons, such as wanting to get immersed in a storyline, connect with friends, or develop a skill. Finding our footing as parents in this vast world is especially challenging if we did not grow up playing video games. Regardless, our children will come into contact with them, and we have to figure out our stance.

Similarly, social media is also ubiquitous. What's your favorite social media app, parents? Are you the Facebook generation, or have you gotten on the TikTok bandwagon? There is no escaping them, especially since so much of our lives are conducted online. The pandemic made virtual events on social media platforms common. Social media is how we find out about our families from afar, keep up on what is going on in our children's schools, discover interesting events coming to town, and even learn new recipes and dance moves. Parenting today means contending with whether we should give our children access to these platforms and, maybe even more important, identifying the right time to do so. These are not simple questions with easy answers.

In developing our parenting philosophy around technology, one of our first tasks is to wrestle with limits. Many of us can remember a time when we waited till Saturday morning for our favorite television cartoon or needed to run to the library to get on a computer. Our parents never had to think about managing our screen usage to the extent parents today worry about it. Something that was never part of our parent generation's vocabulary is now everywhere: *screen time.*

Guidelines provided by the American Academy of Pediatrics (AAP) state that children under two years of age should not have any screen time and that children between the ages two and five should not consume more than two hours a day. However, there are no known specific guidelines that are informed by the unique needs of neurodivergent children. Families are left to figure out what works best for them. Here we share how some parents think about limit setting when it comes to technology use. Factors like cultural upbringing, family values and makeup, and socioeconomic status can influence how parents think about it.

Perhaps surprisingly, many parents raising neurodivergent children of color do not set limits. Meena's family did not see a need to place strict limits: "We found that without limits, they got bored after a point, and my kids are open with us, so they come and tell us the things they were seeing." Moreover, she saw that the iPad allowed her son to understand math in a way he could not at school. It also allowed him to research areas of interest and increased his confidence: "He felt powerful when he could google something or look up an answer on YouTube."

Arica also did not set many limits, because she saw that technology supported her son's emotional regulation, which then allowed him to connect with the world in different ways. "I gave him my phone from a young age to watch videos. He had access to a phone even before he was potty trained." For many neurodivergent people, the digital world can feel safer than in-person social interactions.

Luisa, who unschools her children, offers this fresh perspective: "I did not think it was right to put a time limit when they are researching something that interests them. It is kind of like if I was reading a book and someone said, 'You have twenty minutes.' I would be frustrated not finishing. Initially, when we needed to do a different activity or go to a doctor's appointment, it was tricky. We were able to find a flow, because I learned to respect when they needed time and trusted they would transition. With neurodivergent kids I see they can get very passionate about certain ideas and they follow the tangents to see where it goes. There's so much learning that happens there."

Deepti's experience speaks to the value in collaborative limit setting: "I used to be extremely rigid around screen time limits. I read the AAP guidelines about the negative impacts excessive screen time can have on children, was surrounded by many parents who felt strongly about it, so I rode along and parented almost blindly around technology, without asking myself what I was so fearful about. My daughter pushed against my rigidity, and seeing how mad my limits made her, I was convinced it was technology that was causing her disproportionate anger, and buckled down harder on tech limits. With each iteration our relationship suffered more.

"In hindsight, I knew better, but my fears got the best of me. Deciding something needed to change, I intentionally soothed my own fears. I decided to try a collaborative approach, and together we decided what was a reasonable time limit. And now if she is in the middle of a game or watching a show at the time that the screen timer beeped, I allow her an extra few minutes to complete it. Seeing me relax has also made her relax and has made our relationship stronger."

Mary's experience also speaks to the importance of children beginning to notice their own limits. She says, "Video games are allowed on weekends, but we do realize our child often uses his computer time during weekdays for games. We decided that he would only get into trouble for that if he was behind on his schoolwork. We think it's important that our child is not relying on us to regulate. We are learning too as parents, regarding the right balance of technology use."

Not all parents feel this way about limits on screen time, of course. Molly talks about how if there are no limits and structure in her house, her child with ADHD will have a meltdown. Kids with ADHD can have a challenging time transitioning between activities. For example, she says, "We do not allow electronics in the morning to ensure a quick transition to school after waking up. We are looser about it on the weekends." Malika echoes this as well, and says a big reason for setting limits in her family is to protect sleep and foster creativity: "The children cannot access the screen one hour before bedtime, even if homework is pending. We are worried that there will be a propensity to only be on it. But, on the other hand, we have found that limiting the amount of screen usage has encouraged our children to be more creative with their time."

For better or worse, the struggle with technology does not end with figuring out limits. Parents today need to think about many other aspects of technology use. We also need to weigh the benefits and measure the potential harm.

What brings me joy is witnessing their growth, sharing in their joys, celebrating their success, encouraging their curiosity and imagination, getting goosebumps when they show off new skills.
—Mumbi

Benefits of Social Media and Video Games

We know Facebook can be a reliable way to connect with family and friends in faraway places in the world—how else can we find out if our second cousin has had a baby? This ability to connect far and wide is also true for young people. Many teens have connected with long-distance friends and even found new friends online. In fact, for some kids, these relationships stay purely online. Though our neurodivergent youth often use their devices more for entertainment than for social interactions, social media can be a way for them to expand their opportunities for connection and to try on and practice social communication.

Online interactions can be especially supportive for autistic kids, for whom face-to-face social interactions can be tiring and provoke anxiety. Social media platforms can ease navigating social subtexts in large gatherings and make it easier to distinguish between a joke and what is serious, especially with the use of tone tags, which communicate intention and emotion behind a text. Technology like this also provides much-needed time to process before responding, which real-life interactions do not afford. They can be a safer space, as they give opportunities to socialize without adhering to neurotypical rules of conduct and socialization, which insist that we make eye contact or quickly interpret subtext in a conversation. Meena shares that accessing platforms like Discord has alleviated the stress of social interactions for her autistic son.

Social media also offers bubbles of communities related to various aspects of young people's identities. Some of our favorites include How to ADHD on YouTube by Jessica McCabe and Paige Layle's autism and ADHD TikTok channel. Malika shares how her child has also found communities on Discord pertaining to their interests in music and specific video games: "We can see the benefits of connecting with friends around shared interests. While we are aware of the pitfalls of Discord, we have addressed this in our tech contract* that the new servers they join need to be vetted by us."

Less often discussed is the fact that social media can provide alternative ways to engage in social justice movement spaces, especially for those youth with sensory processing challenges. There are opportunities to limit interactions, turn down sounds, and take breaks.

When it comes to video games, for many neurodivergent youth, gaming offers a safe reprieve from the traumatizing outside world. Additionally, video games are an essential way for many neurodivergent kids to experience autonomy, connection, and competence, all components of self-determination. For many of our kids, the world outside moves fast and is often unpredictable. Video games provide a predictable environment, where they can experience control over their choices. All of us deserve this, our kids especially so.

Mumbi shares that she can see the confidence in her son increasing as he delves into the world of technology. "He is our tech expert in terms of any electronics or technology. He has dissected and put back together multiple forms of electronics. I don't have to teach him anything really. He teaches me everything."

One nine-year-old's observation on video games confirms how games give children an opportunity to be more autonomous. This child told us, "I like playing my football video game because I get to choose my team and decide what team I play against." Another child spoke about his love of *Minecraft* and the opportunity it gave him to challenge himself while playing with others. This ten-year-old boy shared, "I love *Minecraft* because it is exciting and challenging and I get to play with my friends." Luisa also found many benefits in how her son played

---

* A *tech contract* is an agreement that many parents make with their children when they're given access to an electronic device, as a way to discuss the purpose of the device and the expectations for using it and staying safe online.

using technology. Playing *Minecraft* "collaboratively with a few known friends was a big learning opportunity that allowed my son and me to talk about emotions and build emotional regulation skills."

Once we delve behind the knee-jerk reaction that video games are only mindless entertainment, we find many less obvious benefits. Video games normalize making mistakes. Many kids on the neurodivergent spectrum are repeatedly told by teachers, peers, and others that they are not getting something right, which can provoke discomfort in trying new things. A video game is designed such that you improve by making mistakes. It gives neurodivergent kids a space to not have to get it right all the time and can increase their frustration tolerance, reinforcing the value of practice and effort.

Video games, especially those that require strategizing and communication, can offer safer spaces for neurodivergent children to socialize, utilizing asynchronous communication. As a result, it can be a site where our kids find community.

Many neurodivergent children can struggle with hand-eye coordination and fine motor skills. Using controllers while tracking what is happening on the screen can improve these skills. Additionally, video games provide education benefits for neurodivergent kids by supporting math and language skills.

Maybe the biggest benefit is that digital platforms and video games give us an opportunity to connect with our children. Raffael Boccamazzo of Take This encourages parents to think about video games as another form of play and to be curious about their child's interest in a game. We think this can be applied to their interests on social media too! When we go to a park, we follow our kids around as they try the slide and the swings. We explore with them. We caution them of things that may be unsafe. We watch who they are playing with and offer timely interventions when they are hurt. Why should the tech playground be any different?

When we spend time exploring digital worlds with our children, we can begin to understand the value they offer them. In addition, it gives us an opportunity to know our children more by asking them what they are taking away from a particular storyline. For example, how are they feeling about themselves while chatting with others? Can they tell that what is happening in the storyline is not real life?

Valento exemplifies this interest in his child's world. "Half the time, I don't know what he is talking about when he talks to me, but I try to keep eye contact and be engaged. Sometimes I would ask him what something means, knowing that I am opening myself up for a forty-five-minute explanation." Luisa also speaks about showing curiosity in her children's digital world. She says her kids sometimes invited her into the games, especially when they were younger. "I love to hear the stories of what they're building, and they show me what they're building. They know I care about what they're doing in the game. I want to listen and learn, and I want them to share with me. With my kids, it was a great bonding experience. You know, we got to play together and they wanted me to join. They didn't care that I was terrible. It was more about sharing their joy." She delights in their ability and laughs that they were often teaching her.

Deepti found that getting curious about her daughter's online world brought more connection between them. "When I noticed that screen time was causing a lot of distress for me, I actually tried to show more interest in her online world, sat by her, and just delighted in her play, noticing her strengths: her creativity, speed, and knowledge. I asked her if she would teach me. She loves this connection time, and now she routinely asks me to sit by her and watch her play. She would also get hungry sometimes while playing, and I indulged in the request to feed her. Feeding her while she played helped me to reclaim a nurturing cultural practice as I saw how such little acts of nurture traveled straight to my daughter's heart. Now we have many sweet relational rituals around tech, which probably produce more dopamine than the tech itself. At the end of the day, all that matters to me is I now have my daughter back."

Potential Harms When Engaging with Tech

With so many benefits, we can miss some of the more concerning aspects of these technologies. The following section gets into the challenges they pose for our kids and shares how parents have faced these in their homes.

Mental Health

Our neurodivergent kids are already predisposed to experiencing mental health struggles. Data confirms that depression and anxiety are present at a higher rate in this group. Specifically, autistic youth report higher rates of depression, anxiety, and suicidal ideation. Children of color, too, are more likely to struggle with their mental health. The neurodiversity paradigm and an intersectional analysis (as discussed in chapter 1, p. 5) teach us that these higher rates are not a result of individual makeup but rather a manifestation of living in a society that fails to affirm differences that fall outside the standards of normal described in earlier chapters.

Given that our children are more predisposed to mental health struggles, here is what to know about how social media can make it worse. To begin, there is no evidence of causation, meaning we can't definitively point to social media as the reason for mental health decline. However, since the 2000s, teens' mental health has been declining. One study correlated the rise in smartphones, social media, and gaming with declining mental health. More recently, a whistleblower leaked an internal Facebook document showing increased depression in teenage girls who use the Facebook subsidiary Instagram. Whether the emergence and use of social media are directly causing increased mental health concerns is not clear.

While our kids can find community and supportive ways to socialize on social media, these apps can also be a source of distress, as our kids can be bullied and othered. Because this new media has a ubiquitous presence in our lives, what happens online can feel so much like real life it is sometimes hard to tell the difference. Meena talks about her son's experience on Discord and the mental anguish it created: "Someone tricked him and egged him on to get mad and then recorded his voice. This person then put my child getting mad on YouTube. This freaked him out, especially since YouTube would not take it down. This was an excellent lesson about how tech can be used in harmful ways for him."

Social media can aggravate mental health concerns because it distorts our self-concept, which is often constructed through our perceptions of ourselves and how others see us. A healthy sense of self is protective against mental health issues such as depression and anxiety. We see social media sometimes acting as a fun-house mirror, distorting how our kids can view themselves, which is troublesome when they are in a phase of life of constructing who they are. And social media is another place where neurodivergent children of color are exposed to messages from the world around them that they are not enough and are defective.

Social media can also promote unhealthy levels of comparison and a fear of missing out. While it is human nature to compare ourselves to others, these platforms exacerbate the downsides of this urge by creating situations where we compare ourselves to *thousands* of people and end up with unrealistic expectations for our lives. In addition, curated and filtered photos create an unrealistic reality, showcasing only the shiniest, most engaging, or most severe aspects of anyone's life. Research confirms not only that people on the sites tend to compare more but also that these comparisons lead to decreased self-concept and lower self-esteem.

Sleep is another aspect of mental health that can be impacted by the use of technologies such as social media. At the most fundamental level, sleep deprivation or poor-quality sleep affects our ability to feel good about ourselves. Many of our neurodivergent children already struggle with sleep; 50 to 80 percent of autistic youth struggle with sleep disturbances. Add to that co-occurring mental health issues and sleep can suffer more.

Some features of social media that can meddle with sleep include the availability of unlimited content, advertisement engagement, constant notifications, and exposure to excessive blue light from screens. Blue light is part of the visible light spectrum that the human eye can see. In addition to sunlight, blue light is also found in digital screens. Exposure to blue light outside of normal daylight hours can disrupt circadian rhythms.

Cyberbullying

A specific way in which mental health is impacted online is through cyberbullying. Like bullying offline, cyberbullying includes a misuse of power over others online through mean commentary, spreading of rumors, and sharing inappropriate information or images and videos with intent to humiliate and ostracize someone. Unlike real-life bullying, cyberbullying occurs via digital spaces like chat, email, social media, and forums. Here are the critical differences between cyberbullying and bullying in real life:

- A comment online is often permanent and unremovable.
- Cyberbullying can be done anonymously, making interventions more challenging.
- Cyberbullying can be invisible to authority figures.

- Since kids have phones and tend to be hyperconnected, finding a way to escape a cyberbully is even more challenging.

Cyberbullying impacts mental health by increasing feelings of sadness, despair, anger, and humiliation. Many kids feel like they have nowhere to turn. Cyberbullying also impacts schoolwork and relationships with friends and family. For some, cyberbullying can even lead to self-harm and suicide.

Concerns about bullying led Hana to wait till her son was older to let him start gaming and using the chat function. To address cyberbullying in their household, Valento says, "I've spoken to my kid about how online there are going to be people who are nice and playful but with that, there are also 'trolls' who will say and do very mean things in-game just because they think it's funny or you beat them. I always tell him that it's online, and these people are just a power button away from never talking down to you. So if someone is bothering you, just turn the game off or join another lobby."

Body Check

If it feels accessible at this time, we encourage you to plant your seat firmly where you are, or if you are standing, find your feet solidly rooted on the earth. Stretching your body taller, take an in-breath and an out-breath slowly. Take a few moments to notice yourself, your breath, and your emotions.

Attention Manipulation

Imagine sitting in a coffee shop, reading the news on your smartphone and slowly sipping your cappuccino. Out of the corner of your eye, you catch a glimpse of a red-velvet cupcake. The anticipation of the sweet dessert takes you away from the news, and suddenly you are engaged in an internal battle.

Or, imagine you are at work and the company has announced year-end bonuses for the employee who makes the most sales. You feel more motivated to get your reports in and pursue pathways to increase your sales outcomes.

These are examples of dopamine in action. Dopamine is a chemical neurotransmitter, a messenger between the brain and the rest of the body. Once endearingly called the feel-good chemical, recent discoveries in neuroscience have shown that dopamine is not about pleasure itself but connected to the *anticipation* of pleasure. Dopamine is connected to our movement, how we learn, what activities we partake in, and even our propensity to be addicted. For our purposes, we focus on how dopamine is connected to the reward and reinforcement system.

In his work with mice, psychologist, B. F. Skinner illustrated the reward-reinforcement mechanism. Ultimately, when rewards are intermittent, mice continue to engage in the desired behavior. The anticipation of a reward releases more dopamine. Understanding this has been crucial for technology companies to manipulate user attention and behavior.

When people anticipate a reward, the brain releases dopamine to engage in behaviors that might yield more of this neurotransmitter. A reward can be any number of things, including but not limited to a raise, a piece of cake, or sex. Once the reward is attained, the brain then releases more dopamine, reinforcing the connection between action and reward. This helps people learn and change their behaviors so that they experience more of the rewards.

By coupling the understanding of how dopamine works with intermittent variable rewards, social media companies are able to capture our attention, which is the goal. They capitalize on our sense of anticipation when we open up the app. Each time we hit refresh or scroll through, we do not know what we can expect in our mailboxes, social media feeds, or texting apps, so we keep coming back for more. Seeing that a friend has *hearted* something we share or someone prominent has retweeted our messages, or that our TikTok videos are getting a lot of views, is satisfying and pleasurable. More important, it motivates us to go back. It's an effect that can have a particularly negative effect on neurodivergent users—or, at the very least, make it challenging for them to engage with social networks without harm.

Current research confirms a connection between dopamine and neurodivergence. Specifically, dopamine can be in short supply for those who are neurodivergent. We know that lower dopamine supplies can impact emotional regulation, impulsivity, executive functioning tasks, control of movement, and processing speed. While some research associates lower levels of dopamine with autism and Tourette's, more is known about the connection between dopamine and ADHD, so let's consider that example specifically.

We know that the hallmark features of ADHD include impulsivity, distractibility, hyperfocus, and novelty seeking, and that these traits are connected to lower dopamine levels. When channeling attention is already a challenge and there are daily struggles to maintain focus on necessary but uninteresting things (think schoolwork), social media can become a cruel vice. While social media does not cause ADHD, one study found that constant stimulation stemming from these platforms decreased attention span, exacerbating the symptoms of ADHD.

Min, a parent to a biracial teenager with ADHD, talks about her concerns: "I worry that social media provides the opportunities to quickly click, or watch a ninety-second video, or even a three-minute TikTok video, which seems to only sustain his attention for a very short time. He gets bored and seeks instant gratification and immediate results. So this need for immediate gratification I am concerned about is teaching him less patience in working towards a bigger goal."

Persuasive Design Tactics

More generally, social media and video games use a technique called *persuasive design*, which most simply is taking learnings from psychology to design products that are more interactive and engaging. As with dopamine manipulation, there is a darker side. In the context of video games, persuasive techniques that encourage negative behaviors are called *dark patterns*. But regardless of the name, their end goal is to maintain user attention and increase revenue. From manipulating with clickbait to requiring daily sign-ins to preserve the capabilities of their in-game avatar, these tactics profit off our children's vulnerabilities around executive functioning and impulse control.

Ultimately, some of these design tactics remove consent and choice from our kids. For a child who may not experience competency in school and who is experiencing competency in video games by building up an avatar, the possibility of losing this avatar unless they play daily is borderline cruel. As parents we are left to deal with the consequences of these design tactics.

Here are some examples of persuasive designs that are commonly used in many social media sites and video games:

Social Media

- *Infinite scroll:* This allows us to seamlessly scroll through posts or articles without clicking on pages. As a result, we are provided a constant stream of content, some we never asked for. It hooks our attention and compromises our ability to make a choice about whether we want to stay on a site. A decision to leave, then, takes tremendous willpower, which slowly diminishes as the day goes by. Many children stay up well into the night scrolling through, forgoing sleep, because the content keeps coming. One parent tells us she spends inordinate amounts of time on Twitter late at night and can't stop herself, even though she needs to go to bed so she can wake up to send her kids off to school.
- *Push notifications:* A buzz or a chime alerts us to incoming mail, texts, updates to our feed, etc. The alert has trained us to tune into our devices with the anticipation of what might be on the other end. While we might not have any intention of going to the platform, a *ding* pulls us in regardless. The consequence is that we end up diverting our attention and possibly burning the new recipe we are trying.
- *Streaks:* This design feature tracks the number of days in a row a person spends on a platform. The site rewards a user for maintaining a streak, which is designed to keep the user returning to the app, which then, coupled with infinite scroll, means that they are spending hours every day on the platform. Unfortunately, for some teens, breaking the streak can cause severe anxiety. One child, not yet a teenager, told us that he felt stressed if he did not log on to his soccer game every day!
- *Echo chambers:* Platforms can use algorithms to recommend topics and conversations based on a user's profile and interests. While this may seem innocuous on the surface, it limits critical thinking and exposure to diverse opinions and ideas. Algorithm-based content takes a turn for the worse when high-engagement conversations get more airtime. Often these topics are controversial and extreme. They push users to engage more with the topic, thereby increasing the outrage users collectively feel. When we share the outrage, it oils the reward reinforcement in our brains.

Ultimately, we are ushered to the extremes of a conversation, a place where not much nuance and authenticity exists.

- *Clickbait:* Some of these aforementioned techniques are arguably evolutions of the "clickbait" techniques popularized by Buzzfeed. Now an official word in the Oxford English Dictionary, it was introduced by blogger Jay Geiger in 2006 to describe the use of web links intentionally designed to induce people to click on them. Titles like "5 Things Parents Need to Know" or "The Top 10 Kitchen Items Every Home Must Have" promote clicks, drawing users to pages littered with advertisements that increase the site's likelihood of generating revenue. This encourages us to engage with content we did not intend to. In the time of fake news, it becomes increasingly challenging to ensure that our children are not clicking on articles that promote untruths.

Video Games

- *Psychological dark pattern:* This tactic exploits loss aversion, with the understanding that human beings do not want to lose what they have acquired and built. For instance, this strategy encourages players to continue to return to the game so that the avatars and advances they have made are not lost due to inactivity.
- *Temporal dark pattern:* Like "streaks" for social media, this design requires players to sign in every day to preserve the strengths and abilities they've developed in-game over an extended period of time. Instead of being in control of their own time and schedules, players become pressured to play according to the game's schedule. As such, players are made to experience stress and despair if they do not sign in on time.
- *Monetary dark pattern:* Some games give players the opportunity to pay to skip parts that are too hard or uninteresting. Or time-limited features are introduced that require players to spend money to use them, creating urgency and scarcity. Another example is *loot boxes*, sealed containers that players earn through playing, or outright purchasing, that hold in-game upgrades. Their contents are random and unknown until they're opened, which is why they have been compared to gambling: because the player has invested potentially real money and has no control over what

they will receive. These game mechanics have evolved into today's *gacha* games, in which the central game mechanic is spending in-game currency (earned via game time or bought with real money) to receive random upgrades and other in-game items.

- *Social dark pattern:* The tactic encourages players with rewards for bringing in more players to the game, similar to a pyramid scheme or multi-level marketing. More so, games that employ this strategy rely on the effects of peer pressure and the fear of missing out to get the user to spend more time on the game.

Fighting these tactics is hard enough as an adult. Does knowing this change how you think about how your child uses these platforms? How do these aspects of social media line up with your family's values?

Default Whiteness

Initially, social media sites were conceptualized to bring people together and share aspects of their lives. Unfortunately, this noble idea ended up mirroring, upholding, and proliferating structural inequities in our society. They are encoded with the biases of their creators and act as another vehicle for perpetuating White-dominant culture, where the beliefs and culture of White people are considered standard.

To understand why, we consider the role of algorithms, which in the social media context, facilitate sorting data so that it enables a particular type of experience for the user. These algorithms ensure that the puppy videos and the newest dances appear on your feed. The machine learns what will engage you more and feeds it back.

However, algorithms are not free of bias, because people write them. Our lived experiences, including the biases we carry (positive or negative), shape what we create (a good example is this book). As consumers at the other end of the creative process, we are shaped by the ideas, beliefs, and people we are exposed to. While there is more representation recently of different lived experiences, most social media sites have been created and shaped by White, cisgender, nondisabled men.

This means that social media may expose our children to problematic and, at worst, dangerous ideas about what is "normal." For instance, a report conducted by Common Sense Media on YouTube revealed that 62 percent of the videos watched by children under the age of eight had no BIPOC representation. Given that media representation significantly shapes how children of color feel about themselves, the lack of exposure to positive representations of ethnic racial communities is concerning.

Unfortunately, these algorithms also influence and impact the guidelines around what is acceptable and appropriate. And in doing so, it inevitably pushes a set of norms, values, and beliefs. These guidelines, whether intended or not, can perpetuate Whiteness and other forms of supremacy, including misogyny, toxic masculinity, homophobia, transphobia, and US centrism. For example, the same Common Sense Media report states that "videos from the gaming YouTuber VuxVux contained stereotypes including mocking African American and Latino accents and aggressive behavior centered around race. In one example of a video, titled 'Trolling ROBLOX ODERS as Admin' the main character, who is White, taunts and chases a Black female character and kills her with a sword. Notably, the YouTuber also called other BIPOC individuals his 'slaves' in this video."

And since the default is not just Whiteness but also neurotypicality, our neurodivergent children of color can experience a particularly strong sense of not-enoughness. When the world already tells them that they are different and not good enough, it takes extra time and effort to seek out content creators with different identities and perspectives to build an experience beyond what is readily available. Speaking to this, Hana tells us, "I used to worry quite often that he would be absorbed into a White perspective, as this world most certainly centers Whiteness as the default. However, I also take a lot of care; especially now that I teach him at home in a state where critical race theory has been banned, I have the opportunity of telling an unwhitewashed version of history as well as how it ties into our current lives and modern affairs."

We just wonder what these platforms would be like if those who live at various intersections created products for those of us who do as well, especially since 15 to 20 percent of the US population is neurodivergent. We believe that our social locations matter.

Here again, the labor falls on parents to work with their kids to find content producers and games that speak to our cultural and racial locations. Taking on this giant by ourselves can feel daunting. However, there are things we can do to combat Whiteness in our social media feeds, and a comprehensive list at the end of this chapter covers strategies for families.

Video games can also be complicit in perpetuating Whiteness. As with social media, most video games are created by those identifying as White; according to the International Game Developers Association, they make up over 80 percent of video game creators worldwide. Representations of BIPOC characters are often missing or limited. When included, Latinx characters are often depicted as drug dealers and gangbangers, Asian girls are hypersexualized, and Blacks are shown as violent. Games can also normalize a settler-colonial ethos of conquest, the subjugation of minoritized peoples, and the erasure of cultures.

Recognizing that video games can support self-identity development and a sense of belonging, an absence of BIPOC characters as heroes in a story is distressing. All kids need to see themselves reflected in the games they play. As JC Lau, a game producer, states, it is vital for those who hold marginalized identities to see themselves as heroes of a story, which allows people to feel empowered and more immersed in the storyline.

Normalizing Racism

The American Academy of Pediatrics states, "Racism is a social determinant of health that has a profound impact on the health status of children, adolescents, emerging adults, and their families." With children spending more time on digital platforms, we are right to be concerned that their exposure to racism online may compound the racialized stress they are already dealing with in real life.

The racial discrimination Black and Brown kids may experience online includes being excluded, made fun of, humiliated, or threatened for their racial identity. They may encounter racist images, videos, and text, including racial slurs, whether sent directly to them or shared more generally in a digital space they frequent.

Even though we may have put safeguards on digital platforms to prevent our children from experiencing harmful content, protecting them from encountering racism online is incredibly challenging. And part of the challenge with some of our children may be that they do not recognize the words or images they are experiencing as racism—and yet the body registers the harm. More so, some of our children may take racist suggestions literally and/or internalize them. Therefore, we as parents need to have conversations with our kids about racism—why it is wrong, and what to do when they see or hear something harmful—and be available to process with them when they come to us with what they have encountered.

Min talks about how she has approached these conversations: "I think racism online is definitely a problem. There is so much misinformation out there about race, ethnicity, culture, etc. However, I have also seen there is also a lot to learn online about feminist movements, cultural appropriation, and many other topics. To help my kids tell the difference, I've spoken to my children about my values regarding culture, race, ethnicity, and we talk about this on a weekly basis. I make my expectations clear around proper behavior online, and I also often coach them about improper behavior. This I do, not only regarding race, but regarding negative comments, gossiping, etc. My children know to run as fast as they can, figuratively, from racist comments online."

Deepti's experience reminds us that these platforms are here to stay and joining our kids in their interest is essential to counteracting dominant narratives. "The YouTuber culture has really gotten to my daughter. The fascination with watching someone else play a game is something I will never understand. But I have had to learn that this is the culture within which we are raising our children, and if something catches their interest, it isn't their fault. It is simply practically impossible for me to screen everything before my daughter watches it, so I do the next best thing. I join her when I can, or stay close to listen in when I can, to enter her world with her. I may never truly appreciate those YouTubers, but seeing my daughter crack up with laughter because she was tickled by a joke is worth all my trying. I also make it a point to talk to her about whatever we watch—to learn about her interpretation and reaction to it and to help her make sense of it. One of her episodes once contained some internalized racism by a youth of color. We talked about it and why it was problematic. I'm sure we will have to have many such conversations before it truly hits home, but this was an important start."

Today many video games are multiplayer and socially interactive, including popular games such as *Fortnite*, *League of Legends*, and *Call of Duty*. Players chat and talk to each other as they play. And like any site, in real life or online, where human interaction occurs, there is a possibility that these interpersonal communications during video game play can turn negative and ugly. Part of the reason for this is that people who do not know each other, under the protection of pseudonyms, are brought together. Anonymity and access create the conditions for abusive behaviors. While many do find these interactions mostly pleasant, there have also been alarming stories of people being exposed to vitriol.

Hana shares an incident that happened to her child: "There was once where he was playing on the [Playstation 4] in the living room, and I was at my desk station to do some late-night work, and he was playing with the Oculus and in some sort of AR [alternative reality] playroom where he could interact with other players also in the same online room. I heard some random player, another child by the sound of the voice, who just decided to throw out the *n*-word. I immediately jumped up from my seat and started yelling, 'WHAT DID THEY JUST SAY?' (It was rather dramatic, come to think of it.) The second I said that, the other player heard and started running away off-screen and then mysteriously disappeared from the online room. At that moment, I realized they could listen to me and that my son had the mic and headset enabled, to which we then disabled it and set down firm ground rules about playing in online spaces like that again. Not just because of the exposure to racism or to have slurs normalized, but I'm far more worried about what encountering these types of people online will incur. Being on social media for work, I have often seen stories of people swatting BIPOC.* I may have scared one user off, but who's to say another, more intrepid and more aggressive, will not be next? This is not a world where we have the privilege of not thinking about the worst-case scenario. So, if my kid is going to be playing online, there will be hard rules on who he can interact with on it."

Body Check

Bring your hands together in a handshake. As they make contact, explore the sensations of temperature and pressure. What feelings arise as you connect with yourself?

Wise Engagement with Tech

We are parenting at the edge of understanding our relationship to technology, and the reality is we can't escape the digital world. While we have offered you some insights into the inner workings of these

* *Swatting* is making hoax calls to send armed police to a fabricated crisis situation.

companies, we want to propose a wise engagement with tech that brings a *both-and* approach, one that encourages holding complexity and nuance.

We have pointed to some aspects of social media and video games that require more thought and consideration. Navigating these land mines is tricky in any family. With our children, who are more likely to take things literally, be bullied, or have challenges with impulsivity, there is added complexity. We may have to have these conversations repeatedly. We may have to talk about it in chunks. We may have to get creative.

However, we would be remiss without acknowledging that globally stigmatizing and problematizing digital engagement is ableist. The internet provides a way to bypass the demands of in-person engagement and offers opportunities to those who are disabled to learn, play, emotionally regulate, and remain connected. Additionally, some of our kids are also trans, gay, immigrants, and of religious minorities. Finding communities that host these intersections or, at the very least, support the complexity of our identities can be hard to do in our immediate neighborhoods; as such, connecting online becomes vital to the very human need to experience belonging.

It is ableist to attach moral judgment to how the internet is used and what relationships they develop through this medium. Speaking to this shame we impose on tech use, Luisa offers this: "Why does it have to be shameful that we use technology? It's something that we can use to access information, and we use it to connect with people, and it gives us opportunities that we didn't have before. Instead of shaming someone for using so much technology, let's look at the why and what is happening in our lives that push us toward technology."

In the spirit of finding a balance, arriving at a more nuanced approach, we offer the following questions for reflection to support your process in developing your philosophy regarding digital platforms.

We offer some suggestions on the following page for how to navigate this world with your children. As always, we encourage you to rely on your family values and other guiding compasses in making informed decisions about how to keep your children safe and healthy online.

Safety Online

- Install parental controls to block specific sites and/or filter content.
- Teach them never to share passwords with anyone.
- Talk to your kids about your role as a safety manager and explain that occasionally you will be surveying their accounts.
- Talk to your kids about what is OK to share online. In some families, sharing about an upcoming vacation might not be OK. As parents, think through what you are comfortable with and model that.
- Help them identify who they should turn to if faced with unsavory content, bullying, and/or confusion.

Setting Limits

- Determine the amount of screen time collaboratively (depending on your child's age, both chronological and developmental), noting that this will change as they grow.
- Set up computers in more public areas in the home.
- Limit screen usage before bedtime to protect their sleep.

Content

- Speak to your kids about who they are following on social media and what video games they are playing.
- Support them in finding diverse voices from various social locations, and emphasize the value of expanding what information they are exposed to if they are not already.
- Share interesting things (age and developmentally appropriate) you are reading and seeing that disrupt the culture of Whiteness, patriarchy, and ableism.
- Join them as much as possible as they explore these worlds.
- Support your children in trusting their gut if something does not feel right. Encourage them to share if something they see or hear does not sit well.
- Validate their feelings and continue affirming who they are and the various intersections they live at.
- Find support for yourself to process your feelings so that you may be more present to attend to theirs.

Reflection Questions

About Yourself

- What are the benefits and challenges you notice regarding social media and video games for you?
- Are there parts of your child's life that are provoking distress that technology is soothing?
- What are your biases about technology?
- What ideas do you have about what social engagement should look like? Where does that come from?
- What does an empowered and mindful approach to technology look like?

About Your Child

- What benefits and problems do you see social media, or video games, causing in your child's life?
- How are these platforms beneficial to your kids specifically?
- Is this impacting their schoolwork?
- Is this impacting time with family?
- Is this a way of managing anxiety?
- Is this a way to communicate with peers?
- Is it an impulse control issue?

The digital world is neither bad nor good. It is neither helpful nor unhelpful. We know there is a relationship between technology and attention and that digital platforms are intended to have us all spend more time there, as there is a profit motive to do so. Your child may struggle with channeling their attention judiciously. Therefore, we invite you to consider your child, their developmental readiness, and your family values when understanding your child's relationship with digital platforms. It is about accepting that this relationship will change, as most relationships do, and being adaptable and flexible in your position. For example, one parent may not want to give their child a phone at ten and may later change their mind when the child turns thirteen. All of this is to say that there is no script. We are learning as we are parenting. There are no directors to guide us through this, giving us lines from behind the stage. So in the spirit of *The show must go on*, we must be open to new information.

As we close, we return to the experience of a parent who found her way to a more balanced approach. Says Luisa, "With my daughter, she was my first and I was a little concerned. I was walking into new territory. We were hesitant to give her an iPad—at the time she was seven. But then I found this reading app—reading was a bit challenging for her—which read out to you. Also, we loved reading out loud and reading to each other, but I wasn't always available to read aloud to her. So for her to have the joy of independent reading was great. She used it to also watch shows. Once we began engaging with it, it was not so scary anymore.

"With my son, we had a really hard time in his early years. There were a lot of health concerns. We did not know he had sensory issues. He used the iPad to regulate in a space to be present, while still being in a zone that was comfortable and safe for him. This was really helpful, because it got us through doctor's appointments, got us through field trips. I saw that the iPad was helpful to him, like he was able to join us in different spaces that maybe wouldn't have been accessible to him without it. And that made a huge difference with me. Just being like, *I'm totally comfortable with like this. This works for us.*"

Resources for Deeper Understanding

Ableism

Harrison, Greta. "The Importance of Keeping Teens with Disabilities Safe on Social Media." *Mighty*, May 31, 2023. https://themighty.com/2019/11/teens-disabilities-social-media-safety/.

Mental Health

Heid, Markham. "We Need to Talk About Kids and Smartphones." *Time*, October 10, 2017, https://time.com/4974863/kids-smartphones-depression/.

Knorr, Caroline. "Five Ways Social Media Can Be Good for Teens." *Washington Post*, March 19, 2018. https://www.washingtonpost.com/news/parenting/wp/2018/03/19/5-ways-social-media-can-be-good-for-teens/.

Ra, Chaelin K., et al., "Association of Digital Media Use with Subsequent Symptoms of Attention-Deficit/Hyperactivity Disorder Among Adolescents," *JAMA* 320, no. 3 (2018): 255–263. http://doi.org/10.1001/jama.2018.8931.

Rodgers, Anni Layne. "ADHD Brains on Screens: Decoding a Complicated Relationship," *ADDitude*, April 28, 2023. https://www.additudemag.com/screen-time-video-game-technology-dependence-adhd/.

Rogers, Kristen. "Children Under 10 Are Using Social Media. Parents Can Help Them Stay Safe Online." CNN Health, October 18, 2021. https://www.cnn.com/2021/10/18/health/children-social-media-apps-use-poll-wellness/index.html.

Twenge, Jean M. "Have Smartphones Destroyed a Generation?" *Atlantic*, September 2017. https://www.theatlantic.com/magazine/archive/2017/09/has-the-smartphone-destroyed-a-generation/534198/.

Race

Brown, Melissa, Samantha Elizondo, and Rashawn Ray. "Combating Racism on Social Media: 5 Key Insights on Bystander Intervention." Brookings, December 1, 2021. https://www.brookings.edu/blog/how-we-rise/2021/12/01/combating-racism-on-social-media-5-key-insights-on-bystander-intervention/.

Edwards, Lynne, April Edwards Kontostathis, and Christina Fisher. "Cyberbullying, Race/Ethnicity and Mental Health Outcomes: A Review of the Literature," *Media and Communication* 14, no. 3 (2016):71–78. https://doi.org/10.17645/mac.v4i3.525.

Gassam Asare, Janice. "Does TikTok Have a Race Problem?" *Forbes*, April, 14 2020. https://www.forbes.com/sites/janicegassam/2020/04/14/does-tiktok-have-a-race-problem/?sh=646d0b6d3260.

Screen Time

Cherkin, Emily. *The Screentime Solution: A Judgment-Free Guide to Becoming a Tech-Intentional Family*. Austin, TX: Greenleaf, 2024.

Jiang, JingJing. *How Teens and Parents Navigate Screen Time and Device Distractions*. Pew Research Center, August 22, 2018. https://www.pewresearch.org/internet/wp-content/uploads/sites/9/2018/08/PI_2018.08.22_teens-screentime_FINAL.pdf.

Keizer, Kenly. "The Pros and Cons of Screen Time for Kids with ASD." *Autism Parenting Magazine*, August 5, 2021. https://www.autismparentingmagazine.com/screen-time-kids-with-asd/.

Rideout, Victoria, and Michael B. Robb. "The Common Sense Census: Media Use by Tweens and Teens." Common Sense Media, 2019. https://www.commonsensemedia.org/sites/default/files/research/report/2019-census-8-to-18-key-findings-updated.pdf.

PART III

RELATING TO THE WORLD OUTSIDE

8

THE HALLS OF MEDICINE

Navigating Medical Systems

Around the time our child was six, we began to see some behaviors at home that caught us off guard. We noticed increasingly unresolvable tantrums and difficulties with transitioning from one activity to the next. One particular episode led us to begin working with a psychologist, which eventually led to another assessment. It is during this time we learned that our child is profoundly gifted and has ADHD. As most parents do when they learn something about their child, we (meaning mostly me) delved headfirst into researching everything we could about ADHD. Sadly, so much of what I read was about fixing my child.

A thing I started saying to people was that I felt sad and that I worried about my child reaching his potential. I had framed it in my head as an either/or. Giftedness was a blessing and ADHD was a curse. But looking back now, maybe it was really my own sadness and loss I was also experiencing, thinking back to that little girl, newly immigrated, placed in a special education class and told I was broken. I can't quite separate my child's struggles and mine.

In a family where we have medicated ourselves for everything else, my husband and I had charged conversations about medications as a supportive intervention. We hemmed and hawed, and before trying medications, we decided to try some natural alternatives. First, we tried to get our child to meditate. Yes, we really believed that a good dose of pranayama in the mornings could help our hyperactive and inattentive child reorganize his brain structure. It is both laughable and not so much. It is in retrospect sad to me that we were so much in denial. The meditation lasted a day. Then I read up on diets as a possibility of cause and cure. We asked our child to become gluten free. And to his credit, he complied with all that was asked of him. We convinced ourselves that being gluten free improved his focus. Maybe it did a little, but in the grand scheme of things, I am not sure it made any difference.

Eventually, we came around to medications. But along the way, we asked ourselves, Is our motivation to medicate so that our kid can fit into the systems at large? *At the same time, we asked,* If ADHD is a structural and chemical difference in the brain, should we not medicate, as we would with any other condition? If we do not provide medications to help with his focus, then are we not setting him up for success? Then again, whose definition of success? What are we focused on here—wellness or functioning? *These were the questions that animated our discussions.*

It is natural as parents to call on the pediatrician or family doctor to help us understand what is going on with our child when we are concerned. We want to know how to better support our children. We want to help them feel better, whether we're taking them for well checks, a fractured arm after falling from the jungle gym, or something more perplexing such as an aversion to certain foods. But going to the doctor can surface many emotions for us as parents. When we turn to medical professionals to help us understand why our child is not speaking yet, why they are experiencing mood swings, or why they are not making eye contact, we know that we are seeking an answer to a question that feels complex. Certain questions can consume us: *Is there something wrong with my child? And if so, what does that mean for them, and what does it mean to me as a parent?*

Our stories of the medical system matter. Some of us are conditioned to revere medical providers as infallible—their word is truth. Some of us, on the other hand, may be apprehensive of the health care system but may not be quite sure why we have misgivings. Our race, gender, class, ability, and the messages we have received growing up often influence our impression of the current health care system. Naturally, this influences how we may feel about pursuing an evaluation for our children.

However we may personally feel about the medical system, we cannot ignore that this system is forged in the crucible of White supremacy and ableism. Not only does history reveal that the medical institution has been complicit in harming Black and Brown bodies, but we have seen this play out currently with disabled, Black, Latinx, and Indigenous communities and COVID-19. These communities were the most impacted, due to the structural inequities that limit access to health care and reduce affordability, compounding already existing biases many communities of color face, ultimately reflecting the triple pandemic of our times: the virus, racism, and ableism.

This chapter begins with highlighting the stigma, racism, and intergenerational trauma embedded within the health care system to expand our understanding of the context in which parents make a decision to take their children to see a provider. Widening our lens can help situate the nervousness parents may feel as they embark on the process of seeking an evaluation for their child. All too often, we can attribute our hesitation and worries to our own personal shortcomings or to the circumstances of our lives. However, what if the hesitation we feel and the concerns that we experience are indicative of unnamed undercurrents? Let's dive in.

Stigma

Stigma is being seen negatively for certain cultural, racial, and personality traits. Often stigma can lead to discrimination. Yet when we hear of "mental health stigma," what is often meant is that many communities of color see mental health issues as something to minimize and hide. While many communities of color do see anything to do with mental and behavioral health as shameful, we give a voice here to how it reveals itself in many of our South Asian immigrant communities. A common phrase in the Hindi language is "*log kya kahenge?!*" which translates to "what will they say?!" What this reveals is the worry about how others within our South Asian cultural communities will perceive us. Come with us to understand the why behind this worry.

Part of the immigrant musculature is to climb an invisible ladder, which promises us more status and prestige in a White society. We climb by getting more degrees, making more money, buying bigger houses, and ensuring that our kids go to Ivy League schools. We do this to secure our safety and belonging in a system so that we continue to be seen as model minorities.* And as we climb, we also look around to see who else from our community is getting closer to the top. This unspoken competition, this fear of losing status, and this desire to be seen as worthy ultimately all contribute to how we view any differences as something that can quickly cost us our place on this ladder.

To disclose mental struggles or neurodivergence is scary because the underlying belief is that it will compromise our connection to our families and communities. The worry is that our own people may shun us as they continue to strive upward. And belonging within our communities, especially when we are still seen as foreigners in the larger social context, is essential. As a result, many will not speak openly about mental health struggles with family and friends in the community and will instead choose to suffer silently. The stigma then is about avoiding being targeted by the dominant society and also avoiding shaming our families and communities.

Racism

There is another layer to the stigma communities of color experience, which has to do with how the medical system treats us when we seek support. Many experience racism and other forms of discrimination. When we have reached out for support, we are subject to derogatory and/or condescending comments; we are told that our cultural approaches to family, parenting, and healing are the problem; we are not listened to or believed by the provider; we are given an inaccurate diagnosis and incorrect treatment interventions. Clinicians unaware of their biases may seek assistance from the police or law enforcement when they perceive clients of color as aggressive or uncooperative. We do not experience safety.

Naturally, then, this creates a barrier for communities of color from reaching out to get the support they need. As a result, some may characterize behavioral therapy and mental health treatments as too Western or too White, as they fail to incorporate cultural practices and do not take a more holistic approach to healing. What this viewpoint reveals is

* *Model minority* is a term ascribed to Asians for their hard work and socioeconomic success. By collapsing and homogenizing a diverse group, this framework sees to create a racial wedge between Asians and other racial groups like Blacks and Latinx people.

an implicit understanding that this system is racist and therefore unsafe. For those struggling, a real bind exists: they can either seek help within a system that negatively characterizes people of color and be ousted and shamed by their communities or suffer alone by minimizing and trivializing their symptoms. Thankfully, we are seeing an increase in providers of color who are vocalizing a sea change, speaking to the need for more culturally relevant therapy.

> *Implicit biases* are our unconscious and automatic thoughts and feelings. Implicit biases can both be negative and positive, and they are a result of our brains needing shortcuts to make sense of a complex and dynamic world. Many of our behaviors are in response to these biases, even if we explicitly or consciously believe something else. Implicit biases are shaped by the messages we get from our immediate circles and the larger society we live in. Individual implicit biases are the manifestations of supremacist ideologies reinforced through institutions. For example, we have been exposed repeatedly to messages from movies and literature that characterize Black children as older than they are, dangerous, and not worthy of needing protection. This portrayal of Black children can seep into a provider's diagnostic evaluation, resulting in missed or incorrect diagnoses. More severely, an implicit bias can lead to an outcome that puts a child's life in danger.

Intergenerational Trauma

In addition to dealing with stigma and racism, many of us also carry the effects of intergenerational trauma in our bodies. As Resmaa Menakem reminds us, "Many times trauma in a person decontextualized over time can look like personality. Trauma in a family decontextualized over time can look like family traits. Trauma decontextualized in a people over time can look like culture, and it takes time to slow it down so you can begin to discern what's what."

Our uncertainty and concern about seeking treatment can be traced back to the wisdom of our ancestors. When a generation of people experiences something traumatic (like sexual assault, sterilization, famines, or genocide), the effects of it can be passed down to future generations. Trauma also leaves an imprint on our emotional understanding of the world through the messages we have been given by our families. For instance, we learn about what is OK to talk about, how much to express our emotions, who to trust, and how to keep ourselves safe in the world. Trauma then leaves a legacy that reveals itself over time in unexpected ways. Recent studies even show that trauma can alter the expression of genes, in an evolving field called epigenetics. Briefly, epigenetics considers how the environment can impact what markers on the genetic sequence are expressed, illustrating genes alone do not reveal the whole story. So, what if the anxiety you feel before calling a provider might be more than just your individual makeup? What if the anxiety represents generations of stored information, saying *Proceed with caution* or even *Stop*?

Without a layered historical understanding, it becomes too easy to assign blame to communities of color for their coping mechanisms. Removing people's suffering from the larger context of racism and ableism only reinforces the harm already experienced. So, for context, let's look at some of the historical practices within the larger medical system of which the mental health industry is a part. While these practices may appear distant and disconnected to the pursuit of a neuropsychological evaluation for your child, we think the impacts of these practices reverberate through generations to this day and may show up in surprising ways. What you are about to read is disturbing. Trust yourself and decide whether this information is relevant at this time.

- *Forced sterilization:* Informed by eugenics, forced-sterilization laws in the United States largely impacted Indigenous, Black, Latinx, and disabled people. Going in for routine reproductive procedures, people who were deemed unworthy and/or dangerous would be sterilized without their consent, impeding their ability to reproduce biologically. More recently, these procedures are still being conducted on women of color detainees in immigration centers.
- *Medical experimentation:* Black people were subject to medical trials and experimentation without their consent. An infamous example of this is the forty-year Tuskegee study conducted on Black sharecroppers, who were recruited with the promise of treatment for syphilis, but they never actually received treatment

and were actually used to study the effects of syphilis. These experiments have a long history rooted in the grave-robbing-by-night doctors who would steal Black bodies to further advances in medicine. The impacts of these trials could be felt most recently when many Black people expressed hesitancy about receiving the COVID-19 vaccine, conveying a deep and legitimate mistrust of the medical system.

- *Forced removal of children:* Against the backdrop of a racist medical system, the mental health complex has also played a part in deepening the mistrust that Indigenous communities experience. Indigenous children taken away from their families were sent to boarding schools where they have been stripped of any connection to their communities, land, and cultural practices. Recent findings of unmarked graves of children near these schools remind us of the enduring trauma of these practices. By forcibly removing children from their homes, the social-work field has severely impacted attachment patterns for generations to come.
- *Denial of freedom and rights:* Historically, the mental health industry did not think that Black people could experience mental distress, because they did not own property. More so, any attempts by enslaved people to be free from structural violence was itself seen as a psychiatric illness, called drapetomania. In more recent history, Black men's activism in the civil rights movement was read as aggression and led to the inclusion of this symptom as a characteristic of schizophrenia, which led to more Black men being diagnosed with this condition.

Given this tragic and dark history, it is perfectly understandable that some will be more cautious.

Body Check

We invite you to pause here and check in with your thoughts, feelings, and body. Reading about trauma can be traumatizing for some. At the very least, it activates our nervous system.

Reflect on your own experience. How is this information sitting in your body? What does your body need to metabolize this information?

> Reflect on your people's connection to this system. What stories have you heard from family members? Do any memories or images surface?

With this understanding that the medical system is a site not only formed by racism and ableism but also where it is perpetuated, we surface parents' experiences, from recognizing their child is different from others, to seeking a diagnosis, to making meaning of receiving a diagnosis, and then eventually to telling their children. For parents moving through this arc with their children, it can be a tumultuous time, when our past (our upbringing and messages we received about health and normality), present (the challenges of finding the right provider, etc.), and questions about the future (*what does this mean for my child?*) all converge in unexpected ways.

The Differences We See

What are the differences we see in our children? How do we come to recognize them? What does it provoke in us? What factors influence our decision to seek a medical diagnosis? For many parents, it is something we just know; it is a gut feeling fueled by the stuckness, confusion, and overwhelm we feel.

Leela, a South Asian and parent of two kids, one neurodivergent, says, "My instinct told me there was something deeper there than just acid reflux. I felt like my son was having an internal battle with himself. I remember I couldn't sustain the regular classes I had done with my older child, with my younger one. And I remember wanting to give reasons for this by saying things like 'He is just a baby,' or 'He is just one year old or two years old.'" She says when he was two years old, he would shove his chin into the hard places on her body. She relied on "Dr. Google" and identified sensory processing disorder as a possibility. Upon consultation with her kid's pediatrician, this was confirmed.

Valento, too, talked about how he had a feeling it would be autism for both of his children. "I spent hours on Reddit before the appointment. For me, it felt OK; we got a proper diagnosis, and now we can go through the proper channel [of support]." He tells the story of the moment he realized this with his daughter. "I realized my daughter might be autistic when I sang to her and it felt like I was invisible to her. She was in her own world. I cried myself to sleep that night. I wasn't sure I could handle this as a parent, mentally or physically. I wanted to be a good, strong parent and wasn't sure if I could be." He also adds about his son that he "strongly felt he also had ADHD, so we got an ADHD diagnosis before the autism diagnosis." He says it was important to get the ADHD diagnosis first and treat it with medication so that his son could sit through the evaluation for autism.

Similarly, Joy talks about how she saw that something was different from the beginning. Her son "was obsessed with lights from birth and experienced challenges with sleep. And at eleven months, he started talking, but it was difficult to understand, though I knew what he was saying. At thirteen months, he stopped talking."

Mumbi, a mother to twins, says, "One of my kids would run away, not respond to their name or make eye contact. The other child would walk on their tippy-toes and would bite themselves and others. I did not know what to make of these behaviors, and so I initially thought it was ADHD. But eventually, I learned about sensory processing disorder and had to shift my attention to figuring out how to support my kids and how to keep them safe." Eventually, both her kids did get an ADHD diagnosis, though the kids presented very differently.

Arica is a Black, disabled, and Jewish mother to one child who is biracial and trans, and who has a diagnosis of autism, ADHD, and giftedness. Arica says, "I knew from the time he was little. With my experience in preschool, I just knew from observing him. At two, he would separate himself, playing all the time parallelly. People around us would excuse this behavior by attributing it to his giftedness. He also walked on his tiptoes and did not get potty-trained till four and a half years old." Luisa recounts that her son had a lot of health issues in the beginning and many of his behaviors were attributed to them. She says, "One day, it just clicked and I realized it was not just his physical health and that there are other things going on." With her daughter, she could see her struggling in school and starting to lose her self-confidence.

Mary tells us how challenging it was initially, because some of what she was seeing did not make sense. Desiring an explanation and wanting to help her children, she sought a diagnosis. "There are many nights that

I found myself crying and feeling hopeless trying to figure out why and what I did wrong. I remember taking him to the community learning center, thinking it was fun, but he cried on the car ride back. I remembered picking him up from preschool, and he insisted on me making a left turn while our house was on the right. I remember him sitting in the garage for a long thirty minutes crying and would give up the trip to the park just because he didn't get to press on the garage opener that day. Many things that seem like the right choice for a kid are wrong for my child. I have so many memories of him crying, and I felt stuck."

For some other parents, the recognition that their child is not like the other kids can be retrospective. Anamika states that "in hindsight, there were so many cues. The speech delay was most striking. He had poor eye contact, a lack of joining attention, and he would not point at things. He was good at spinning and could spin anything."

For others, it comes from teachers. Hana explains how she saw that her son would need to be reminded to put on his shoes many times and that the teacher finally recommended that he be tested. Meena says about her son that "reports came from the daycare around the age of two, stating that they were noticing echolalia and that he was not engaging with peers, and also not making eye contact." With Sanvi's child as well, it was the teacher who first identified that her daughter needed some intervention with reading. "Her second-grade teacher told us she thought my daughter was a little behind in reading. We had her hearing checked, because she was not listening to oral directions. When she got to third grade, the teacher confirmed that she was not reading at level."

Noticing differences in our children naturally provokes a response in us. Malika says, "When I was in those early parenting groups like our library storybook hour, I would sit in a circle with our baby propped in front of us, amongst other exhausted sleep-deprived parents. Between the spit-up clean-up, Cheerio grabs, and the occasional diaper blowups, the conversation inevitably would turn to comparing notes about when our child rolled over, when they sat up and walked. Being around anxious parents would fuel more worry."

For some parents, differences can threaten safety, both physically and emotionally. Remembering Elijah McClain, a young Black man who was identified as different by his family and was forcibly injected with ketamine by police, Joy tells us what it meant for her to notice a difference in her child. She was not necessarily concerned he was autistic. To her, the deeply ingrained fear she felt was about the safety of her Black autistic boy in the middle of racial unrest and the rearing of explicit White supremacy in our nation. "How am I going to keep my Black autistic boy safe?" she asks. The criminal justice system already criminalizes Blackness, and his autism may add another layer of complexity to interactions with the system. She worries his autism increases his potential to be further problematized by a society with narrow definitions of socially sanctioned behavior.

When the world is unaccepting of difference, it is not fully clear whether receiving a diagnosis of autism for a child is protective or not for the child and family. Elizabeth speaks about the balance between standing out and fitting in. "We don't shy away from talking to our son about his differences (skin color, neurodiversity, two moms, privilege, etc.). I think the instinct to fit in is strong in a society like ours, so there's a balance of consciously or subconsciously trying to fit the mold while also being proud (and sometimes loud!) about what is different about our family. Being Brown, queer, and neurodivergent, we have a lot to work with in terms of navigating how and when to fit in or not."

Noticing differences can often lead us to seek an evaluation. We'll hear from parents about their experiences with making this decision. But first, to help explain what to expect in this diagnostic process, the next section explains how the medical system thinks about disability, and then provides an alternate approach called a *social model of disability.*

Body Check: 5-4-3-2-1

This exercise, invoking our senses, helps with grounding when you are feeling activated.

- Notice five things you see in your environment. You can adapt this, to five round things or five green things, for example.
- Next, name four things you can touch.
- Name three things you can hear.
- Name two things you can smell.
- Lastly, name one thing you taste.

Approaches to Disability

Medical Model of Disability

The medical model—that is, the one that emerges from the field of medicine—seeks to find a cause for illness and accordingly treat the illness with a cure. In psychology, the medical model sees neurodivergence as a variation from the brain function that is intrinsic to a person and as something that can be fixed or cured. Part of the problem with this approach is that the diagnostic standards used to assess well-being are normed against White, male, and nondisabled populations. As such, when someone's brain works differently, it gets labeled as atypical and in need of intervention. This approach aims to get neurodivergent people to perform more neurotypically. Interventions can look like teaching patients how to communicate in socially sanctioned ways.

It is worth pausing here to note that for many, engaging with the medical model is what provides the diagnosis of neurodivergence. The process of identifying how one's brain works, receiving an autism or ADHD diagnosis, can be hugely valuable. More so, for those neurodivergent folx with high needs, interventions geared towards basic physical safety are crucial. Where we think the medical model misses the mark is in seeing many neurodivergent traits—like hyperactivity, lack of eye contact, and stimming—as negative, maladaptive, and requiring intervention. While this model may offer clarity to people in the form of a diagnosis, it also sadly perpetuates a limited understanding of human expression and furthers ableist notions of wellness and functioning. It becomes another mechanism through which the unideal body and mind are named.

A concrete example of what we mean can be seen in the fifth edition of the *Diagnostic and Statistical Manual of Mental Disorders* (commonly called the *DSM-5*), which is the mental health clinician's guidebook. ADHD, a common type of neurodivergence, is identified by the following symptoms (this is not the full list):

- "Often fidgets with or taps hands or feet, or squirms in their seat."
- "Often leaves the seat in situations when remaining seated is expected."

Identifying naturally occurring body movements as symptoms is the first indication that the medical model problematizes behaviors that step outside the lines of a limited definition of normal. And without the wider analysis of how White supremacy, capitalism, and ableism contribute to defining these as concerning behaviors, the system quickly defaults to wanting to fix them.

Social Model of Disability

As opposed to a medical approach, a social model of disability states that disadvantages faced by disabled individuals are a result of societal barriers. An important distinction the social model of disability makes is between *impairments* and *disabilities*. According to this model, an impairment is a difference in functioning that results from inherent variation in the human species. The actual disability arises from the experiences of discrimination and oppression due to societal barriers.

Let's take processing speed as an example. Some people take more time to process; this is variation. The disability comes from the social environments that make slower processing speeds a problem needing an intervention. We surface this distinction to clarify that neurodiversity (variation in the human brain) is not inherently problematic. Variation only becomes divergent when certain standards of functioning are not met, which is usually due to lack of social, cultural, and systemic support. We thus sit with the tension of championing the neurodivergent identity while also recognizing that someone is only considered neurodivergent because of our fidelity to normal. We have found it helpful to remember that this idea of normal is constructed through the prism of racism, ableism, and capitalism.

Considering the same ADHD symptoms listed in the previous section, a social model of disability asks what situations dictate an expectation of being seated, and who decides what these situations are that require this level of decorum? Why is tapping hands or fidgeting something that is worth medically intervening in? Most important, what are these societal conditions that make seeing these variations in human expression something to be fixed?

Should We See Someone?

Should we see someone about this? is a natural question that might arise when you, a teacher, or well-meaning family members notice that there is something different about how your child interacts with the world around them. But before we even enter a provider's office, for many families of color, the decision to seek a diagnosis is rife with complexity, and there are many factors to contend with. Let's look at some of the more top-of-mind factors that parents think about.

Cost

A serious consideration for many families of color is the cost of assessments. Costs range from $3,000 to $8,000 and depend upon where in the US one is located. They also depend on whether the testing is done in a private practice, hospital, or training clinic. It is worth noting that evaluation by trainees is associated with lower costs.

Additionally, health insurance does not always cover testing. For instance, psychological evaluations that are deemed medically indicated, like assessing for ADHD and autism, are often covered, while testing to assess for learning differences often is not. When insurance covers a type of testing, it also can mean that only certain types of *treatments* are covered. For instance, Joy asks, "Why is it that the government and insurance only fund ABA (Applied Behavioral Analysis)?" Indeed, insurance companies seem to favor behaviorally driven interventions such as ABA (informed by behaviorism, which values shaping humans to conform and produce) over alternatives that are more relationship-driven such as DIR Floortime, music therapy, dance/movement therapy, play therapy, or animal-assisted therapies such as hippotherapy or equine-assisted mental health therapy. Moreover, Hana reminds us of yet another barrier: "We learned of my daughter's giftedness through the therapist she is seeing, but we cannot afford to have her formally tested by a psychologist. Testing is costly."

Time

Getting a diagnosis also takes time. Scheduling an appointment can take anywhere from months to a year, with extensive waitlists. The testing process itself can take two to four visits, depending on the nature of the assessment, spread out over weeks or months. There are many factors that impact the amount of time the process can take, including academic research, evaluation, collecting collateral information from other adults in the child's life, and writing the report itself. From the waitlist period to the time we receive a diagnosis, parents are left to figure out how best to meet their child's needs, so naturally, this can be an anxious and stressful time.

Geography

Where families live also makes a difference. Wait times are longer in remote areas, and research shows that when there are no adequately accessible community resources or public transportation, it is harder to physically get to the necessary services. More so, there are minimal support systems for parents of children with disabilities to rely on for transportation or other logistical help in more remote areas.

Mumbi shares, "Living on an island that does not have much access to services, we had long waitlists, high co-pays, and a lack of knowledge about which care would offer benefits. There were so many care needs for my child, and it seemed like taking them to all services would be a full-time job. Although we were initially lucky to find available services, it was brief, and now we have been on the waitlist for nine months."

Culturally Competent Care

After addressing the initial concerns of cost, time, and location, parents can also struggle to find providers of color, or, at the very least, those who exhibit cultural competency. This can be a particular problem in remote areas. But when a patient *does* feel a connection to their clinician, it can greatly support the efficacy of the treatment.

Having providers of color can help to support families in having more trust in the process. A provider from the same background can mean that patients do not have to do the heavy lifting of explaining their cultural and ethnic backgrounds and how that may inform their experiences of the diagnostic process. For many, there is also the worry about whether White providers will have biases toward their families and whether those biases will pathologize their child further. Moreover, to have providers of color can mean that the provider may be able to connect parents to resources that exist within their community and that incorporate cultural ways of healing rather than solely depending on the Western psychological model.

Leela talks about the Asian pediatric neurologist who was affirming and able to connect her to a local community organization for families of color. Similarly, Mumbi, though living in a more remote area, was able to take one of her children to a woman of color neuropsychologist. She says, "She was a woman of color, and she came across to me as someone who had wisdom. And I feel like she gave me the entree to the resources I would need for my toolbox."

Additionally, clinicians of color who speak our language are necessary when accessing care and services. Josefina found that having Spanish-speaking providers has made the process of obtaining a diagnosis for her child easier.

Provider bias and lack of cultural competency can lead to inaccurate diagnoses and inadequate treatment, further perpetuating mistrust in the system. Safety and trust are built when race, culture, and other differences are made visible as a fact of the lived experiences of the patient. Unfortunately for Joy, all the providers for her son have been White. She talks about the burden of being a mom and a professional in those settings as she does a lot of legwork to research and advocate for him. "I am advocating all the time," she says. Furthermore, as a doctoral student in an equity and education program, she is making the connection between how little energy is given to intersectionality in the research process, which is impacted by what types of studies are funded, which then impacts the best practices on how to work with communities of color.

Hana tells the story of the first time they saw a provider who was White. The interaction felt clinical, and she did not receive support after the process. "He did not sit down and talk and explain the findings, and there was no follow-up."

Reader Alert: This next anecdote contains a graphic description of a suicidal attempt.

Janne shares the story of her son's prescriber, and her experience gives voice to how unchecked implicit biases in providers can be serious and deadly. "What makes me the angriest is the psychiatrist attending to my son before his suicide attempt. The doctor had him on Strattera, explaining that many of my son's issues were with ADHD. I noticed my son was not doing well. I called the doctor and said we should take him off it. The doctor responded with, 'Let's wait and see.' The next day my son hung himself. Would he have been more concerned if he had been a White child?"

Experiences like these are all too common and heartbreaking. For families who already feel alone in navigating this process, provider bias only creates further isolation for families of color. How nice would it be to, at the very least, have providers who can understand the complexities of our experiences?

Getting the Diagnosis

After navigating these many barriers, if families do choose to pursue a diagnosis, this will involve neuropsychological testing and assessments, which vary depending on the symptoms present. Some parents never question whether to pursue a diagnosis, because they want frameworks for moving forward, especially if there has been a lack of clarity. These families articulate that early intervention, getting support, and having a name for their child's experiences feel empowering.

As Sophia says, "I draw on mythology and believe that if you have an enemy and you know its name, you can defeat it. I am the kind of person who would rather know than worry about the unknown, so having the diagnosis was comforting to me. I have a name, I can deal with it. Some parents will mourn, but I was relieved." It was similar for Joy: "Getting a diagnosis has never been a question for me. Diagnosis matters. It is a system and form of communication. It is the subjective meaning that can be problematic, the ways we attach a picture of what something means."

She also adds that getting a diagnosis for her son prompted her to seek an evaluation for herself as well. "I want my Black autistic son to have another reference point for what it means to be Black and autistic and not just what the world says it means." Sophia, too, was able to learn more about herself and her family with her child's diagnosis. "Neurodivergence, as we know it now, was unknown in my country. I did know my family was strange, and I was considered a smart but weird girl. Getting my children diagnosed opened my eyes to understanding myself and my family more."

Getting a diagnosis was important for Leela, because it helped her to advocate for her child. "I am not a fan of the label, but it does help to have a label to explain to the world what my child needs and helps me in advocating for him." She provides an example of taking him to a trampoline place and how naming that he was autistic helped him get extra time to transition out of play and out of the building at closing time.

And Josefina reminds us that while diagnoses are helpful, no two people with the same diagnosis are the same. "As a mother, it has been very useful to know his diagnosis, although for me, the diagnoses are not conclusive, since I feel that no person is the same as another, despite having the same diagnosis."

Getting a diagnosis creates many pathways to multiple supportive services such as occupational, speech, and mental health therapies, which can be accessed either within the educational system or outside it. Even if parents decide initially not to opt for a diagnosis through the medical system, the question of diagnosis resurfaces in the formal public education system (for children who attend public schools), giving parents an opportunity to (re)consider a diagnosis in the light of supporting their child with learning or behavioral challenges.

Hana says, "Diagnosis became more important in working with the school. I don't know if it is because we are a BIPOC family—the school wrote us off when we asked for support. Having the diagnosis legitimized us and what we were asking for." Kim's experience also speaks to the need for diagnosis to access services within the school. "Initially, a diagnosis helped our family feel seen. It helped us know that our struggles were not unique, that many families were dealing with the same differences, and that it would be OK. We were looking at traditional public-school options at the time, and a diagnosis was geared toward that. The neuropsychiatrist we worked with specifically gave one diagnosis because it would open doors for the types of help [our son] needed, working backward from the type of environment she thought he would succeed in and what diagnosis would get there." She also notes that not being in the traditional school system has made the diagnosis not as important. "Now that we homeschool and plan on continuing that, a diagnosis means very little to us. Sure, it helps in a pinch to explain certain behaviors to others or a new doctor, but they cannot possibly reflect the richness of our son."

Josefina also speaks to how having a diagnosis facilitates getting the right services. "I feel that having my son's diagnosis helps me to find the best way for him to learn and to help him express his thoughts and needs." Mumbi's experience with access to services also surfaces the role parents have to play in case management. "Diagnosis can be valuable and helpful to offer the kids greater access to needed services like early intervention, speech therapy, OT (occupational therapy) or even ABA (applied behavioral analysis), etc." She adds, "However, when parents are thrust into the role of case management, to find the available services while not knowing the steps, or the 'best practices,' it is overwhelming and confusing. Every child's needs are different as the spectrum is vast."

Getting a diagnosis can also be extremely important to keeping our Black and Brown children safe within systems. Rupa attests to this, saying, "We are raising a Black boy, and we believe the diagnoses will be crucial for him. We can tell teachers that he is not aggressive and doesn't have an oppositional defiant disorder, which can help stave off the preschool-to-prison pipeline as long as possible."

Unfortunately, many children's symptoms are missed or get misdiagnosed due to providers' implicit bias during the diagnostic process. Misdiagnosis of ADHD can feed the *misdiagnosis-to-prison pipeline*, as coined by Natalie Cort. According to Dr. Cort, when we miss the diagnosis, behaviors that are attributed to conditions like ADHD can get miscoded as defiance, which then leads to responses from teachers and administrators that are more punitive than necessary. And even if they receive the appropriate diagnosis, biases can impact the course of their treatment.

Black and Latino children are less likely to be diagnosed with ADHD than their White counterparts, even though they display symptoms to a greater extent. Black children are instead diagnosed with oppositional defiant disorder (ODD) and bipolar disorder, which leads to incorrect treatment. Black children in particular face at least three years of delay in assessment after parents raise concerns about language, development, and behaviors. The impact of a delay in seeing a professional can contribute to higher rates of intellectual disability, according to data from the CDC.

While the families we spoke to all had a formal diagnosis for their children, we want to acknowledge that not all families pursue a diagnosis, which is a choice worthy of celebration. Other families take longer to get diagnosed because of the label. We want to normalize the paths we take and the choices we make. All of us are doing the best we can.

Meena tells us that the fear of the unknown, the fear of having her child labeled, especially when her journey to motherhood was replete with struggles, delayed pursuing a diagnosis, despite noticing some differences. She acknowledges, "I recognized that my fears were valid, and that they got in the way of me being able to show up for my son."

Making Meaning of the Diagnosis

Receiving a diagnosis can provoke many feelings. We want to normalize and validate that what shows up does not make you a bad parent or mean that your love for your child is any less. While it is ideal to take time to process feelings, we know that it is hard to find the time for yourself. Sometimes parents, like Joy, just have a car ride home to get themselves sorted. She says, "We are pioneers, and we have to create a path for ourselves when it comes to figuring out how to support our children." She tells the story of how alone she felt while receiving the diagnosis. "It hit me like a ton of bricks. I don't even know how I got home. I pulled into my driveway and could not get out of the car. I cried and cried. I then had to go and tell my husband by myself."

Joy's story speaks to the loneliness many parents of color feel already and how receiving a diagnosis can compound these feelings. The following stories from parents demonstrate the many ways we can respond.

- *Problem solving:* After receiving a diagnosis, a typical response is to shift into research, problem-solving, and advocacy mode, because we are left to find how to parent a child with neurodivergence. When Valento learned of his child's diagnosis, he wanted to address what his child needed head-on, and part of that was to educate his family. He states, "People said to me, 'I pray for this to go away,' and my response was always, 'Don't pray for this to go away; pray for me to have the strength to deal with this.'" He also recognized that he needed to be strong for his wife. He assured her that "there is nothing we can do to change the diagnosis except give our child the best life we can give."
- *Seeking an explanation:* Many of us will go down the path of seeking explanations for the diagnosis to understand whether we did something wrong. This may especially be true for gestational mothers, wondering if that hike we did during our second

trimester or the sushi we ate near the end of our last trimester contributed to this. Seeking an explanation is a natural part of the human condition, as we are meaning-making beings. Valento shares that his wife felt guilty initially, believing she was the reason their children were autistic. He was able to support her through these initial feelings by finding information and support in Reddit communities. "It helped us to know that we were not alone."

- *Navigating cultural messaging:* The messages we have received from our families and culture about differences can play a significant role in how we come to terms with our child's diagnosis. Min's experiences learning about her son's ADHD reflect how our cultural upbringing informs the sense we can make of diagnosis. "Growing up, anyone with any type of learning disability or difference was seen as 'less.' Asian culture is all about assimilating into the group, assimilating into a whole, either a family unit, a community, a neighborhood, a church, etc. Having a child that was different than others was very hard to deal with. However, being a parent means that you love your child unconditionally. It also means you understand that one child is never identical to another. Whatever die is cast your way, you make the best of the situation."
- *Relief:* After all of the appointments and researching, sometimes having a label, knowing what is going on with your child, can be a relief. As parents, we know what we need to do, instead of throwing darts aimlessly. Mumbi experienced tremendous relief in being able to know what was happening to her children: "I am relieved. I know what I need to do now, and I can see what I have to work [on] as a parent to be there for them."
- *Grief:* A common response parents experience is sadness and grief. We think grief is so prevalent because the diagnosis challenges parents' narratives on health, success, belonging, and well-being. Grief should prompt us to critically question what we have actually lost. Julie's experience speaks to this fear of not belonging. "We were worried that we weren't welcome or belonged in our communities. It has been a great deal of worry and anxiety. It's full of grief and pain." Her worry speaks to the mental health stigma in our communities of color discussed previously and how being seen as different can cost us our places of safety and

> connection. Anamika talks about the grief that hit her when she received the diagnosis, and how part of it had to do with the efforts it took for her to have a child. "I broke down at the doctor's. I had spent so much energy trying to have a child, and then I did not know what the future would hold. I knew autism as a word and did not know what it meant. I did not know how much more would be needed." Sanvi also confirms feeling grief initially. She says, "I really wanted my daughter to be a part of the highly capable community, and the thought that her learning disability would keep her from it was hard on me. Over time I have realized I have made it about me and not her."

The messages we have been given about what it means to be normal and to be healthy influence our meaning-making. We want to honor that in our process toward liberation, a place on the developmental journey for parents is coming face-to-face with our own internalized ableism and oppression.

Telling Our Children

After we know the evaluation results, a big question is whether to tell our children and, if so, how to tell them. We acknowledge the concerns about telling our kids. Some parents hesitate, not wanting their children to feel different, think something is wrong with them, or worry that other kids might bully them. Others want to tell their kids, because they feel that by withholding this information, they are reinforcing the belief that being neurodivergent is a problem. Each family knows the best way to tell their child and the right time to do it.

Here are some examples of our parents telling their children.

Mumbi says, "Yes, we have shared the diagnosis, but he has been unable to understand what that means other than being special. We had a family meeting to gently talk about it uninterrupted.

Elizabeth states, "Yes, we told him. We kept it light (he was eight!) and explained that everyone's brain works differently and that he'll need to learn to use the brain he has been given."

Kim's experience reminds us that we can build up to telling our children, giving them an opportunity to process information. She offers, "We did not tell him right away. We read books about neurodivergence and with neurodivergent characters. We pointed out traits that seemed to be particularly similar between a character and our son. We celebrated those traits and talked about their challenges. I think he knew what we were getting at, but we did not push it. One day, he asked if he was like the characters we read about. And we said that he was."

Luisa's approach underlines the importance of giving our children a choice in identification. She recounts, "So after getting the diagnosis, we told the kids that the doctors have identified these traits and think that you fit this identity. We also told them they get to decide if they also identified with it so that they could experience some empowerment in that too."

In considering whether and how to tell our children, one outcome parents can be prepared for is the child choosing not to identify with it. Sanvi shares how her daughter has chosen not to identify with her diagnosis at this time. She says, "My daughter wants to be like all the other kids at her school and feels the burden of a label." This can create a challenge for parents in figuring out how to provide support and services that might be useful in the face of a child stating they do not need it. Speaking to this, when Deepti's daughter had a hard time accepting her diagnosis, she listened and gave her the space she needed. She spoke to class teachers about broaching a conversation around neurodiversity in class. "It turned out to be valuable for her, as hearing many of her peers accept their differences helped my daughter feel less alone and share about her own."

A big consideration in telling our children may also be their developmental age. Rupa offers, "We have not quite told him because he's only two and a half and has limited receptive language skills, even though I know he understands more than we think. I also think that given how things are in our home, and the pandemic, I doubt at this stage he has a sense of normal and therefore needs to be informed explicitly of a deviation from normal."

As we near the end of this chapter, we leave you with the following reflection prompts. As always, if it feels accessible, check in with your body and notice the sensations.

Reflection Questions

- What are some of your first memories of being at a doctor's office or being in a medical facility? What are the sights, sounds, smells, and textures you remember? How did you feel?
- How did your family think about well-being? How do your cultural upbringing and racial and other identities impact your thoughts?
- What do you remember about how the medical professionals treated you, your parents, and your support systems?
- What do you want to teach your kids about navigating the medical system? What is something you wish you were taught?

Resources for Deeper Understanding

Constantino, John N., et al. "Timing of the Diagnosis of Autism in African American Children." *Pediatrics* 146, no. 3 (August 24, 2020). https://doi.org/10.1542/peds.2019-3629.

Frye, Devin. "The Children Left Behind." *ADDitude*, March 31, 2022. https://www.additudemag.com/race-and-adhd-how-people-of-color-get-left-behind/.

Morgan, Paul L., Jeremy Staff, Marianne M. Hillemeier, George Farkas, and Steven Maczuga. "Racial and Ethnic Disparities in ADHD Diagnosis from Kindergarten to Eighth-Grade." *Pediatrics* 132, no. 1 (July 1, 2013): 85–93. https://doi.org/10.1542/peds.2012-2390.

Smith, Kylie M. "How Bigotry Created a Black Mental Health Crisis." *Washington Post*, July 29, 2019.

9

UNLEARNING THE SCRIPT

Educating Our Children

One of the most compassionate teachers I had the pleasure of having during my middle school years was Mr. R, a young, hip physics teacher with just the right ratio of fun to serious. He was passionate about his subject and his students. He was the kind of adult who was fully present with you if you were talking to him and would always make time to listen if you approached him in the teachers' room, on or off the clock. He was a teacher that I could turn to without fear of judgment or shaming. It is sadly comical that for the teacher that had the most impact on me during my secondary school years, I delivered the most abysmal grades. The thing is, though, I didn't hate physics. In fact, I actually enjoyed it. I enjoyed learning about particle mechanics, thinking about projectile motions, and deriving Galileo's equations of motion from scratch. I looked forward to Mr. R's lessons. I felt like I could take small risks in his class and would occasionally raise my hand to ask a question. I felt safe approaching him after class to ask clarifying questions. To me, emotional safety in my environment was of paramount importance to my learning. When a teacher made the effort to create a climate of emotional safety, I let my guard down, removed my masks, and revealed myself more. When I felt emotionally safe, I felt more connected, and my brain was better positioned to learn. And so any teacher I had had the power to make or break my interest. Mr. R was certifiably a maker.

Interest has always been a significant factor of my traditional academic success, but it has never been enough to overcome the neurotypical educational system. Throughout my life I have heard variations of assumptions based on "interest":

- *"If you were interested, your grades would reflect it."*
- *"If you are truly interested, you can put your mind to it."*
- *"If you are interested in something, you will create time and discipline for it," or the reverse:*
- *If you are not disciplined about it, you are not interested in it."*

I have been met with these statements in any area of pursuit, be it academics, music, a new hobby, or an exercise regimen. As an adult, I have finally come to see and name these statements as being ableist toward me and the neurodivergent community. To those who have said or thought this of others, I implore you to enter into a space of critical self-reflection. The creation of time and focused discipline are the very challenges that define the ADHD experience and yet often the only attributes that are cherry-picked to gauge one's interest in a subject. Other learning challenges can make this divide more pronounced.

And so it was quite possible for me to enjoy physics and for my grades not to show it. My teenage confusion was palpable. I failed to understand why my hard work never translated into good grades. At the end of one particular examination season, I wanted to make my parents proud and couldn't let them down yet again on my next physics grade. I knew my physics grade would not be prideworthy, and I was right, but an internal flame appeared to be fueled by a fight—a fight to redeem my sense of worth and dignity.

With my physics paper in one hand, I stormed into Mr. R's office the following day. His ever inviting, listening presence welcomed my gush of tears that choked back any attempt at words. Within a few minutes, I could begin to make some sense, and Mr. R leaned in to ask about my thought process behind my test scribbles—and felt called to award me points on its basis. A safe, connecting, and nonjudgmental presence to talk a subject matter through with me was all that I needed to get my neurons firing. When Mr. R provided empathy, encouragement, and a second chance at my examination, he helped me feel and think well. He became my therapeutic agent of change.

But I was one too. Perhaps Mr. R's agency activated my own. But my agency was spiraling to the surface. It was so enmeshed with helplessness, guilt, and self-defeat. The internal tug of war between agency and powerlessness was relentless and exhausting, never quite translating into self-advocacy. In hindsight, with each iteration of this internal spiral, it felt like I was getting closer. At that moment, my agency was alive in the legs that walked into that office, and in the heart that desired to be seen as able and whole. But it coexisted with the dire helplessness in my voice, my desperate cry for help. But that impulse to reach for support held a glimpse of my agency too.

And little did I know then that my helplessness was a legitimate response to an ableist system.

My rage was their rightful lovechild.

My storming into Mr. R's office was not desperation—it was my rising.

The Landscape of Education for Neurodivergent Children of Color

Education. At the outset, it feels like a regular word every parent contends with, something that we take for granted as a part of all our lives and our children's, often without question. But taking a minute to *feel* this word, we notice its depth beyond its utilitarian meaning in the dictionary. The word is drenched in the richness of story, braided together by personal biography and intergenerational history that shape the meaning and the values we attribute to education. Given that our parents and grandparents did not always have opportunities for education, the opportunity to educate our children takes on renewed meaning, and our educational decision for them gets embedded with increased tension. This decision lands differently on someone who may have been the first in the family to be formally educated or to graduate high school, or earn a GED or go to college; or the first to break the cycle of poverty or the preschool-to-prison pipeline in their family; or the first in their family to find safety from war or healing from historical, intergenerational trauma.

These stories, if left unacknowledged, can allow messages, myths, and negative or limiting self-beliefs that we have been conditioned with to persist in our parenting and our children. One way in which we can start our own reflection is to ask ourselves, *what did education mean to our parents or parental figures?* A few parents share their answers here.

Leela shares how the values instilled in her about public education from her dad weighed heavily on her decision-making regarding schools for her child. "My dad, who didn't do schooling here in the US, always said how lucky I was to receive a free education. The education may not be the best, but no one said I couldn't do it. We were a poor immigrant family, and the immigrant mindset that schooling is free, and a right, is so strong." Deepti shares how her father, who was the first in his family to travel out of India and settle abroad, instilled in her the value of education: "Education was the best gift he gave me, and it was such an important value for him—he often remarked how it was the best gift he had received from his own parents. It shaped his drive to ensure that his daughters received every educational opportunity they could."

For many of us, when the first knowing of our child's neurodivergence takes us on a personal journey through grief, one of the biggest things we're grieving is the loss of our educational aspirations for our child. We may hope that our child would carry the torch forward with our passions or realize our own unrealized dreams and potential. We may hope they achieve success by a capitalistic metric as we did or did not or make others proud in ways we did or couldn't. We may want to instill in our children the educational values that our ancestors fought for. All these feelings that sit deep within us are challenged, or simply crushed, by our realization that our child's neurodivergence may be a barrier to their educational success.

However, in our parenting journey, we are often not awarded time at this juncture to sit with our grief. We are asked by society to box it up and move on, because there are checklists for our child that we must contend with. Grief that has not been allowed to stay or be felt, processed, and integrated into our nervous system may quickly fold into fear. We fear the unknown that has yet to unfold, especially given the COVID-19 pandemic and its ramifications for our children's education. It seems as though the pandemic has unmasked and exacerbated the systemic oppression already present within public schools, especially for low-income communities of color across the nation. The failure to respond equitably in the face of racism, classism, poverty, and state-sanctioned segregation to our children's learning and health has only deepened the mistrust that communities of color (especially Black and Latinx) have felt toward the public-school administration.

Given the history and present-day state of the education system, it is understandable that we worry about the ways in which our neurodivergent children will develop and the ways in which the oppressive world will treat them. We worry if our child will:

- Be seen and celebrated as a child of color with neurodivergence but not singled out for it.
- Be supported with all the learning complexities of the neurodivergent brain.
- Be bullied for their racial and learning differences, or other differences.
- Be disciplined in harsh ways.
- Have caring teachers who believe in their abilities.
- Receive enough individual attention and connection.
- Be safe.
- Belong.
- Thrive.

Sometimes our fears, like our hopes, are tangled up with our own experiences around education. Leela asks, "Is my fear based on my own experience of being different as a Brown kid in an all-White classroom growing up, just not in a neurodivergent way? I didn't want to be called at or called on; I just wanted to be right here, under the radar. I feel like I'm taking on the worries of my child even before they happen."

Deepti, too, shares how she recognized that her fears for her daughter were conflated with her own experience of education in childhood and prevented her from making an important decision around the school. She consciously worked on her fear through a Hand in Hand Parenting tool called the listening partnership. "When confronting a decision around public schooling for my child, I choked back tears and could feel the heat in my body rising as images of my own rigid education haunted me. This was my cue to take a break from what felt like a confrontation and continue at a later time. In the meantime, I decided to share my feelings with someone I trusted. Prompted by them, I got to share what education was like for me as a child with undiagnosed learning difficulties, how the public-school system had failed me, and how I was worried that that might happen to my daughter too. I cried and raged, and my listening partner nonjudgmentally held space for my feelings. Over the next few days, I felt a powerful shift in my body—I felt less fear and a renewed sense of energy and confidence with which I re-approached my decision-making."

Because our arrival at our children's education is a cultural legacy, pregnant with the hopes and dreams we hold for them, we invite you to give yourself permission to feel the present and the past and to dream into the future. Feeling allows healing. We know that reflecting on our childhood stories, creating a coherent narrative, and allowing ourselves to feel the sadness or the rage that our younger self felt when they were bullied years ago is an act of healing that paves the way for confidence and clarity in our parenting today. Healing our wounds affords us a healthy degree of separation between our children's experiences and our own and allows us to access the confidence and clarity we need to identify our child's needs, find a way to meet them, and be able to dream into their future, for dreaming gives us hope. Envisioning a liberated future for our children gives us something to hold on to as we weed through the barriers ahead of us and them.

Making Schooling Choices

Figuring out how to educate our children is one of the most significant decisions we make as parents. The context in which we make this decision is with the understanding that the public education system is designed, in theory, to guarantee education for all children regardless of race, gender, ability, sexuality, religion, etc. In practice, however, our BIPOC and disabled children are still often not afforded the right to a free and appropriate education. We are still fighting for our BIPOC and disabled children's civil and educational rights, which raises valid concerns for us around our children's safety and well-being at their schools and creates understandable tensions and emotional distress in our decision-making around their education. We know that emotional safety provides the necessary conditions for learning. However, the impacts of toxic stress (see chapter 3) resulting from systemic oppression make finding emotional safety harder for our children, contributing to a wider achievement gap between White nondisabled children and our disabled children of color.

For those of us who decide on formal education, our children spend 13 percent of the waking hours of their life away at school. We entrust the school system, a community of adults, to care well for our children during that time. Considering the needs of our neurodivergent child of color, we approach this system not only with our own intuition of what our child needs in an educational environment but also with what advancement in brain science confirms what we know to be true—that any child, our child included, benefits from more play and movement; more opportunity for connections with caring adults who take the time to know, love, and celebrate our child's strengths and support their struggles and needs; less academic standardized testing; less homework; more intrinsic motivation than extrinsic motivation like token rewards; and no punitive discipline. For our children, then, these aspects become even more critical, as neurodivergent children may need extra time and care from their adults to think and learn well.

Many of us are forced to ask ourselves if public schooling is the right fit for our children. Depending on the time, energy, values, financial resources, and support system available to us, we navigate this question in many ways, as highlighted later in this chapter.

No amount of checklists can appease the emotional tug-of-war that plays out internally. It is a test of our grit to weed through all our unresolved educational baggage to arrive at a decision that offers us promise for our child. It tests our ability to release our children into the world, to trust that their needs will be met. The race of our child and their neurodivergence make decisions around schooling complex. While factors such as educational methods, academic curricula, and extracurricular activities are valuable to educational decision-making, we are concerned more about the safety of our neurodivergent BIPOC children, and rightfully so. How we channel our chronic fear around a chronically hurting educational system and children depends on the perception of whether we can counter the challenge ahead of us. How we access this perception in the face of chronic fear lies in the permission we give ourselves to feel our fear, fully, and to dream of a better future for our children.

As Carmen puts it, "I don't trust the school system. I'm going to be honest with you. I don't trust them. I don't trust anything about them. I don't care how much they smile to my face and tell me how much they love my kids. I don't trust them. Because I've been in a predicament where my son was hurt. And nobody said nothing."

Factors Involved in Decision-Making

When parents are deciding on an educational model or type of school for their children, the factors that typically play a part in such a decision include personal resources (money/income), teaching/learning philosophy, student-teacher ratio, parental engagement and input, proximity to home, and school transportation. Our desire to make an informed decision about our child's education stems primarily from our desire for safety, inclusion, and respect for our children's learning differences.

In this chapter, we explore the many aspects of public education that parents contend with for their neurodivergent children of color: inclusivity in education; racism and ableism; bullying; special education services; relationship-oriented education; discipline; and alternatives to public education. While public schooling, despite its challenges, is a natural and valid consideration for most parents, often the inability of the dominant public education system to meet our children's core educational needs and values leads us to consider various alternatives.

Inclusivity

Will my child be seen and celebrated as a Black/Brown child with neurodivergence but not singled out for it? Will my child fit in?

It is of utmost importance to Leela that her son's autism and sensory processing differences are normalized. She is afraid of what will happen as her son enters the public education system. "At some point, somebody will need to label him so he can function in the system. What would it feel like to be separated from his neurotypical peers for instruction throughout the day? Would he feel different, or would he not care?"

We emerge from the ashes of a painful history of cultural genocide, exclusion, and segregation in the education of disabled and BIPOC children. The impacts of boarding schools or residential schools reverberate in Indigenous communities to this day. These educational institutions, designed to forcibly assimilate Native youth into White culture, too often were the only choice of education for Indigenous families. The residential schools separated Native youth from their families and subjected them to physical, emotional, and sexual abuse. The schools were instrumental in the erasure of Indigenous cultures.

The monumental *Brown v. Board of Education* desegregated schools in name only. Today, we continue to see segregation along racial, ethnic, and class lines. This modern segregation, due to practices like redlining and school secession,* keeps disabled and Black, Indigenous, and Latinx children from accessing equitable education.

One way that segregation continues today in the educational system is evident in the enforcement of special education laws. While the current special education laws state that students should be excluded or removed only to the extent necessary to implement the student's education plan and meet individually designed goals, the reality is that children of color and children with disabilities with extensive learning and support needs continue to be removed from their peers in general education. While these classrooms promise increased instructional resources, it has been found that segregated children in fact experience higher levels of distraction and lose critical instruction time.

Our parent community experienced this firsthand. Elizabeth, a public-school teacher herself, desperately wanted to believe in the public education system's ability to meet her autistic son's learning needs. But with her son shuffling between the general education classroom and the special education classroom for his social-emotional needs, she quickly found that he was not being challenged enough to match his growing level of learning. "The special education classroom became his comfort zone, rather than the general education classroom, because he learned that he did not have to work hard in the former. It is difficult to see how low the expectations for my son were." She also observes how her son's special education classroom is disproportionally more Brown than White, while the teachers in the classroom are more White. She questions what this means for the messages that Brown children like her son are internalizing in this environment that appears difficult for her son to transition out of. Data supports Elizabeth's anecdotal experience in that "students from nondominant groups tend to be overrepresented in special education in the United States."

"My daughter was not challenged academically. She was deemed incapable," says Angela, another public-school teacher, who recalls her horrible experiences with public-school education for her daughter, now an adult. "I understand how much is put on teachers, and how

---

* *Redlining*: to mark, sometimes literally with red lines, a minority neighborhood as high risk for mortgage lending, thereby reducing the ability of residents there to obtain financing. *School secession*: when White neighborhoods create new and separate school systems to move tax funding to White-only schools.

unsupported they are, but I would walk into her resource classroom, and she would be by herself, and her teachers would be chitchatting. They were failing her."

Even when a child with disability is technically sharing a classroom with their nondisabled peers, what they are taught may veer significantly from the general lesson plan and goals that the rest of the class receives. Carmen shares how her son's learning was not equitable. "Regardless of my son's disability, he has the right to receive content somewhat similar to the rest of the class. But he was just given something completely basic to just pass time while his (nondisabled) peers learned."

Such stories are a painful reminder of the deep inequities embedded in the education system for our children. We acknowledge that there are countless teachers and paraprofessionals who care deeply for our children and go that extra mile for them. But when the education system does not support teachers in making education equitable for our children, stories of equity for our children are the exception, not the norm. As parents, we cannot afford to rely on the heart of individual teachers to catch our children, making educational reform paramount.

In response to recognizing that students of color and students with disabilities were not receiving equitable access to education, a movement emerged to push for *inclusive education* for all children. Inclusivity goes beyond the ideas of *desegregation* (where students of color and differing learning abilities were now allowed to learn in schools with White and nondisabled children but in separate environments) and *integration* (where children with disabilities were invited to join general education classrooms if they were able to learn with the instruction provided by the teacher). *Inclusivity* ensures that all types of learners are included in the education system, and that all teachers are supported and equipped to teach all children. This approach to education makes clear that inclusivity is not necessarily about including children with disabilities in a shared space with nondisabled children but more about ensuring systemic change so that the learning needs of children with disabilities are justly and equitably met by the system.

There is strong evidence that inclusive education enriches the educational experience of all children, regardless of disability. Specific benefits include:

- Improved quality of friendships.

- Equitable instruction of all children.
- Enriching academic content.
- Opportunities for increased literacy.
- Fewer referrals for discipline and more opportunities for socialization.
- Better outcomes after graduation from high school.

Despite these benefits, with quality inclusive education across the nation still being a far-reaching goal, many alternative schools and programs have emerged to meet the needs of children who are not rightfully served by the public-school system. We touch on these toward the end of this chapter.

Supremacy: Racism and Ableism

Will professionals at school treat my family with positive and kind regard? Will my child and family be treated equally? Will the history of my people be taught to all children, or will our history be erased?

Many stories throughout this chapter highlight examples of racism and ableism in the educational system. As a reminder, racism and ableism are not just interpersonal; they are embedded within institutions and are ideological. It manifests overtly sometimes, and at other times it is less visibly woven into the fabric of the educational establishment.

Here are some critical examples of overt racism and ableism felt by parents and children within educational institutions both public and private—because racism does not discriminate by institution. As a BIPOC parent reading this, you may resonate and see your own story in these too. We are tenderly holding all our stories among them.

"Black people can't be smart, but it must be the Jewish in you!" Arica, a Black mother with mixed Jewish roots heard this from their private school director about her highly gifted biracial child.

"Your boy must not be loved [because he is part Black]." The bullying experienced by Janne's biracial Black autistic boy prompted a professional's unwarranted assumption that his White father must not love him.

"No amount of speech services for your daughter can help her learn." Angela, a single mother and public-school educator herself heard this from a speech-language pathologist at her daughter's IEP (individual education plan) team meeting upon her advocacy for her child's speech

services. "I looked at the head of the meeting in shock, seeing this professional feel emboldened to speak her ableist mind in front of other professionals. I couldn't believe what I had just heard." Angela shares how she allowed herself to unpack this. "At the end of the meeting I sobbed in my car, enraged. But it was a defining moment for me, as it lit a fire in me. I resolved never to let anything bring me down, and that I was going to continue fighting for my child's needs without worrying about what people say and think." Allowing herself to acknowledge and feel her rage helped Angela connect with her inner power to sustain her advocacy for her daughter.

But often we get hit even when we are able to access our inner power. Carmen speaks to a time when her young son got off the school bus with a sizeable injury. "None of the adults in charge could tell me what happened; they told me the bus cameras weren't working. I was furious. It was their responsibility to know, because my autistic son with a speech delay certainly could not communicate this to me. How did my son's injury go unnoticed? Not only did they not take any responsibility, the bus driver was also nasty to me and threw my son's bus bag at my face with force. That was the last time he traveled on that school bus."

"You are being a difficult mom." Joy also shares how an experience of having to advocate for an inclusive learning environment for her child at public school was met with racist microaggressions by a White service coordinator. It is sadly not uncommon that Black mothers passionately asserting their child's rights are quickly judged as being "difficult."

To claim what is rightfully ours, against an establishment that holds a legacy of refusal and erasure of BIPOC rights, comes as a grave threat to the establishment itself. It is important to see these examples of individual responses as ones that emerged from having marinated in the values of institutional racism.

Carmen shares Joy's experience of being seen as difficult. "It's sadly true that it's not until you basically go completely off the radar for them to understand, 'Hey, don't mess with my kid.' You know? They just don't get it until you go there, until you are forced to get big." Corey shares how he is perceived as "getting big" even when not attempting to do so: "I am a Black father. Schools do not expect to see me. And when I show up at an IEP meeting, they have police officers stationed outside. If I raise my voice even a little, they tell me to calm down or otherwise they will have to have the police come in. This shows that these educators don't have the cultural training to understand different forms of communication and because of that are quick to call the police."

Pitting BIPOC people against one another is another way that a system steeped in White supremacy retains power. Hana reminds us that when questioning school police and authority, racism can shift focus away from us, landing on the next easy target—teachers and staff of color. Hana describes the guilt that her rightful advocacy brought about: "When an unjust policy I questioned ended up getting our favorite teacher (also BIPOC) in trouble, I didn't want to throw her under the bus, so I stopped pushing on that policy."

It is tragic that educational racism and ableism can create multiple barriers that prevent us from advocating for our children's needs. The system counts on our differences, on us not knowing our rights, not having the resources and the support system to help us and our children move forward. Hana and Carmen speak to different ways in which they access their strengths in advocating for their children's needs.

"I remind myself every day that despite being a woman of color, due to my ability to pass as White, I hold color privilege and a responsibility due to my proximity to Whiteness," says Hana, who identifies as Asian. She shares how she used her privilege to advocate for her family within the system. "My child's school treated my Hispanic husband differently than they treated me. They were willing to hear more of my demands than if my husband went in, because they see me as acceptable." Despite that, "it adds a lot more pressure on my shoulders. I remind myself that if I need to advocate for my child, then I will use the small amount of privilege I have to do it."

When Carmen noticed that her son's learning needs were not met by the school, she first relied on her family for support: "My mom's a teacher, and we worked with my son to supplement what he was missing in the school system, because they were not giving it to him." Carmen also shares how it quickly became clear to her that she needed external support to advocate for her son's educational needs when the school was not taking her concerns seriously. "I found myself desperate to understand how to support my son in his learning and hired a special education advocate [someone trained to support parents in navigating special education services for children]. My advocate was a godsend. She had the information and authority needed to get my son the services he deserved. She knew the laws, asked for support that I did not know I could ask for, and helped bring me respect. The school authorities listen to me now and are meeting my child's needs adequately. I can see the difference in my son. He has made important strides with support—he actually likes to read now."

For many parents of BIPOC children with disabilities in this country, English is not their native language, and they require translation of documentation into their native language in order to communicate effectively with the school. In response to these language barriers, a community came together in Washington State to fight unjust educational policies and procedures that posed a significant barrier to a quality education for our children. This program, led by parents, enforced the language-access bill requiring effective access to education-related documentation in a parent's native language. Quoting a parent from their report, "When I get emails, they're only in English, and when I try to get them translated, I am ignored or never answered. I went into the school one time to get some documents translated into Spanish. The principal treated me very badly and told me, 'This is the USA, English, English, English.' And then the other staff present began to laugh and make fun of me."

Another barrier parents of BIPOC neurodivergent kids encounter is the internal bias inherent within evaluations and support services. Evaluator biases are an important factor that can impact the accuracy of the evaluation process, resulting in children not receiving a correct or comprehensive diagnosis and, as a result, missing out on the support that would help. Here are some ways in which evaluation biases show up toward Black and Brown children:

- Lower academic expectations.
- Focusing on their "problems" not strengths.
- Adultification of Black children, who are seen and treated as older chronologically or more advanced developmentally through a skewed lens.
- Harsher, more punitive consequences.
- Denial of services, even with special education plans in place, such as a 504 plan or an IEP (discussed in more detail on p. 218).

Our parents share how they experienced the weight of evaluation bias, especially in the context of giftedness. Anamika says, "My son's IEP goals only center on his 'deficiencies' and where he needs to catch up, and less on his strengths and how to develop them. He has become so advanced with math that I fear that because it's too easy for him, he is losing interest and engagement in class."

Arica's experience of special education services for her son exemplifies how the school system is primed to deny the needs of neurodivergent students of color. Arica shares how her son's genius IQ and giftedness diagnosis has made it harder to receive all the learning support that his neurodivergent brain needed. Ironically, she says, "Giftedness has been a barrier to his learning."

Malika agrees as she shares how difficult it has been for her and her partner to seek the accommodations necessary for their gifted child's educational success because of the internalized bias and misconception that giftedness precludes a child from requiring any academic support. Their experience of asking for a specific addition to their child's 504 plan was met with a countersuggestion rather than acceptance. Malika also highlights how the burden of working through such a bias falls unfairly on the shoulders of the parents. "While there may be accommodations like fidget toys and extra time on assignments for those identified as neurodivergent, what it inherently communicates is that one must do the labor of asking—pushing—for them. It also means that without the medical establishments certifying a diagnosis, these accommodations are not available. I long for school systems where there are many ways for students to engage with the material and showcase their learning in various ways that are conducive to their learning styles. Ultimately, I desire that the system is accessible to all ways of being in the world without putting undue labor on those deemed different to fight for their educational rights."

Implicit biases also show up as lower expectations when supporting children with cognitive delays. Angela shares her experience of seeing how the system's low expectations of her nonspeaking autistic daughter manifested in the supportive services she received at school: "As a communication tool, my daughter would only be given three choices to pick from to express herself: [I'm hungry, I'm not feeling well, I need to go to the bathroom]. It made me so mad that they were limiting her communication rather than expanding it. I resisted and advocated for a different approach."

Stories like these surface the crushing power of implicit biases from teachers and administrators working within a racist, ableist, capitalist educational system. Despite educational laws to protect the rights of our children, these overt experiences of racism and ableism land piercingly on parents who already have their hands full navigating the barriers of the special education system, making it that much harder for them to meet the needs of their children within the system. Such stories affirm the urgent need for anti-oppressive educational reform.

While there are many stories of racism and ableism toward parents and children, there also exist important stories of collective support, advocacy, and hope rooted in community relationships. Systemic oppression is meant to divide and isolate us, so any opportunity we may have to lean on one another in service of collective strength and spirit is an opportunity toward collective liberation.

When Joy was called out for being "difficult" when advocating for her son with passion, another teacher of color had her back. She stood up for Joy with an important reframe: "When I encounter a difficult parent, it means they care a lot." Joy recalled how validating it felt to hear this.

Jasmine, too, shares a story of hope. "When my son was wrongfully disciplined and placed on the school-to-prison pipeline for an incident that occurred outside school premises, other parents in the school community approached the principal at school together to advocate for him and demanded that his disciplinary actions be dropped." Such stories remind us of the power of community and how imperative it is that we parents and teachers stand up for those who unjustly get caught in the system.

Body Check

We invite you to gently stretch your body. Notice where you feel tight, where you feel looser. Move your body in any way you feel called to at this moment.

Bullying

Will my child be bullied for their racial and learning differences?

"In his first year of middle school, my son was getting acquainted with the new environment," recalls Jasmine. "The teachers didn't understand him or what he needed, or his accommodations. During that year, when he got sick and stayed home, he got way behind and really struggled to catch up. These teachers, instead of trying to help him, met him with aggression, because he was still there and because he was not understanding it at the pace they wanted him to get it. Of course, he picked up on that energy. So he responded negatively to that energy too. When I asked this teacher, who was White, to help him navigate his assignments to get him caught up, she was very rude to me. She would whisper in her colleague's ear and laugh in front of him. Just made him feel really bad. Basically, he was being bullied by the staff there."

Many of us are apprehensive that our neurodivergent children of color may be singled out for their differences by their peers, but as this story shows, adults, too, can participate in this othering, and our children can become subject to racism and ableism, from subtle microaggressions to overt oppression and bullying. Bullying is a severe school issue that causes lasting emotional and physical distress. In the playgrounds, classrooms, bathrooms, and locker rooms, and even in the less visible terrains of online chatrooms in the form of cyberbullying, children racialized as Black and Brown and with disabilities have been subjected to bullying and rendered powerless.

Reader Alert: This next anecdote contains a graphic description of a suicidal attempt.

Janne's son experienced persistent bullying in schools, and the price of it was an attempt to take his life. "One day after track practice, I went to pick my son up, and he was not there. I found out from school that he was at the nearest hospital. Two girls had accidentally found him hanging himself." Janne connected the suicide attempt to the torment he experienced from a group of kids at track. "My son was on a ventilator for two days and suffered permanent nerve damage that resulted in an anoxic brain injury. He received a lot of incredible support postinjury, but still struggles to live independently, and he has not worked in two years." Janne shakes her head. "I don't know if I am through it. I will live with this for the rest of my life."

Stories like these make us wish we could turn back the clock and provide the deserving interventions to all children involved.

In Janne's story, it is easy to see bullying as an interpersonal, individualized problem where "hurt children hurt children" and learned behavior gets propagated through children. But Jasmine's story of adult-propagated bullying behooves us to take a step back to see the bigger picture and understand bullying as more than an interpersonal problem.

In fact, Aaron Kupchik, author of *The Real School Safety Problem*, makes a daring observation: even when teachers do not directly bully kids, the punitive behavioral-modification measures they enforce resemble bullying in ways such that it is not surprising that students learn to emulate them. Within such a frame, we see that bullying is no longer just an interpersonal social problem but one rooted in the larger power dynamics of crackdown education.

Special Education Plans

Will my child's needs be covered through special education services and followed according to law?

When parents are thinking about special education support, an enormous incentive to consider public education are the federal laws designed to protect children with disabilities: the Individuals with Disabilities Education Act (IDEA) and Section 504 of the Rehabilitation Act of 1973 (commonly referred to as "504"). These laws are meant to ensure that children with disabilities are granted the support they deserve in order to claim their right to free and appropriate education comparable to their neurotypical or physically nondisabled peers.

Supports under IDEA include special education (SPED) services such as a SPED resource classroom, a SPED teacher, and a general education teacher and related services such as physical therapy or speech therapy. A 504 plan, on the other hand, offers less involved accommodations, such as the use of a fidget, particular testing conditions, or a specialized behavioral intervention plan. Such a plan, ideally cocreated by parents, teachers, and the child, may stipulate the use of behaviorist strategies such a token reward system to decrease behaviors deemed undesirable like distractibility or meltdowns, or it may require more relationship-based supports such as requiring that a teacher offer a child a one-on-one check-in at the start, middle, and end of the day to support their emotional state and needs. Overall, IDEA is a stronger law than 504, with greater safeguards for our children and, in theory, greater accountability measures for the administration to follow. To receive the protection of these laws, children must receive a formal diagnosis from professionals like school and developmental psychologists.

While these laws have provided and continue to provide an important educational edge for countless children of color with disabilities, the system is still riddled with educational stories of marginalization and exclusion, owing to the structural barriers inherent in the educational system. One of the ways this came to a head was during the pandemic. The online classroom format made the mistreatment and sidelining of our children more visible to parents like Hana, who found out that her son's 504 plan was not being met. She witnessed her son's strengths and struggles during online instruction and gained insight into his classroom dynamics, seeing how he is taught and treated.

"During the pandemic, all I heard was that he was not doing his work, but I didn't know how badly he was struggling until I saw it myself at home. Yes, it was true that he was not doing his work, but he needed help. He needed someone to check on him. Unfortunately, he doesn't ask for help—he feels like if he does, there is something wrong with him." She wonders if his tendency to not ask for help could be a part of his South Korean cultural messaging absorbed unconsciously.

"*You are your son's 504.*" This was the advice a school psychologist gave Hana when she inquired about the lack of support from the school around her son's 504 plan during the virtual schooling phase of the peak of the pandemic. Even well-intentioned teachers doing their best under a blanket of toxic stress can contribute to increased racial and disability microaggressions towards our children if not well supported to keep their biases in check. "I fully support educators and know how hard it is. The school system as a whole relies on parents not knowing what to ask for or know what they can push back on, because they are already strapped for resources, so it is easier to say no. Teachers will say no, administrators will say no. So I took the psychologist's advice and quit my job so I could be my son's 504."

Though not intended, Hana's financial privilege to devote her full time to her son's education and opportunity to implement the 504 plan virtually during the pandemic brought immense benefits to her son's education. Knowing her son the best, she was able create a truly child-centered special education plan to meet his unique needs. She could start and end school at any time, take breaks as needed for movement and rest, and provide him with emotionally attuned instruction. "My son is a night owl, so if he needed a break during the daytime, we could leave home for a hike and return to work in the evening," Hana shares, attesting to the significant mental health benefits her individualized 504 support and virtual schooling provided him. "I'm not going back to his clinical suicidal depression ever again because he cannot keep up [with the level of instruction at in-person school] and having him internalizing failures. Never again."

Many of our children have ended up not receiving the emotional and learning support they deserved, forcing parents onto various paths, from advocating for their children within the system to leaving it. We chant our favorite mantra once again, that all choices we make in the best interest of our child's needs are valid.

"I don't hang my hat on it." Being an educator herself and knowing how public educators are overloaded by the system, Elizabeth takes a practical approach to meeting her son's learning needs. "The IEP is just paperwork to me," she says. "I focus on where the rubber meets the road, ensuring good communication with the schoolteachers and that appropriate action is taken to support my son's educational needs." Frustrated with the system, she, too, decided to quit her job to attend to her son's learning needs through homeschooling.

"There is no time for the IEP." Molly, parent of an autistic child with ADHD, speaks to the challenges of underfunded schools in high-poverty districts. "My son recently entered kindergarten with an IEP at an under-resourced neighborhood public school where teachers are stretched so thin that they often forget to check if there is an IEP."

"If you don't know, you don't get." Angela goes by this motto and shares her experience during her daughter's school education: "Despite having an IEP, the burden of knowledge and advocacy of services fell on me. I had to stay aware, educated, and constantly vigilant." Time and again it has been seen that the public education system relies on parents not knowing their child's educational rights and not knowing how to navigate the special education system to advocate for their child. And tragically, most often, the system wins. To meet this gap, educational advocacy programs have emerged to support parents.

Cheryl Poe, founder of Advocating 4 Kids, an educational advocacy organization based in Virginia, shares how having an informed advocate can "help parents feel less alone and more empowered" when walking through the special education maze and fighting a mammoth of a system. "You don't have to do this alone."

Relationship-Oriented Education

Will my child have caring teachers who believe in my child's abilities? Will my child receive enough individual attention and connection?

When you think back to your school days, what do you remember the most? A teacher who was particularly caring? A friend who welcomed you to sit next to them when no one else seemed inviting? The sense of community you felt with a club you joined? Or the specifics of your fifth-grade math curriculum? Chances are, it wasn't this last one. That doesn't make math any less important, but it does illustrate that what our internal psyche values first, foremost, and in the long run is how an experience made us feel and if it felt safe or not, rather than what specific content we learned, as exhilarating as that may have been at the time. This feeling is created in a nurturing relationship and has the power to make or break our self-esteem and our desire to learn. And in school, the relationships that can have the biggest impact are often with teachers, like Mr. R in the chapter's opening anecdote. Being in an affirming relationship creates a sense of emotional safety to help us feel, think, and learn well. All children deserve this.

Unfortunately, the reality of much of public education is that it prioritizes production over relationships. A production-oriented education system, deeply embedded in a capitalistic and ableist ethos, sees the role of schools as integral to cultivating future workers to serve capitalism. As such, the focus is teaching children to behave so that they conform and produce efficiently, which strips away the creativity and passion our children hold in their hearts.

Malika's experience speaks to what happens when schools value conformity and operate from a narrow definition of productivity: "Luckily, our twice-exceptional child qualified for the gifted program in our school district at the end of his first-grade year. We were excited about this because we thought it would provide him with the needed services and support his insatiable appetite for learning. However, during one parent-teacher conference, the teacher politely informed us that our son had failed the math test, because he had skipped several pages to focus on one problem where he had provided a way to solve this problem in twenty different ways. We thought that this program would foster our child's creativity and out-of-the box thinking. Instead, it was just an alternative path to making them conform within the box."

Malika's anecdote illustrates behaviorism, the idea that behaviors that do not conform to normal social expectations are to be fixed with rewards or punishment. In this case, a child was punished by failing them on their test without a semblance of curiosity for the way the child brought creativity to the table. It is tragically antithetical that a teacher within a program designed to support neurodivergent thinkers, a goldmine for creativity, is conditioned to stifle creative thinking. Perhaps if this teacher's own creativity were encouraged and they were better supported within the system, Malika's child's strengths would have been seen and appreciated too. But such experiences are exactly by design and hence expected of a production-oriented education, in which a relationship-oriented partnership between teacher and student is replaced with a stack of instructions, some brownie points or a fail grade, being sent to the principal's office, or often a ready suspension.

For change to occur such that education becomes relationship oriented, the whole system would need to be reorganized. Policies would change, a fundamental shift in values, attitudes, and beliefs in relationship-oriented education would transpire, teachers would receive more care and support to do their incredibly challenging jobs, and parents would be free to expand their definition of their children's success at school. Then, our dream of a relationship-oriented educational environment that would nurture and celebrate the uniqueness of all children, including children with differences, could be realized.

Despite the existing systemic barriers, we hear heartwarming stories of particular teachers who have gone the extra mile, and continue to do so, to affect our children in important ways. Here we share some stories of teachers who, despite their busy and challenging jobs, have committed to remaining relational as they teach. As we enter these stories, we hold the reality that these relationships are more likely present in well-resourced schools with well-supported teachers and usually a luxury within the current public education system available to us. But it is important that these stories be told and heard so we can be reminded what a difference relationship-oriented education can make for our children. Quality education for our children is meant to be a right, not a luxury.

Molly shares, "With an inclusive White teacher who understood ADHD because she had it too, my kid flourished. She celebrated our cultural holidays at school and advocated for him at the IEP meetings. As a result, he jumped three reading levels in her class." Sophia feels similarly about her children's public school. "So far, I have had a lovely experience with my school district. They have been very supportive, and the teachers and aides are like an extended family for my children." Meena also shares how her child's private school was like her second home. "Teachers and para educators* and families were incredibly supportive of both my child and us."

Janne recollects how her child had a magnificent first-grade teacher who knew he was a little quirky and saw his strengths and challenges. "She believed in his potential. She had a way to calm him down and was patient with him." As Janne says, "Teachers have the power to make or break a desire to learn."

Valento beams, sharing his experience of his children's schooling: "Every teacher is amazing and has worked with them and their needs. At one point, I was getting daily strengths-based reports about [my daughter's] day. They value partnering with parents and take care to staff IEP meetings well, including five other teachers and staff in there with me. It is teamwork, and they do it very professionally and take it very seriously." Valento's experience at this school greatly validated his decision to switch school districts upon noticing how his children were not thriving in their earlier setting. "My son was only there for three months, but you could see that he regressed in his education there, because the teachers there did not lean in, and it didn't help at all." Valento was grateful he leaned on his intuition to seek a school where relationship-driven education was valued, because that allowed his children to thrive.

These stories, along with the chapter's opening anecdote, remind us not only that relationships are critical to the emotional well-being of children, but also that relationships prime children's brains to learn at their best. But one nurturing teacher during one particular year of school can only do so much. Our children deserve such relationships throughout their education. We envision that at the heart of relationship-oriented education lies a whole nurturing school community that commits to connecting with and affirming every single child's strengths and learning needs, bolstered by a systemic culture that supports such a practice.

---

* Professionals who work alongside teachers to provide extra support to students with higher needs.

Punitive Discipline

Will my child be disciplined in harsh ways?

Tapping foot, repetition of verbalized thought, lack of eye contact, loud vocalization, nonverbal communication, nonresponsiveness, inability to sit still, overwhelm, impulsivity, stimming, aggression. These are some behaviors commonly correlated with neurodivergence that we see in our Black, Brown, or Indigenous children in classrooms or at the playground—or at the principal's office. These behaviors serve an important function to help our children regulate, but most often they are misunderstood as willful defiance and cause for punitive discipline.

Malika, one of many parents who routinely experienced reports of their children's behaviors in school, shares how her child's ADHD-related behaviors were repeatedly seen through the ableism filter as wrong. "We would get communications from the school about his 'disruptive' behavior, including his inability to sit still in the chair and his lack of interest in following rules when it comes to standing in a line. It bothered me to hear that just being a fidgety kid meant he was getting notes sent home. He was being told something was wrong with him."

Jasmine tells us about experiences with her son's school that speak to the role racism plays in what behaviors are coded as delinquent. "It started when he was in kindergarten. My son was hyperactive, would not stay in his seat, and would get under his desk. Instead of getting him support or testing him to find out what was going on, they put my kid out in the hallway. They just got him out of their hair and did not want to deal with him. Now in middle school, the teacher, who was White, thought my son was being disrespectful during the Pledge of Allegiance, because he stopped in the middle of picking up his books to say the pledge. She pushed him with her hands from the classroom into the hallway. When I confronted the school about this, they did an investigation led by the school resource officer [police officers stationed at public schools] and the principal. It is no surprise that they concluded that there was nothing else to pursue and that the investigation was closed. I kept asking for a copy of the report, and they would not give it to me. If my son, as a five-foot-nine Black male, had done anything like what the teacher had done, he would be in handcuffs."

Speaking on special education programs that remove children for their behaviors, Corey says, "These types of programs are aggressive. My daughter had a medical emergency one day, and instead of responding to her medical needs, the teacher insisted she finish her task and then continued to ignore her pleas. Eventually, my daughter started kicking and crying. In response, they pinned her down on her back and held her down for over seventeen minutes. My daughter had bruises from being pinned down. Three hours after my daughter said she was not feeling well, they finally called my wife to come and get her. In this program, my daughter was denied medical care, ignored, bruised, and disrespected. After this incident, I did not want her to go back to this school. Since she did not go back, they suspended her. She is now finishing her schooling online."

These examples illustrate how our children's regulatory behaviors along with their race determine the consequences imposed on them. While some punitive discipline is highly visible, typical punitive consequences frequently show up in small doses to disrupt a child's education. Children of color with neurodivergence are more likely to miss recess, do extra homework, be sent to the principal's office, be sent home with parents early, and interact with a school resource officer than their White counterparts. Each time a child is removed from their educational setting to receive behavior correction interventions, a.k.a. punishments, they are impacted academically and emotionally. This reinforces the preschool-to-prison pipeline.

Ideally, to discipline is to teach, but sadly, punitive discipline teaches our children nothing good. Instead, it induces fear and presents a threat to our children's nervous system, eliciting a survival response that looks like revving up or shutting down, with learning new information being the last priority. When punitive discipline becomes the norm, so that our precious children experience it every day, many times a day, and see other children experiencing it too, they become conditioned to respond to it as an ongoing threat to their emotional and physical health. Emotionally, our children internalize shame, embarrassment, a feeling of inadequacy or worthlessness, isolation, or low self-esteem and may experience anxiety and depression. These feelings often live in their bodies and show up in physiological ways such as stomach, head, or body aches; sleep issues; and increased meltdowns and shutdowns. If our child was already falling behind academically, punitive discipline only makes it harder for them to catch up. For some of our children, these health impacts, along with the persistent threat that induces them, may result in a refusal to attend school—a big challenge that parents and schools must contend with. Parenting at this juncture can be a confusing and helpless experience. When our neurodivergent child is unable to communicate their internalized experiences to us, we are placed with the grave responsibility to be vigilant for these external signs of distress and trauma to clue us in to how our children may be experiencing their world and how they need us to support them.

Sadly, as we have shared previously, an unsafe environment can make our children's regulatory behaviors more visible as they work extra hard to regulate through their fears. And it is the same unsafe environment that can make our children feel even more unsafe under egregious discipline, making this a vicious cycle. There comes a point when our children's nervous systems get so triggered that they may react in ways that are misunderstood as defiance or as a threat, triggering extreme consequences from the school authorities. What is more frightening than our children's behaviors is the authority that our school administrators have to exercise undue force over our children in ways that are not overseen effectively by federal law. This package of behaviorism, adultism, and racism lands on children as a sit-down with the school resource officer, surveillance cameras to scrutinize children, juvenile detention, suspensions, restraints and seclusion, expulsion, and even death.

Elizabeth shares how her son's elementary school responded to his unsafe behaviors toward teachers: "They would pull him out, make him sit in the administrator's office, and try to calm him down within two hours. If they couldn't, they would call us parents to get him. As an educator, it is tricky, because I can see from the educator's perspective. But as a parent, if you pull him out, he misses out."

Janne shares how her child, diagnosed with what was then called Asperger's syndrome but is now seen as a part of the autism spectrum, would fall victim to group bullying. At one point, he became dysregulated and threatened his peers. This yielded a suspension. However, Janne notes how the school failed to see the entirety of the situation. A group of kids had tormented him before he lost his temper. In missing this critical big picture, her son was further marginalized.

Hana speaks to the consequences of the school failing to provide the necessary educational support to her son, resulting in emotional and behavioral difficulties, specifically with impulse control. She states that the school immediately wrote him up as a delinquent. "Writing him off as a delinquent is probably the worst thing they can do for him. It would impact how he was treated all remaining years in school," she says. "This is the impact of being BIPOC and neurodivergent—you don't get a lot of chances."

Cheryl Poe also reminds us, with historical context in mind, that sometimes it isn't our children's neurodivergent behavior but other aspects of their disability that are cause for punitive discipline. She says, "I know that many kids get suspended because they're asked to read aloud by a teacher and they are unable to, because of their disability. Coming from a history that criminalized Black people for being able to read, it is ironic that we now criminalize Black and Brown children for not being able to."

It is no wonder many parents of neurodivergent children of color entering the school system sit with fears about how their neurodivergent child will be treated for the differences inherent in the ways they behave, which are often misconstrued as intentional noncompliance or defiance. This normative culture of behaviorism in school, seeing children as needing to be fixed and brought into alignment via rewards and punishments, has been stretched to the point of partnerships between schools and the police state.

What's more, the crisis of school shootings has perpetuated a climate of fear of children for adults. An unreasonable and unfounded response has been to employ police in our schools to ensure safety. Predictably, children of color with disabilities are seen as a threat to this safety.

Systemic responses to behaviors of our children perceived as dangerous include restraints and seclusions. An extreme byproduct of behaviorism, *restraints* restrict a child's body movements with a tight hold, and *seclusion* confines a child alone in a small place. Both these methods have proven to be dangerous, leading to serious physical injury, trauma, and even death. While they are to be used if a child is a grave, imminent harm to others, they are used more often than needed in response to minor behavioral problems from children of color with disabilities. "The problem is that there is no federal law today banning seclusion and restraints. Each state is left to address it on their own. There is no evidence, data, or research that shows that restraints and seclusion keep behaviors from happening. Staff feel bad for putting their hands on a child, the child who is restrained is traumatized, and other children who witness this are also traumatized." says Cheryl Poe.

Reader Alert: This next section contains descriptions of unjust deaths resulting from systemic punitive discipline.

This is how Grace, a fifteen-year-old Black girl, was sentenced to juvenile detention for not completing her homework. This is how a school principal repeatedly caged Jaleel Williams, an eight-year-old Black boy in Washington State. This is how Michael Renner-Lewis III, a fifteen-year-old Black boy on the autism spectrum, was restrained for "noncompliance" and killed on the first day of high school. And this is how Cornelius Frederick, a sixteen-year-old Black boy, died after being restrained for twelve minutes for throwing a sandwich.

These gut-wrenching stories are just a few examples among many. Let us breathe for the precious children we have lost in this way to such senseless injustice.

While it may rightfully feel like a powerless place to be as a parent educating our children in a system infused with behaviorism, in chapter 10 we will share some practical ways in which we can advocate for our children and keep them safe, in the context of protecting our children from the preschool-to-prison pipeline. You don't have to do this alone.

Body Check

Think of a place where you feel calm and relaxed, a refuge from the demands of every day. This can be a real or imagined place. Maybe your favorite room from childhood or a place in your house today, a place in nature, in your car, by the water . . . Let yourself be there, recall the sights, the sounds, the smells, and how the air feels on your skin. Notice your breathing. Stay as long as you need, and leave when you are ready. Please know this place exists as a resource in times of stress.

Alternatives to Public Schooling

What if public school is not a fit for my child?

With the numerous barriers preventing our children from receiving an equitable, respectful, and child-centered education in the public-school system, it is no wonder that so many families seek an alternative path. The last few decades have seen prolific growth in the number of alternative schools that specialize in teaching neurodivergent children, as well as in the reach of grassroots efforts: parents coming together to create their own communities of learning that cater specifically to their children's unique learning needs. Learning concepts such as "homeschooling" and "unschooling" have entered our collective daily lexicon. These efforts reflect a deep yearning in our society to advocate for the numerous children who fall through the cracks of public education. While some of these alternate environments are inclusive of many types of learners, some are more specialized, e.g., for dyslexic children. Despite the benefits that inclusive education offers our children, by bringing an affinity group of students together under one roof, difference is readily normalized. At their core, these alternatives exist for our children who yearn to show up unapologetically in the world, to be seen and celebrated for their strengths, and to be supported adequately in their challenges.

As we approach this section, we recognize the privileges that are inherent in the decisions made alternative to the public-school system. Privileges of financial means (a high or adequate household income), time (one parent may need to give up their formal career to take up a new, unpaid job as teacher or colearner), and resources (a two-parent household, literacy) make alternative schooling decisions more comfortably possible. We highlight these options to validate the stories of many parents at the intersections.

Private School

Private schools are an important alternative option for families that can afford to consider it. They offer many benefits that public schools do not and are often sought out by parents who have ruled out the public education route.

Unlike public schools, private schools come in many shapes and sizes. Some cater to the general population, others to certain types of learners. Depending on our child's learning needs and our values and preferences, we may gravitate toward one option over another. For example, a school that specializes in teaching dyslexic children can be very affirming for a dyslexic child. To be among other children who think like them, who experience struggles and joys like them, can be immensely normalizing to children and families. Neurodiversity-affirming private schools that cater to all kinds of thinking and learning styles can provide neurodivergent and neurotypical children the opportunity to learn and play together. We have seen the benefits these kinds of inclusive learning opportunities provide.

Parents of neurodivergent children turn to the option of private schools for a variety of reasons. Some parents come to private schooling after trying out public schooling and learning that it did not meet the needs of their child. Others with the financial means have tried private schooling throughout their child's elementary years. Dolores shares how she knew early on that public school would not be a good fit for her son: "As a professional, I have advocated for many clients with special education needs in the public-school system that quickly informed me that public school was not a place where my son would thrive. His private school with a small classroom and a great teacher-to-student ratio has been a great fit for him. The current school supports his learning by accommodating his needs, just like the 504 plan in the public school without the paperwork, and the teachers are very understanding. We work together as a team."

Meena also reflects on how private school was a wonderful fit for her son in his early years. She noticed that her son thrived in an environment designed purely for children with unique learning needs, and how it supported her son's sense of belonging and self-esteem. "The advantage of this school is that he grew up without any shame, because all learners are neurodivergent."

Deepti shares how her daughter's private school has offered her many benefits that public school could not have. "A private school's ability to offer any child generous amounts of time for outdoor play and movement, multidisciplinary learning, connection with teachers, and extra support from a learning specialist team, all while prioritizing their emotional health, their strengths and preferences, to offer a truly child-centered education is any parent's dream for their child, not just parents of a neurodivergent child of color."

Serena decided on private school for her daughter because she was very worried about bullying in public schools. She says, "I wanted her to be in classrooms where there are low student-teacher ratios and more attention on her."

Private schools, not bound by state laws and rules, have much freedom to shape their programming to suit neurodivergent learning needs. When done well, private schools have the resources to properly invest in areas that would serve all children's diverse learning needs, including access to technology and continuing education. True, the bells and whistles of private schools are attractive, but the backbone of these perks is the systemic support (care, community, resources, training) provided to their teaching community that in turn help them to be able to support their students well in the here and now and to sustain their energy and good thinking throughout the school year. As pointed out by several of our parents, the low student-to-teacher ratios make it conducive for teachers to create meaningful relationships with children and foster a climate of emotional safety through their learning environment.

Homeschooling

Many families of color are turning to homeschooling for their neurodivergent children to carve out a learning path that does not exist for their child in public-school settings. Factors of financial ability, parent readiness to educate their child, low teacher-to-student ratios, flexibility in routine, and parent educator's knowledge of their child as a learner are very attractive to many families. As we wrote this chapter during the pandemic, we saw a significant rise in the percentage of families of color opting to homeschool.

Homeschooling, however, is not a contemporary trend. It has been a long-standing act of social resistance in US Black history. Dating back to the 1930s, hundreds of Black families chose to withdraw from public schooling in search for a better, just, and honest education, reflective of the needs of Black children. This movement was spearheaded by a Black mother, Sister Clara Muhammad, in response to the unjust restricted education provided to Black children in adherence to Jim Crow laws. This movement resulted in the creation of independent elementary and secondary schools for Black children, only to have those schools be criminalized by the state, eventually leading many families to homeschool against the laws.

Elizabeth speaks to her grave disappointment of seeing her adopted multiracial son straddled between two settings of general and special education ineffectively in his public school as she shares that "there is no place that catches my son's needs in the system. As an educator I am seriously thinking about homeschooling. Why should I have to do this? I'm feeling resentful."

Another adoptive parent, Kim, shares how she knew from the start that traditional schooling was not going to work for their son. She shares, "Homeschool has given us so much flexibility. I started a homeschool co-op with another mom, who was a special education teacher, inclusive of all learners. We structured our co-op outside, with a lot of open and free play, and made lessons shorter and interactive. Our son is able to do clay, chew gum, eat snacks, or draw to regulate himself during a lesson, and the parents stay during the co-op to support the children in their social interactions."

For parents entering the homeschooling arena, there is not much recognized access to critical information that would help parents educate children with special learning needs at home. For example, many homeschooling parents of color are left unaware that their local public-school district is obligated to provide a special education evaluation to their homeschooled child at no cost to parents, and to provide any teaching consultation and support if possible and within their means.

Hana, who took to virtual schooling from home during the pandemic as her son's primary teacher, reaped the benefits of homeschooling with the support of her home state's public-school curriculum and structure. When she decided to continue virtual schooling despite schools opening up after the first years of the pandemic, many asked if she was denying her son the opportunity for socialization. "I know there is the weighing of social interactions, but I'm more than willing to pay for social groups [to supplement]." Many adjunct programs exist around the country to support homeschoolers, such as homeschool networks for social bonding and experiences.

With the rise of homeschooling's popularity for children at the intersections especially, it is also valid when parents decide against homeschooling for important reasons. Malika shares a perspective many of us will resonate with: "We considered homeschooling and spoke to other parents about how it works. Where we live, the homeschooling community is mostly White, and we decided that, at least that in the public-school gifted program, there were kids of color that our kid could connect with. Also given our kid's need for structure, we did not know if homeschooling would meet his needs."

Deepti shares how despite her draw to homeschooling for its benefits to our children, she had to decide against it: "Being neurodivergent with my own executive functioning challenges, I can barely keep my receipts organized, let alone organize and execute a curriculum to teach my child. I knew I would not be setting ourselves up for success if I attempted to homeschool."

Unschooling

Unschooling is a type of homeschooling that is founded on the premise that children have the wisdom to direct their own learning. It has been defined by Earl Stevens as a "unique opportunity to step away from systems and methods, and to develop independent ideas out of actual experiences, where the child is truly in pursuit of knowledge, not the other way around." Iris Chen, author of *Untigering*, calls unschooling "an act of resistance," specifically against White supremacy, racial/gender stereotypes, ableism, and other forms of oppression that target marginalized voices.

For many reasons similar to homeschooling, unschooling declares itself as a legitimate response to traditional education that has been so oppressive to children of color and children with disabilities. Parents come to this option mostly upon rejecting the notion of homeschooling for philosophical but also practical reasons. Practically, many parents do not feel that it is possible for them to wear the dual parent and teacher hats, making homeschooling less desirable. Philosophically, unschooling parents see homeschooling as providing the same learning curriculum, structure, and standards set for children by Whiteness. Many parents that look to unschooling have already traversed the path of traditional schooling and perhaps even homeschooling. They are drawn to unschooling for values that resonate with them, including disruption of time and urgency and full trust in a child to be leaders of their own learning, empowerment, and liberation.

Joshua shares how his family decided to carve out an entirely different path for his child: "When we saw our kid struggle in the traditional school environment, we began to look at alternatives and did not see any good options anywhere. We decided against homeschooling because needing to be a teacher and parent was not what we wanted to do. We wondered what we did before current social norms and technology.

We did not worry about learning, grades, and performance. Traditional schools have created a sense within children of not being good enough. So we decided to go the unschooling route: It allows children to trust in their genius and to feel self-motivated to follow their curiosity; they learn faster and better. Traditional schools, on the other hand, squash children's true sense of self."

Luisa shares this sense of freedom when she decided to pull her first child out of formal school after her first kindergarten year in public school, and there was no turning back. She recollects, "My daughter was having a tough time with learning in kindergarten. And here I come from a special education background, and seeing her struggling at school at such a tender age with a negative view of herself, where her self-confidence took a hit, was hard. It prompted me to start looking and searching for an alternative. At first I was drawn to homeschooling, but the educational philosophy of 'unschooling' really resonated with me. I have since unschooled both my children, and it has been the best decision for us."

Thus far we have explored what concerns parents, the choices available, and the barriers to equitable education. In working to ensure that our children are equitably and properly educated, it may be that our own experiences in the educational system will resurface, resulting in many feelings for us. We find value in slowing down to understand how our stories intersect with our children's and how our unhealed/unprocessed wounding might get in the way of clarity. Here we offer a few prompts as an invitation for reflection.

Reflection Questions

- What are your memories of your own education?
- What were some inherent strengths and challenges in your own education journey?
- Where did the values you hold about education come from?
- What is the connection between your perception of your child's strengths, challenges, and needs, and the values you hold about education?
- Who was your favorite teacher growing up and why?
- What are some fears you hold for your child's education?
- What do you need in your support system to be able to advocate for your child's learning needs?

Resources for Deeper Understanding

Advocacy

Advocating 4 Kids. https://www.adv4kidsinc.org.

Alliance Against Seclusion and Restraint. https://endseclusion.org.

Down Syndrome International. "A Brief History of the Concept of Inclusive Education." YouTube, 4:04, March 23, 2022. https://www.youtube.com/watch?v=Ed9Nc4ayQ-A.

Olympia Therapy. "The Weight of Distance Learning." December 9, 2020. https://www.olympiatherapy.com/post/the-weight-of-distance-learning.

School Choices

Robinson, Sir Ken. "Do Schools Kill Creativity?" TED, January 7, 2007. YouTube, 20:03. https://youtu.be/iG9CE55wbtY.

Wilson, Betti. "'Homeschooling? Really? We Didn't Think We Could Do It, But . . . .'" *ADDitude*, April 6, 2022. https://www.additudemag.com/homeschooling-autism-success-story/.

Legal Resources

Wright, Peter W. D., and Pamela Darr Wright. "The History of Special Education Law in the United States." Wrightslaw. Updated October 18, 2021. https://www.wrightslaw.com/law/art/history.spec.ed.law.htm.

Ableism

ACLU Washington, "Pushed Out; Kicked Out: Stories from Families with Special Education Students in Washington." https://www.aclu-wa.org/pages/pushed-out-kicked-out-stories-families-special-education-students-washington.

Disability Rights Education and Defense Fund. "A Comparison of ADA, IDEA, and Section 504." https://dredf.org/legal-advocacy/laws/a-comparison-of-ada-idea-and-section-504/.

National Council on Disability, *IDEA Series: The Segregation of Students with Disabilities*, February 7, 2018. https://ncd.gov/sites/default/files/NCD_Segregation-SWD_508.pdf.

Punishment Issues

Kupchik, Aaron. *The Real School Safety Problem: The Long-Term Consequences of Harsh School Punishment*. Berkely: University of California Press, 2016.

10

DISMANTLING THE PIPELINE

Protecting Our Children from the Legal System

"My son and his friends made a bad decision. They were playing with a clear toy plastic gun with an orange tip, and they should not have been joking that way. There were four kids; one was White, and the other two were mixed race. My son is Black. The White kid has been friends with my son for years, playing with Nerf guns. The joke they decided to play was to prank this White kid by startling him with this toy gun and then recording him. I have my son on video coming into the house to get the toys, and then he leaves. The video shows them playing in front of the house, and at some point, they run down the street, getting ready to implement this joke. My son calls this kid's name, and the kid sees the toy gun, gets scared, and runs home to Mom. Another friend is following this kid, saying, 'Come back, it's a joke, it's not real, calm down.'

"This kid's mom calls the police and tells them there is a revolver. This mom did not come to me, talk to me, or try to find out anything. She just went to the police. All of this happened in the afternoon, but the police came to my house at ten o'clock at night. They try to enter my house, saying my son has a gun. Number one, I'm a Black woman in America. You are not coming to my house at 10:00 PM. For all I know, you could come into my house and say something that didn't happen and hurt my son and me. No way. That weekend, I got a call from the principal, telling me my son couldn't come back to school, though none of this happened in school. They automatically took the word of this White family. And my son was automatically guilty. And so the police tell me

that 'We want to give him a brandishing a firearm charge' at thirteen years old and take him in." —Jasmine

In this chapter, we get into the legal and criminal justice system, a complex, challenging, and confounding topic.* For many families of color, this chapter may be painful and, at the same time, validating. However, if you are not Black, Latinx, or Indigenous, you may think this chapter has nothing to offer you and your family. Regardless of how our specific communities are impacted, we think this chapter is essential reading for all parents raising children of color with neurodivergence. Our collective freedom is dependent on all of us caring and acting. This is our shared history. This is also, unfortunately, our shared future. We are interconnected; when one child is hurting, all our children are hurt.

If you feel disconnected from this topic for whatever reason, whether due to overwhelming pain or the idea that this chapter does not impact your child, we think it is worth pausing to notice your response. You may see that the disconnection within your response reflects the systematic disconnection underpinning the larger legal system. Unmistakably, this system thrives on severing connections between families, friends, schools, and communities. If it helps to know, even as authors of this chapter and as therapists, we needed time to arrive here. Just reading and researching the subject, we felt overwhelmed, angry, confused, and sad. To live at the mercy of this system with our children is unfathomable. We even wondered if this book could get by without this chapter. But finally, by giving ourselves time, we have been able to bridge our heart and intellect, reconnect with our body, our breath, our feelings, and most important, reconnect with you, for this invisible relationship we have with you is the *why* behind this chapter.

We hope you will allow yourself the time and space you need. Sitting with brutal truths and moving through them connects us more deeply

* A note on language: You will notice that we use the word *disability* more in this chapter. While we situate neurodivergence as a disability, the data and stories of young people pushed into the legal system use the word *disability* to capture the varying experiences within this identity. It does not distinguish between children in the system who are disabled physically versus cognitively.

to those with varying experiences, restoring the collective humanity that the criminal justice system is designed to steal.

Introduction

In 1944 a fourteen-year-old Black boy, George Stinney Jr., was electrocuted for allegedly murdering two White girls. He would be and remains the youngest person to receive the death penalty. His body was so small that George needed to sit on a Bible to fit in the electric chair, and the mask on his face kept slipping off, revealing the tears of a terrified young child. Finally, some sixty years later, the case was reopened, and George Stinney was found innocent.

Ten years later, Emmett Till, another young Black boy, was bludgeoned to death by vigilantes who thought he behaved inappropriately towards a White woman. Emmett, who had suffered a bout of polio as a young child, developed a disability, most evident in his stutter. His mom taught him to whistle to clear his vocal passages. This brilliant adaptation would be read as a catcall, resulting in his life ending tragically. The image of his brutalized face in an open casket was a powerful act of resistance by his mother, who insisted that the world see and confront what happened to her beloved son. Many years later, the White woman who accused Emmett Till admitted to fabricating the story. And unsurprisingly, the men who murdered Emmett were found innocent.

Pause. Breathe. Notice your body. No child or human being deserves to die in this way.

Today, we have a painfully growing list of names of children of color with disabilities targeted by the juvenile justice system. The data shows that most of these children are Black, Latinx, and Indigenous. They have been restrained, assaulted by police officers, arrested, placed in chokeholds, removed from their caregivers, and called despicable and cruel names. Some have sadly lost their lives to the police and legal system—tragedy after tragedy.

Our children's entry into the juvenile justice system often begins with run-ins with police in their neighborhoods and contact with school resource officers (SRO). SROs are armed police officers placed in schools to act as law enforcement, mentors, and counselors for youth. Encountering them impacts our children profoundly—emotionally, physically, and socially. Corey says, "On one side of the freeway, the police in schools are there to protect. On the other side, the police are there to arrest," speaking to the racism inherent in how law enforcement is leveraged against students in the school, depending on what "side of the tracks" a school is located on.

The impact of criminalizing our children is seldom isolated and bleeds into their families. For example, we know that when parents are incarcerated, children experience psychological distress, can develop unhealthy coping mechanisms, struggle in school, and face an increased risk of being incarcerated themselves. Most damaging, the incarceration of parents gravely impacts how families find connection and safety over generations.

Similarly when children are incarcerated, members of their family are also significantly impacted. For parents and family members to be disconnected from their children for a prolonged period is unimaginably painful. In addition, the systemic lack of transparency in the legal process and the legal rights of children and families throughout this process keeps caregivers from adequately supporting the needs of the whole family. It destroys families within a generation but also well into the future.

Acknowledging that this is a monstrously big topic, in this chapter we focus on our children's vulnerabilities due to race and neurodivergence and explore preventive strategies related to police encounters. A special thanks to Cheryl Poe of Advocating 4 Kids for her contributions to this chapter, specifically the prevention section.

To situate the discussion, we begin by providing a brief overview of law enforcement history in this country.

A Historical Context of Policing

We begin with history because we need to know our past to reshape the future. However, we recognize that many of you already know this history in your bodies. This is not new. Instead of educating or informing, we present this condensed history as a political act: the more we speak this truth, tell the story, and make it plain, the more we unsettle and disrupt mainstream narratives about policing. For those who do not have similar relationships with the police, there is something to be gained in a more conventional sense from this condensed history.

Encounters with police have a long and torturous history dating back to the settler-colonial occupation of this land. Policing has taken many forms over the years, but underpinning the drive to police has been the domination of a land and its people in the name of building capital. With Indigenous communities, we cannot separate that the logic of elimination has dictated policing and continues to be an occupying force. In fact, data shows that more Indigenous people die at the hands of the police than any other group. We cannot separate that policing is intimately tied to continuing the settler-colonial project.

Policing expanded during slavery to control Black bodies so that wealth accumulation and land acquisition through cheap and free labor could continue. And it only grew from there. From slave patrols, a group of self-appointed White men who took it upon themselves to return enslaved people who had run away using vigilante tactics; to the Black Codes, which limited the freedoms of Black people and increased the parameters of what constitutes criminal behaviors; to Jim Crow laws, which denied civil rights by instituting separate-but-equal policies; segregation was enforced by police, and breaking these laws led to further criminalization and punishments. The process continues with today's mass incarceration, in which the overcriminalization of petty offenses (for example, marijuana possession and minor theft) has increased racial disparities in our criminal justice system. Mass incarceration of Black and Brown people in our prison system is an avatar of the system of slavery—it is a way to control and exert power over Black bodies.

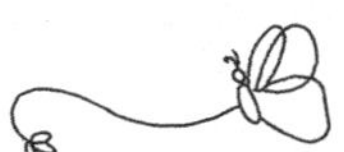

The cause of the problem of police abuse of African people is that Black communities are effectively domestic colonies in the United States and the police serve as an occupying force in those communities.

—M Adams

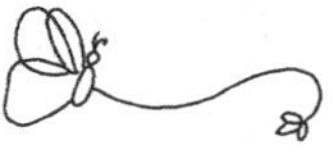

The policing of disabled people is also both historical and current. Disabled people were institutionalized and sent away to poorhouses and sanitariums to keep White, wealthy, and nondisabled people comfortable and safe. The "ugly laws" of the 1800s sanctioned the removal of poor, disabled, and immigrant people away from urban centers to create a "more beautiful" environment. While largely seen as positive, the deinstitutionalization movement of disabled people did not include structural shifts to address housing, health care, and employment of disabled people. As a result, many disabled people, especially those of color, have now been subject to increased policing and criminalization. Today, disabled people of color are overrepresented in the justice system. Equating Blackness and disabilities with criminality has devastating consequences. This does not account for the additional stress some may have of being poor, LGBTQ, and an immigrant.

Data from the American Civil Liberties Union plainly illustrates the disparate criminalization of students of color and students with disabilities.

- Students with disabilities were arrested at a rate 2.9 times that of students without disabilities. In some states, they were ten times as likely to be arrested than their counterparts.
- Black students were arrested at a rate three times that of White students. In some states, they were eight times as likely to be arrested.
- Pacific Island / Native Hawaiian and Native American students were arrested at a rate two times that of White students.
- Latinx students were arrested at a rate of 1.3 times that of White students.
- Black girls made up 16 percent of the female student population but 39 percent of the girls arrested in school. In addition, Black girls were charged at a rate four times that of White girls.
- Native American girls had a school arrest rate of 3.5 times that of White girls.

While policing is promoted as a way to keep our communities safe, it is in fact a tool for the systematic criminalization of those perceived as a threat by identifying delinquent and criminal behaviors within our communities. So, when SROs are placed in schools, the motivations and goals of the larger policing system inevitably inform the assessment, perceptions, and engagement with our youth. Sadly, the system is evidence of the harmful ways White supremacy, ableism, and capitalism intersect.

We briefly pause here to say that while we are talking about policing as part of the criminal justice system, we see that the "policing" of marginalized kids transcends this system and trickles down to schools, doctor's offices, technology, community settings, and the home. The fear of our child's entanglement with the external systems can unknowingly pressure us parents into becoming the first enforcers of policing. If we keep our child in check, we believe, the system won't need to. But, of course, we cannot keep the system from criminalizing our children. That our children's behaviors are a rightful response or manifestation of living under oppressive systems is grossly missed—instead, they are seen as criminals and end up in a system that perpetuates the trauma of living under these systems. It is a tragic loop.

Listen to your kids. If they say something weird that puzzles you, listen more.
—Carmen

Vulnerabilities

There is no justification for the brutality enforced on children by law enforcement and criminal justice systems, regardless of the crime committed (and often, there is none). Racism, ableism, and adultism, stemming from supremacy, are deeply embedded in the structures of the criminal justice system, and as a result, neurodivergent children of color become natural and easy targets. Here, we list some of the most significant vulnerabilities of our children that play out at the interpersonal, institutional, and ideological levels.

"We talk about how this country treats people with Black and Brown skin differently, says Joshua. "We talk about racism; we are more at risk of being put in jail just because of our skin. I carry the fear of my child being pulled into the criminal justice system, and it impacts how we parent. We worry about emotional explosions towards us or our property. Suppose he does not learn how to do something different with his body. That worries us. We work on emotional regulation as the most important thing to remember, because it can keep him safe. We told him if you don't understand this, you could get into big trouble with the law and be thrown in jail. It truly breaks our hearts to name this. We started talking about this after the murder of George Floyd. The truth is, with kids of color, this is part of their education on how to stay safe in a world not designed for them."

The Invisibility of Neurodivergence

We know our children and we know their behaviors and what they mean. But often the very behavior that communicates needing support is read as willful and uncharitably characterized by the external world. This is because some of the disabilities like autism, ADHD, and learning disabilities are not immediately visible upon first meeting someone. And even if someone knows that a child is neurodivergent, many people are ignorant of how these disabilities manifest, leading to interactions with neurodivergent children that lack understanding and respect. This often shows when our children are treated according to their chronological age rather than their developmental age. Because our kids develop asynchronously, when they are not doing what is expected of them at a particular chronological age, they are shamed for not knowing.

- Behaviors such as stimming, inattention, lack of eye contact, and impulsivity get misconstrued as defiance.
- Obsessive behaviors can look like boundary violations. Many of our children have special interest areas that lure them in with a single-minded focus. For instance, a child could follow a person obsessively because of their interest in the Pokémon characters on their backpack. The following behavior, uncontextualized, looks like an intentional boundary violation.

- Expressing intense emotions like anger can be read as intentionally threatening. Recall the incident shared in chapter 9 in which Janne's son lost his temper after constant bullying at school. "Some kids would torment him every day," Janne says. "And one day, my son reached his breaking point and yelled back, 'I'm going to kill you!' and ended up getting suspended. But, unfortunately, nobody took the time to understand the bigger picture, the *why* behind my son's anger, or the lack of ability or intent to follow through on his 'threat.'" This example illustrates how children of color with disabilities are not afforded the benefit of the doubt.
- Our children do not receive comprehensive sex education and, as a result, may struggle with questions about their sexuality in isolation, leading to unwarranted and even harmful behaviors.

When these behaviors lead to a law enforcement response, interactions with the police can create sensory overload, possibly leading to even more emotional overwhelm. For instance, the hold of the handcuff, the lights or sirens, the threatening demeanor of the police, and the constant questioning of the officer can create a cumulative traumatic impact on our children's nervous system. To cope, they might rely on regulatory strategies like stimming, which can further be misread as defiance and delinquency.

Adultification Bias

In chapter 6 we discussed adultification bias, by which children of color, especially Black children, are seen as older than they are. This phenomenon can lead to disproportionate disciplining of BIPOC kids and an increased likelihood that they will be referred to the juvenile justice system compared to their White peers. Because they are seen as adults, they are also less likely to be seen as capable of change and growth. Sadly, by imposing standards we use for adults, Black children are not afforded opportunities to make mistakes and learn from them, an integral part of childhood. Their mistakes can instead result in jail time, injury, and even death.

For instance, a nine-year-old Black girl, handcuffed to the back of a police car, was pepper sprayed as she was having a mental health crisis. As she cries for her dad in the now publicized video, the police officer responds with "You did this to yourself."

"I do not think the police are safe," says Zion. "They are another gang. I tell my child not to interact with them at school. They are strangers until we meet and know them. I have told her that if you need to talk to them in an emergency, give them your name, age, birthday, and nothing else. She is twelve, five foot eleven, and two hundred pounds. She is going to be seen as a threat. I have to do a lot of role-playing to help her understand how she should engage with the police."

White Supremacy in the School System

In another incident captured on video, a sixteen-year-old Black girl was slammed to the floor by an SRO. The video captured the audible thud of her head crashing onto the floor. This is just one example of how adultification bias intersects with policing in our schools. Unless our children are homeschooled, they spend most of their time in school, and with students struggling in overcrowded and undersupported classrooms, schools increasingly turn to the police to manage our children. This makes the education system one of the primary sites for encountering law enforcement bias.

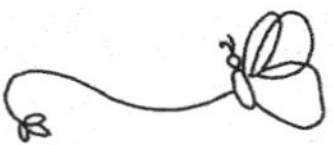

It is important to find community, because raising a child with support needs or who is neurodivergent can feel so isolating—but there are so many of us who exist.
—Molly

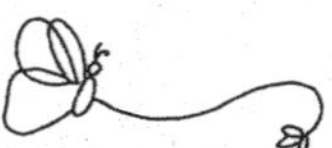

Jasmine speaks to the racism and ableism of how educators can contribute to criminalizing disabled children of color. "My son's teacher accused him of being on the phone when he was not on it. The teacher said she saw his phone was under his desk and that she saw the light lit up as they were getting ready to transfer to different classes. She reported asking him to give her the phone and that he responded with 'If you want it, then you need to come to get it from me.' My son told me he never said that and that he asked the teacher to call me. This resulted in an automatic referral for my son. A referral is like a ticket in your educational record where this incident follows you to every school you attend and remains a mark on your record. They never discussed it with him. The principal told me that the teacher was nice to give a referral and that she would have suspended him if it was her. I couldn't believe they threatened to suspend a child when he did not raise his voice or yell at anyone."

Whether a child's behavior in school is considered delinquent and punishment worthy and whether the police respond reflect the internal biases people hold against certain groups of people. How a teacher or an administrator responds to a fight between students is, unfortunately, dependent on whether the child is Black or Brown and/or disabled. The very act that lands a White child with only a warning for poor behavior would criminalize a Black or Brown child.

This is the reality of the preschool-to-prison pipeline, which the ACLU has labeled a "disturbing national trend." Suspensions can begin as early as eight months old at childcare programs. A staggering 250 preschoolers are suspended from preschools throughout the country, roughly three times the frequency of older children.

Zero-tolerance policies, an artifact of the war on drugs during the Reagan administration, were designed to discipline children for presumably dangerous behaviors to ensure school safety. But schools use suspensions, expulsions, and referrals to the police for the mildest behaviors, such as lateness, possession of an aspirin, public display of affection, pretend-playing with an imaginary gun, and questioning authority. The result is, at best, exclusion from learning. Nearly every state in the country has had some form of zero tolerance. Unsurprisingly, the children disciplined under these policies are primarily children of color with disabilities. Stories of mistreatment, restraint, seclusion, and cruel and unusual punishment are tragically too familiar. Making headlines, a Black child with a developmental delay in the Florida school system had her arm pulled by a teacher, resulting in a sprained arm. The teacher accused this child of stealing a cell phone.

Jasmine tells us about the punishment her own son received around the incident with the phone. "The school wanted him to do detention, but I disagreed, because it was unclear what it was for and I did not trust the school to keep him safe. Despite my wishes, one day I got a call from my son saying that the school was making him stay back for detention till much later in the evening. I told him that he was not doing that—I did not feel comfortable with it because of the sequence of events leading up to this, because there were not enough staff after school, and because there was history of other terrible things that had already happened in this school to kids. So I pulled him out. In response, they gave him a second referral for the same incident. These referrals paint this picture of my son, who they think he is."

It is tragic that parents are forced to be more vigilant to protect their children from the in-built systemic supremacy and ableism in schools—a place designed for learning and growth. And when things go wrong, like in Jasmine's experience, parents are left alone to support their children with the trauma of being handled like a criminal. Often, not only does such trauma reside in the child directly criminalized, but its vicarious effects also ripple through to family members, peers, and the whole school community.

Body Check

Notice where you are tight and practice gently unclenching. Maybe you open up your jaw and move it around. Maybe you shrug your shoulders and release. Observe what it is like to do something different and break a habitual stance.

Protective Factors

While some of our children are more susceptible to the grips of the juvenile justice system, there are, thankfully, many protective factors that can mitigate their entry into it. For example, in chapter 6, we identified that parent-child connectedness is a protective factor for children encountering adversities. Understanding that she needed to be an attuned presence in her son's life, Jasmine worked hard to go back to school to reorganize her work life to meet the needs of her and her son's life. "I knew I could not keep working twelve-hour shifts as a single mom, so I went back to school to get my bachelor's. I am able to now work from home for the health administration. I have always had a plan with my child in mind. I want to make decent money to do whatever it needs to be there for him."

Other essential elements that can keep our children out of the juvenile justice system include access to:

- Resourced adults who can provide healthy attachment.
- Play without the specter of criminalization.
- The arts.
- Nature.
- Animal companions.
- Ancestry / spirituality / ethnic heritage.
- Intergenerational stories.

Unfortunately, the inherent vulnerabilities children experience, coupled with the many structural barriers, can prevent children and families from benefiting from these protective factors, rendering them susceptible to the predation of the legal system. Additionally, the structural barriers placed upon parents make accessing these protective factors for their kids even more challenging. For example, supremacy culture criminalizes the very things that are protective, and productivity culture also disrupts access to them.

Think about the Black family in Oakland, California, who was enjoying a family barbecue at a lake and had the police called on them because they looked "out of place." Think about Tamir Rice, gunned down at twelve for simply playing. Think about family relationships severed by incarceration, leaving children disconnected and abandoned, not knowing their entire histories. Think about the underfunded schools in many communities of color, where routinely, music, arts, and dance programs are cut due to lack of funding, deemed as being extracurricular. Think about the parent dependent on a job with inflexible schedules and tough working conditions, struggling to be home for the precious connection time when their kids leave for school and return from school. Burdened by racism, ableism, and capitalism, parents have less time, energy, and resources to attune to their children. Being called on to parent against the systematic erasure of our children's protective factors is unjust, defeating, and relentless.

These structural factors don't just hinder us from leveraging the protective factors discussed above that help prevent children from entering the legal system in the first place. They also make it harder to exit the system once inside it. In the face of these vulnerabilities and barriers, we turn to prevention at the family and societal levels.

Prevention

"I know as my son grows, he will want more independence," says Dontea. "The world is not safe for Black children, especially those with autism. I worry that even if [a police officer] tries to help, he may not respond correctly and be seen as defiant. My son will be six foot four, and if he does not respond appropriately, this is a recipe for disaster. I can't afford for there to be a misunderstanding. As he is getting older, I am teaching him to be safer. How do I keep him safe? This is definitely a worry."

Dontea's concerns reaffirm the fact that this is a systemic issue and not a problem of a few bad apples. Focusing on just a handful of problem cops strips policing away from its historical roots and fails to connect the supremacist, ableist, and colonial principles embedded in its structure. It is our dream to see processes of restoration that are not rooted in punishment, exile, and a monopoly of power but in community accountability.

At the same time, as we work to realize this dream as a society, parents at the intersections are forced to ask: How do we live and help our children live in a system blatantly designed to criminalize and kill them? How do we protect them from the harm we know is coming? Perhaps the most effective solution for our children is to help them stay out of harm's way (the legal system) in the first place. In this section we surface a variety of prevention strategies that can help us keep our children from getting entangled with this system.

Note to Reader: We understand that you may not resonate with all strategies presented here. Some of you may see the police as perpetrators of violence and not as a solution to community safety. Others may see the police as a necessary part of society and the conversation around community safety. In full transparency, we the authors champion the abolition of the carceral system. Knowing that this goal is something we are dreaming into, and we still live in a society that utilizes policing, we surface a variety of prevention strategies that support parents in navigating the current system. We invite you to take what fits.

Attunement to Protective Factors

As parents, we are naturally vigilant. We are wired to keep our children safe and do what is needed to protect our children from threats 24/7. But the truth is, most often the best we can do is prepare them to have the strength and perspective needed to overcome challenges themselves. In other words, we have the power to build their resilience through access to the important protective factors identified in the previous section. We invite you to consider how you can attune to your children's protective factors by prioritizing access to healthy experiences with adults, play, arts, nature, spirituality, and racial, ethnic, and disability cultures. These are all essential elements of life that help human beings regulate and connect back to their inner self. When connected to such strengths, it cannot but reinforce a perception that this life is worth living—the fundamental perception that fuels resiliency.

"I always want my son to have a safe place with me, where he can feel whole as a person," shares Jasmine. "Having a safe place for children to land in and be themselves can help reduce their anxiety and depression, because they're not holding everything in and not feeling like they got to conquer it all by themselves. A safe place can help them find their courage."

My son is a profoundly good person. I love the conversations he and I have about life.

—Janne

Police Meet and Greets

"I worry for my kids as they grow up, especially my son, who has poor boundaries and is projected to be six feet two," says Sophia. "I plan to introduce the local police to him as soon as I'm able to, for them to understand he is neurodivergent and know that he is not a threat or carries a gun. I do not own any firearms or plan to."

Let us make no mistake that it is and always will be the responsibility of all adults to treat our children with respect and dignity within any system. But unfortunately, the stakes are too high to entrust our children's safety to the adults of the legal and criminal justice system. And thus, regardless of the cognitive/intellectual capacity of our neurodivergent children, we attempt to engage them in an endeavor to do all we can to keep them safe when it comes to brushes with the police. As such, many parents choose to take a proactive approach.

Taking your child to the local police station to meet the police before they randomly encounter your child on the street is one such approach. That is precisely what Sophia did. It was about safety for Sophia's daughter, as she was often quick to escape to the streets without supervision. Sophia allowed her children to experience and learn about the police in a few critical ways. She says, "My child got to meet the officers when she was not in crisis, and that made a positive impression on her, I think. I wanted her to know that when she ran away, these people could be a help to her. The police officers also learned about my autistic daughter, and they could see that her behaviors were communicating something and not threatening." This planned interaction with the police was crucial in ensuring her daughter's safety.

We recognize that some of you may feel inspired to take a proactive approach with the police introductions, and some of you may cringe at it. There is no judgment on how you choose to keep your child safe. Thinking about these choices provides a good opportunity to reflect on your values and choose what feels right.

Neurodivergent Identity Cards

Another proactive strategy can be to have your children carry an identification card with critical information about them for the police or first responders.* This concept has been around by different names: medical ID cards, wallet cards, autism alert cards, and communication cards. Below, we list helpful information that can go on these cards to keep your child

* For more information on wallet cards and similar safety measures, see the website of the Asperger/Autism Network (AANE): https://www.aane.org/resources/wallet-card/.

safe. It is important to have discussions ahead of time with your child about how and when to use this card. Sometimes, even having a role-play in front of willing first responders can be beneficial.

- Child's name.
- Parent name and contact information.
- Child's diagnosis, if one exists, with description.
- Their go-to regulatory behaviors (i.e., pacing up and down, repetitive smiling, stimming).
- Behaviors they may exhibit that can be interpreted as aggressive (flinging arms).
- How they appear when under stress and their needs from the police/responder (no touch, no sudden movements, explanation of intervention before exercising it, less bombardment of questions, etc.).
- Medical information such as medications and allergies.

Despite the many benefits these cards bring, autistic author and criminal justice system survivor Nick Dubin offers a significant limitation: they are only as effective as the first responder's reflexes during a crisis or high-stress situation. An officer's reflex to protect their own body over a civilian is often a split-second internal decision driven by their deep-seated biases. Only officers in low-stress situations and those who have done enough inner work to slow down the reflex process during high-stress situations can have the mindfulness to ask for or notice and read what the card says.

The "Other Talk"

"Yes, there have been issues where police have shot people of color with mental health issues and just assumed they are dangerous or purposefully noncompliant," says Valento. "Honestly, I don't know how to approach this, because I don't want my children to fear every police officer, especially since my best friend is an officer himself. I have explained to my son that there are issues of racial profiling from the police, but I don't think he understood the talk, so it's an issue I have to come back to."

We know that many parents in this country raising Black and Brown youth are forced to have a conversation with their children, one that sets them apart from the experience of their White peers. Given the disproportionality of the engagement of Black youth in the juvenile justice system, it is a sad reality that most Black parents are familiar with this "other talk" they are forced to have with their children. Whereas the "talk" around the birds and bees holds more hope and promise, this conversation is fueled by imminent fear for a child's safety.

Like all conversations parents have with our neurodivergent children, no one size and shape fits all, and it need not be verbal. We also heard from parents like Carmen and Corey that even though they are raising Black autistic children, they do not talk to them about the police for various reasons. Carmen tells us she has not done so, to protect him at this young age: "I do not feel the need to talk to him about the police. My kid does not watch the news. He does not know what the police do. I want to protect his innocence as long as I can." Corey reminds us that parents have to be advocates and protectors when our children can't fully comprehend the implications of the police. "I have not talked to my daughter about the police because she can't fully understand due to her cognitive capacities. Instead, I have to be vigilant that she is safe from them, because I understand how they work and how they see us."

While many families of color who are not Black or Latinx may not necessarily think to have a conversation about police interactions, we believe there is value in talking about it with all our kids. Here is an example from Malika that speaks to the different layers other families of color may address in their version of the "other talk": "One day, I was driving with my two kids. In my rearview mirror, I noticed a motorcycle cop. I knew right away that he was going to pull me over. And within a minute, he did. I knew I had done something wrong, driving without a renewed license plate. As he walked up, I immediately told the kids not to talk and turned down the music. Something about the uniform and maybe what they have learned about police over the years, my usually talkative and curious kids immediately became quiet. The officer informed me that this interaction was getting videotaped and recorded. He asked about my plate, and I explained that the motor vehicle department told us there was a backlog in plate production. Stating, 'I am going to choose to believe you,' he let me go with a warning. Taking a deep breath, I drove my car over to a nearby lot to have the talk with my kids. I explained to my kids that it is important to narrate everything you are doing with your hands and body (getting a license out, reaching over to get the registration, etc.) when dealing with the police. And then I told them we were most likely let go without incident because we are Indian. This would not have played out if we were Black or any other group of people seen as a threat. At this moment, I wanted to normalize the fear response and also help them understand that our experiences are not the same."

This conversation is hard, particularly for children and parents at this intersection, and there are many ways to have it, or not, as these stories illustrate. We trust that, as a parent, you can arrive at a decision best for you. Perhaps connecting with yourself around this topic and reflecting on your intention can illuminate the path forward:

- Do you want to teach them about safety when interacting with the police?
- Do you want to help your child know their rights?
- Do you want to help them build more body awareness and develop their advocacy skills?
- Do you want to teach them about police brutality toward people of color and people with disabilities?
- Do you feel ready? Do you think they are?

Document, Document, Document!

Jasmine's experience with the school and law enforcement highlights the necessity to document religiously. She says, "I document everything. I do not erase voicemails; I hoard paperwork. People will ask why I was keeping things, but I think this is from my health care background, which teaches you not to get rid of paperwork. Keeping everything has helped with the process of getting my son the services he needs, and has kept him safe. I have a a paper trail from the present day all the way back to 2016."

As parents of children with supportive needs, our plate is more than full. It becomes very challenging to keep abreast of our child's educational progress, know whether the school is honoring their accommodations, or track how many times this month the school has called us to pick our child up early. But it often falls on parents to equip ourselves with the information necessary to advocate for our child's learning and safety—by ourselves or with external support.

Somewhere along the way, our child's behavior can trigger a disciplinary action so quickly that they are suspended, expelled, restrained, or arrested. Parents responding at such a time of crisis are tasked with a seemingly impossible mission—to fight for our children against a system fortified by law enforcement and the criminal justice system. It is hard for us to fathom how our child went from being a kid to a delinquent, and eventually a numbered legal case. We find ourselves needing to be our child's emotional first responder, advocate, and lawyer—all at a time when we are weighed down by pain and cannot think clearly. At such a point of crisis, it can be incredibly difficult to pull together the documentation necessary to support your child. "So that parents can avoid finding themselves at this place, it is so important to take a proactive approach to documentation," says Cheryl Poe, an advocate for children and families. For a list of these recommendations, please see appendix A, p. 299.

We want to acknowledge that for many of us neurodivergent parents, documentation may not be our forte due to our own executive functioning challenges. If financially affordable, outsourcing this support to a professional special education advocate can help decrease stress for us and create confidence knowing we are held as well as our child. And for those for whom this may not be possible, the *Autism in Black* podcast has an episode that walks you through documentation strategies (see p. 318 for the link).

Emotional Support

Place an oxygen mask on yourself before placing one on your child.

Walking through an unknown and chaotic process is scary, and taking the time you need to support yourself is critical to the energy and thinking you can bring to your advocacy and your child. Find support for yourself in your community to help you deal with the trauma your family is experiencing. When you can prioritize your own ability to regulate your emotions, you can better help your child to regulate theirs. Tending to yourself and them in this way can help them feel less alone and scared, think better, and sustain the attention and energy needed to survive a very confusing and chaotic process. In this spirit, we start with encouraging emotional support for yourself.

- Who nourishes you and gives you strength? (Think family, friends, community, pets, etc.) You may wish to reach out to the school social worker for help in identifying community resources your family needs.

- Are there local or online support groups that can help you feel and process your emotions? Meeting people with the same lived experiences reminds you that you are not alone in your journey, and they may have ideas for your consideration.
- Are there activities and practices that help you feel more like yourself? (Think faith, music, nature, etc.)

Advocacy in the Criminal Justice System

You know your child, so there can be no better person to offer context and relevant facts. Parents are highly encouraged to advocate for their child at school by communicating directly with school resource officers, administrators, and teachers and requesting that in the event there are challenges, parents or trusted family and friends be the first point of contact. Advocating for our children becomes more complex when they are detained after an arrest.* Please see appendix A, p. 300, for some critical ways parents can support their children in such a situation.

Utilize Non-911 Resources

While it may feel more convenient to dial 911 and get police to respond to crisis situations, we know all too well that Black and Brown families' encounters with law enforcement can be risky to their lives. By moving away from the police as the immediate response to emerging needs and challenges, we can create opportunities for us to know our neighbors better and also to meet their critical needs directly.

Many organizations supporting families of color have a list of non-911 resources to access various individual and community support. But it is important to note that many community resources, especially those involving mental health crisis support, partner with the police and are not entirely independent of police intervention. One resource that points to local alternatives for multiple cities across the US is the site Don't Call the Police.†

* *Detainment* refers to temporary confinement until the determination of innocence or guilt.

† https://dontcallthepolice.com/.

Systemic-Level Interventions

Not all of this labor to keep kids safe should fall on hardworking, already exhausted parents and their immediate communities. Broad-scale systemic efforts are necessary to see long-lasting changes, so that parents are not solely left to do the work to keep their kids alive and safe. We need to move upstream to the source of the problem, rather than trying to fix and address the impacts one student at a time. With that in mind, we suggest reforms in the following areas.

Promote Inclusive Education

Inclusive education asserts that all children learn differently and, despite these differences, can learn together. Being together can decrease the isolation and seclusion neurodivergent learners experience and foster a sense of community, and it also allows non-neurodivergent students to enjoy their neurodivergent classmates' ideas and contributions. These potential benefits spread beyond the academic domain into the social-emotional environment. When there is awareness and appreciation for neurodivergence and neurodiversity, our children feel more welcome and less othered. In such an environment, our children are less likely to be singled out or treated harshly by peers and teachers, and thus less likely to find themselves in the hallways of the criminal justice system.

Prioritize Comprehensive Sex Education

Comprehensive sex education is a highly critical protective factor for our children, for whom navigating sexual development becomes infinitely complicated due to the many gaps in sexual education, as discussed in chapter 6. Nick Dubin emphasizes the paramount role that sex education plays in supporting the sexual health of autistic individuals and keeping them from entering the criminal justice system. Dubin discusses how comprehensive sex education, effectively communicated with autistic children and youth (and we extend that umbrella to all neurodivergent individuals), keeps them from looking to other external sources like unregulated internet sites and adult movies for their education and awareness and thus getting into legal trouble.

An important aspect of comprehensive sex education is the availability of mentors who can guide our children in accessing and processing the appropriate information. When they turn to the internet or peers for sex education, it may have dangerous consequences, from receiving heavily skewed lessons, to discovering and consuming child pornography, to engaging with unsavory people who may take advantage of our children's social vulnerabilities.

Remove School Resource Officers

There is no conclusive evidence that shows school resource officers make schools safer. In fact, research reveals that the presence of SROs does little to prevent mass shootings in schools. As a response to school shooting incidents at Columbine and later Sandy Hook, more police were placed in schools as a means to keep children safe. However, the reality is that school shootings have declined, school police have not been able to thwart the shootings that do happen—and, most devastatingly, the presence of school resource officers has contributed to the criminalizing of students of color and disabled children for typical childlike behaviors. The mere presence of SROs harms these kids, because they are more likely to be targeted for minor infractions, leading to more suspensions and arrests. As discussed earlier in the chapter, SROs contribute to pushing students of color and disabled students into the juvenile justice system by criminalizing childhood behaviors.

Invest in Solid Police Training

We know the police are here to stay in our larger society for some time to come. Police officers have not received training in working with young people, differences in neurotypes, defusing crises, and alternatives to physical interventions. They are not trained in the rights of students with disabilities. Given these gaps, an essential preventative measure is ensuring that our law enforcement officers are adequately trained in many aspects of our neurodivergent children of color. However, Morénike Giwa Onaiwu, an autistic self-advocate, cautions against any run-of-the-mill training program to "meet the hours" for police officers. She emphasizes the need for holistic, strengths-based learning and experience with autism or other neurodivergence, as deficits-based training can only further serve to harm the community they are trying to serve better.

Many training programs around the nation have tried various creative approaches to support police training, including role-plays, virtual simulations, and debriefing police roles, that help officers put their learning into practice and receive and build on feedback. If the police are here to stay, we recognize that they need to be better trained to be in contact with our children. Many advocates and programs worldwide have tried various successful approaches. In the appendix, we present some critical components necessary for effective police training to protect children at the intersections of race and neurodivergence.

Restorative Justice Diversion Program

After an arrest, between the intake process and a trial, there is a critical time to advocate for our children. This is the stage of a pretrial diversion, where our children, typically seventeen years and younger, are provided with supportive community-based options outside the criminal justice system to meet the critical needs that likely led them to their arrest in the first place. This is a way to help divert them out of the system. To understand the full process from arrest to posttrial, we recommend the Office of Juvenile Justice and Delinquency Prevention's flow chart, as describing the entire process is not within the scope of this chapter.

If our child commits a delinquent act, diversion programs informed by restorative justice can be an appropriate intervention. It is a strengths-based, community-oriented approach to supporting both/all parties of a crime. These programs provide supportive case management to meet children's underlying needs, help them understand and acknowledge the harm they created, and work with them to repair it.

Some of our kids might struggle with understanding and acknowledging the harm due to cognitive and communication differences. It is important to recognize a child's inability to participate to the extent needed should not be used to name them as unwilling, uncooperative, and irredeemable. Ideally, the diversion program can be an option for our children and can prevent many of our children from slipping into the trenches of the criminal justice system.

In summary, colluding with schools, law enforcement has entered the hallowed halls of learning, where the biggest questions for our children should be about recess, lunch, and homework. Instead, the presence of police in our educational institutions has placed a target on the backs of our beloved children, making the attainment of education an impossible hurdle. To parent in this context means having to make impossible choices between safety and learning.

No parent should have to do this, and yet so many do. We hope that the prevention strategies give you some sense of power in a cruel and unjust system. We hope that they work enough that your child will never come into contact with law enforcement in harmful ways. We hope that one day we change the system so that this chapter is irrelevant and unnecessary. Until then, may you and your children be safe and whole.

Reflection Questions

- What are some memories you have about getting into trouble as a child? What were those experiences like?
- Did your family talk about the police, and if so, what were those conversations like?
- What are some protective factors for your children?
- Have you had the "other talk" with your children? Why or why not?

Resources for Deeper Understanding

Criminal Justice System

Children's Defense Fund. "The State of America's Children 2021: Youth Justice." https://www.childrensdefense.org/state-of-americas-children/soac-2021-youth-justice.

Juvenile Law Center. "Youth in the Justice System: An Overview." https://jlc.org/youth-justice-system-overview.

Maruschak, Laura M., Jennifer Bronson, and Mariel Alper. "Disabilities Reported by Prisoners." Survey of Prison Inmates, 2016. Bureau of Justice Statistics. US Department of Justice, March 2021. https://bjs.ojp.gov/content/pub/pdf/drpspi16st.pdf.

Youth.gov. "Juvenile Justice." https://youth.gov/youth-topics/juvenile-justice.

Community Policing Alternatives

Adams, M, and Max Rameau. "Black Community Control over Police." *Wisconsin Law Review* (2016). https://wlr.law.wisc.edu/wp-content/uploads/sites/1263/2016/06/4-Adams-Rameau-Final.pdf.

Don't Call the Police. "Resources by City." https://dontcallthepolice.com/.

May Day Collective and Washtenaw Solidarity and Defense. *12 Things to Do Instead of Calling the Cops*. https://not911.me/12things-screen.pdf.

Not 911. Seattle Tech Bloc. https://not911.me/.

Smith-Stewart, Tim. *What to Do Instead of Calling the Cops During Mental Health Crisis: And Why They Might Show Up Anyway*. Daisy Chain Press. https://not911.me/alt2police.pdf.

Parent Supports

Association for Children's Mental Health. "Navigating the Juvenile Justice System." http://www.acmh-mi.org/get-help/navigating/the-juvenile-justice-system/.

Center for Parent Information and Resources. "Juvenile Justice Resources Collection." Statewide Parent Advocacy Network. https://www.parentcenterhub.org, https://www.parentcenterhub.org/juvenile-justice-resources-collection/.

Justice for Families. https://www.justice4families.org/.

PART IV

BUILDING A BETTER WORLD

11

FINDING WHAT FEELS LIKE HOME

Building Our Village

Our community has looked different over the years, reflecting what we have needed at specific moments. We have gone from a village of international families sharing toddler playdates, to a community of parents of gifted children from South Asia, to a community of parents with no unifying identifications.

A through line for us has been my parents and my sister. When they learned of my child's ADHD diagnosis, it did not affect the ways they continued to delight in him as he was growing up. In the throes of my journey, knowing that my family was there in the ways they knew how was a profound source of comfort.

Whether it was watching our kids, preparing food for the week, or brainstorming on strategies, my parents specifically were ready to help. It has also been curious to see their approach to him, which is to not see him as different. While I hold the position that differences must be visible and celebrated, I also understand their perspective as a historical remnant of being an immigrant in this country, where difference is dangerous.

I have also been lucky to have friendships with women who generously love me, which has allowed me to be there for my children. It has been learning that a community does not have to be a large group of people; community is a feeling. I remember conversations with my dear friend Amanda, who has been a steadfast and compassionate witness to my process. And on our many walks, I would talk to her about struggles at home with parenting. As a true friend, she witnessed my motherly concerns while gently reflecting love and compassion for all of us.

My other friend Jill is my constant companion in parenting BIPOC neurodivergent kids. I can text her late at night and vent my anger and frustration:

> **Me:** *Omg! Can this day be over? Why can't something be simple with the kid right now, and why is he growing up so fast?*
>
> **Jill:** *Oh, love, I know, they grow fast, and you are doing a great job. You are just what he needs, even as he pushes you away at this moment. I love you both so much.*
>
> **Me:** *Thanks. I needed to hear that.*

On our parenting journeys, we all need friends like this, friends who will love our children and us fiercely, offer wisdom, compassion, and humor, and bring over our favorite drink on a tough day.

They say it takes a village to raise a child, but for parents like us, raising neurodivergent BIPOC kids, finding a village is not always easy. We often find ourselves isolated, lonely, and exhausted, which makes it hard to find the best parent in us. We get by with the bare minimum sometimes. The drudgery of the mundane weighs on us. It can often feel like our children are just too much, and then we feel guilty for thinking so. Even when we think we may be able to seek some respite at an *abuela* or an auntie's house, we remember how our last visit ended: with our yearning for our children to be accepted for who they are in their full glory. We wonder if the kind of village that lives in our imagination exists, where a consistent group of people is invested in our children, in celebrating them, in calling them in when they are up to no good. And the kind that is invested in us—in holding us and seeing our goodness amid our mess-ups. We all deserve such a village, where we can be fully known, accepted, and supported. Humans were never meant to raise children alone.

Creating a community is hard. If we don't have one already, it takes much intention, time, and effort to contend with the pressures of productivity culture to make it a priority. Without a systemic safety net that guarantees our fundamental human right to health care, many of us are participants in a corporate model of work where we are tied to a forty-hours-a-week job, often much more, in order to qualify for health care benefits. It feels unfair to have to choose between our access to employment benefits and our access to time to nurture relationships in the community.

In this chapter, we explore how we can experience community, naming the joys and struggles it entails, and share things we learned along the way! Finally, we encourage you to engage with the reflective prompts and hope they are helpful for your parenting journey.

The Many Faces of a Community

Many of us have an opportunity to find community among our families, friends, and neighborhoods. Finding people to support our children in these spaces can offer breathing room for parents.

Family and Friends

We begin with some examples of parents who have found community and support in their families and friends. Rupa states, "I'm lucky that I came into parenting with a strong community of aunties and uncles for my kiddo—almost all my friends don't have kids, and if it weren't for the pandemic, I know they'd be very involved in my kid's life. They're a source of stability for me too."

Meena shares that finding some support from her parents and in-laws did not come immediately—it took several years. She believes that part of the reason for this was their denial that her child had autism. Over time they have come to accept the diagnosis. She says, "Having the grandparents at home has been helpful overall, and the kids have developed a good relationship. They are supremely patient with the kids, and that is great, because I am not always patient." This anecdote reminds us how we need people in our lives who believe in our reality. Molly echoes the value of grandparents spending time with the kids. "My parents live with us. I am glad my kids are getting a chance to have a relationship with their grandparents, as I never had that." Valento also shares his gratitude to his in-laws who reside with them and the resulting bond his children have forged with them.

Leela makes a cultural distinction between the support from her own family and the support from her husband's White family. For example, she says, "My mom just comes and takes the kids when I need, whereas with my husband's family, we need to be more intentional around scheduling, and support becomes harder to coordinate." Leela's anecdote reminds us that our cultural backgrounds shape our understanding of community.

In Arica's family, her White husband's family has been more accepting of their child, especially about their child's trans identity. But she says, "I am estranged from my mother, as she refuses to call my child by their name and pronouns and uses their dead name instead. My mom also does not believe in these conditions [their neurodivergence] and thinks it is something made up."

Mumbi says, "All around, there was positive feedback for the kids from the family. My family approaches kids with great patience and calm. The family believes I have acquired superpowers as a parent—they provide their full support and know I am doing the best I can." Joy shares how her parents played an intimate role in supporting their grandchild in play and play-based interventions. She says, "My parents would help me by taking my son to play therapy, group play, speech, and OT (occupational therapy) every week for one and a half years. They were also my childcare while I worked."

Support and community are not readily accessible for many in their families, and that can sometimes feel complicated. Sophia speaks to this complication: "So far, my friends and family from the Dominican side have been supportive and understanding. They have joined me in my journey with my children. My ex-husband's family was just not very supportive, which is one reason we divorced. It is easier for me to raise our children without their interference."

Elizabeth says, "Parts of our extended family were fantastic—willing to support our boundaries and have our son over so we could have respite. Other parts of the extended family were scared of him and wouldn't have him over unless we were there to supervise." She describes feeling alienated by her family when they got scared of her son's aggressive play. "They didn't fully understand what we were dealing with (violence, dark tendencies)."

After a trip with extended family, Malika became more careful about who she trusted with her children's care. "On a trip with some extended family, we left our kids with an adult family member while we went for dinner. When we returned, he immediately said my son was being a problem. While I knew my kid's neurodivergence could present as loudness and a challenge to authority, it did not feel good to hear my child be framed as a problem. I learned I needed to leave my child with people who truly understood their neurodivergence and were accepting. While I can't always shield my kid, I wanted the time with my family to be a safe experience."

Hana connects how cultural differences make it hard to find support from her and her husband's family. "I can't talk about it with my mother, because as an East Asian woman who experienced racism, neurodivergence is one more thing that makes us a target. She sees it as a failure in parenting. My husband's family, who come from Mexico, tend to sweep things under the rug." Valento says, "I don't like going over to my extended family members' house or get together, because sadly they don't get it and yell out at my children for being too hyper or playing with things that aren't meant to be played with. So while I'm there, I am usually more stressed out than if I wasn't since I have to monitor them even harder. There is also a lot of unasked advice about how I need to raise and discipline my kids. They tell me to correct their behavior, which hurts to hear, because it shows such a lack of understanding. Even when I did try to explain my kids to them, it still led back to discipline. Sadly, I just don't feel comfortable taking my children to places where they tell me I need to spank them."

Deepti shares how her extended family would respond to her daughter's emotional expressions during a phase when her emotional outbursts and sensitivity to rejection were high. "When pushed to the edge, my daughter would be quick to use rude language. I knew and trusted that she was blowing off steam and needed to, and it was the adults' responsibility to hold that perspective. But coming from a South Asian culture where respect for elders is paramount, my parents did not see it that way. They took it personally and saw it as disrespect."

Kim says, "When my child was younger, there were a lot of eye rolls, distance, and silent pleas to take him outside and get him 'under control.' The family would not engage with him too much, though some did better than others. Now that he is older and his physicality has mellowed out a bit, there is more engagement. However, there is still a disconnect, because he does not always respond as they expect. As a result, I am seen either as an amazing hero who 'deals with this kid' or someone to be pitied, neither of which is true. Friends who were enthusiastic when we adopted him became less so in time. It is the hardest thing we have experienced."

Other Communities

When support is unavailable in our immediate circles, the school can be a place many of us find community, especially if that school is designed for students who learn differently. Meena says, "The school my child attended was designed with neurodivergent kids in mind and has been hugely supportive. The teachers and paraeducators were part of our family. Unfortunately, when my child graduated out of it, we felt the loss of this community." Mumbi says, "The homeschool community has been the most helpful, as a mom and homeschooler, though not neurodivergent specific."

Religious or faith-based spaces can also be a source of community. Carmen, who identifies as Christian, has found the church to be a safe place to be with her kid. She says, "When he was born, he was in the hospital, and the church rallied and prayed for us. Today, during services, if he acts up or needs to move around, they respond with a lot of grace and patience." Speaking about finding religion supportive, Dontea states that knowing that God forgives her and that she can start each day anew in God's eyes gives her the strength to parent her child. However, while religion can offer sanctuary, it can also be a place where ableism is reinforced, specifically when there are narratives about how praying can cure someone of a disability.

We can also find community at organizations we join intentionally. Julie shares, "I have found community at all stages of my parenting journey. Places like early parent groups and the school's parent teacher student association have been a source of support for me." But Julie also points to the tension of how these spaces can be helpful until your child's differences are too uncomfortable for the group. She says, "We are all in it together until we are not." But she continues, "Community keeps changing, especially since your kids are always changing, and you need people to be on your side. You need community."

Meena tells us about finding support while participating in a community theater play. "Putting on the show was an intense process, and I spent a lot of time with this group laughing and crying together. After the show, we continued to stay in touch, and when I learned of my child's autism diagnosis, I reached out one night to everyone, sharing my struggles. Everyone showed up differently, and that was OK." Meena's story also reminds us that sometimes it can be helpful to ask for support.

Mary found a community in a local school organization that supports families of gifted kids. She says, "I remembered attending the seminar this organization hosted, educating parents about what it means to be gifted and how they perceived the world differently. It was the first time I understood my child's thinking and emotions. I truly wished I had been told about this and known way earlier. For example, I wish I had known that most of his tantrums were amplified because he did not know how to handle his intense feelings. It was not because he was trying to be difficult."

Leela describes how valuable it was for her to connect with a local organization that supported and connected families of color. "It was so great to know that I was not the only Brown parent raising a neurodivergent child." And Deepti shares how connecting with a nationwide parent-support organization was critical to helping her feel at home. "It is uniquely beneficial to find an organization that you believe in—for the values that you are likely to share with other parents you connect with. I have made nurturing friendships in person and online, set up regular calls to exchange listening time, and created a text chain with parents who I have reached out to during moments of helplessness and isolation. This community has provided me with encouragement and love, which has given me the needed confidence. In this space, I have felt deeply supported."

Anamika says, "I am part of at least a dozen online groups supporting special-needs children, and they have been a wealth of information. Some of the [virtual] talks/meetups are also helpful. I wish there was a community to provide in-person help to parents like us, to give us a much-needed break from time to time. We need a lot more awareness and acceptance of special-needs kids in the mainstream population. We need support/peer groups for our special-needs kids, not just for parents/caregivers."

My Black, autistic child is full of joy and wonder. I think about how blessed I am that I've been forced to ask really hard questions about what I've assumed about how to parent, the role of school, and the role of others. I wonder if I would have been otherwise complacent and my eyes would have been closed for so much longer, at the expense of raising free humans.

—Rupa

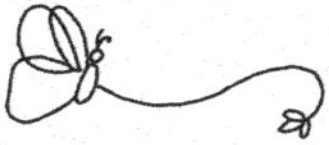

Sometimes support shows up in unexpected places and when we least anticipate it. Finding people who get our kids and us is the release valve we did not know we needed. Rupa found their community online, specifically on Facebook groups. "I joined a Facebook group about language and speech, and it became an unexpected community, because of the commitment to constantly learning and growing. They are oriented to asking questions and providing suggestions. It helped that there are a lot of similarities to my kid's experiences and many of the parents are in a similar position with public schools not meeting our kids' needs. This is where I found out about unschooling. From there, I found a group for parents who unschool their neurodivergent kids. That was my next 'warm blanket' of a group. Many parents there have kids who, like my son, scored in the bottom percentile on their preschool evaluations and still said, 'Fuck your system.' Every day that I've had doubts, they're the ones who have lifted me back up."

Meena tells us how isolating parenting an autistic child is and that she looked forward to the visits from the applied behavioral analysis (ABA) therapists. She says, "If I am isolated, I can't do much for him, and having the ABA therapists in the house Tuesday, Thursday, and Friday felt like a holiday. It was helpful to have another adult in the house who I could talk to."

Our Learnings

Here are some insights from our collective journeys and prompts to help you on your way as you build community. Notice how the following prompts invoke the body. Remember that returning to the body is part of healing and moving towards anti-oppressive, decolonial parenting and community building, and that it's OK not to notice anything immediately. Give yourself time, space, and patience as you tap into your innate intelligence. We are in this together with you.

Rethink Our Parenting

We believe it is helpful to start by critically examining our notions of parenting, including the messages our families and the larger societies we live in have given us around what it means to parent. For instance, both Priya and Jaya have had long conversations about the impact of adultism in our Indian upbringing. It's not easy; we are simultaneously confronting how we were parented and also understanding our parenting styles, which reveals the places where there are opportunities to shift and do something differently.

Furthermore, living in the modern world, where many of us live in nuclear families and shut the literal and figurative doors to our lives after work and school, it is hard to imagine receiving and providing support on a larger web. Many of us do not know our neighbors. Many of us live far from our extended family. Many of us have internalized that we need to do this alone.

We are here to disabuse you and us (this is an ongoing lesson!) of the notion that parenting is to be endeavored alone, with only the occasional meetups with family and friends. We are not meant to do this alone, especially when we are raising kids who live at many intersections of identity and experiences.

Essentially, we do not have to rely on old templates prescribed to us by the larger culture, which is often in service of fueling capitalism and White supremacy. So, to imagine a different future for our children and ourselves, let us examine our familial and cultural inheritances about parenting, and notice what is unhelpful and what continues to be relevant.

The Invitation

Pull out a journal or voice recorder. Ask yourself the following questions. These prompts also offer an anchor for conversations with our partners and trusted friends.

- What messages did my parents or caregivers give me implicitly and explicitly about parenting, and how is this keeping me stuck?
- How did my parents or caregivers show care?
- Who were the support systems that my parents or caregivers relied on to support them? What did I take away from this?
- What expectations do I have of my children that are inherited from my parents? Do I want to continue to hold on to them? Why or why not?
- What are the similarities and differences between how you parent and how you were parented?

Know Yourself, Know Your Child

Understanding your needs as a parent in this current moment and your child's needs is also critical. Sometimes these needs align, and sometimes they don't. Conversations with your child, your partner, a therapist, a trusted mentor, or another parent can help gain more clarity. Getting clear on the needs is the first step on this journey of community building. And it's OK that not all spaces and groups will fit where your and your child's needs are.

The Invitation

Use the following prompts in a journal or voice recorder or in conversation with someone you trust.

- What are your top three needs at this moment as a parent? Some examples include intellectual stimulation, physical activity, spiritual growth, monetary support, and friendship.

- What do you think are your child's top three needs now? Some things can include needing more play, friendships, mentorship, intellectual stimulation, or a hobby.
- Are there spaces that already exist in your lives where what you and your child need can be met? If so, what keeps you from accessing these spaces?
- We believe imagination is play for adults. Imagine now what a space that addresses your needs would look like. Identify the smells, sounds, and sights. Name who would be there and how you might dress. Describe how you might show up in this space.

Find Your People

We talk a lot about community, but what is it really? Used broadly, *community* can mean many things: it can be a place, a feeling of belonging, a social commitment, a connection to our values, or a connection to our cultural roots. When it feels right, it feels like *home*—the kind of home that helps you feel safe, seen, and supported. And this experience of finding and being in one is very different based on our positionalities and intersections.

Speaking to this, Joshua shares, "Community has looked different for us, because we live at many intersections. Being queer, Black, and neurodivergent, I never quite fit anywhere. Finding community has been hard, and I spend a lot of time looking for others at our intersections. Parenting is a lonely and difficult experience, in addition to providing for kids and trying to adult and be a human in this world."

Entering a well-meaning neighborhood community organization with no structural and power analysis as a BIPOC person is a different experience than attending an organization that explicitly attends to race, equity, antibias, and the impact of oppression trauma.

The Invitation

Here, we invite you to slow down and explore how you know when you have been in community. Here are some prompts to get you started!

- Go back to when you were with a group of people and recall when you felt most alive, most like yourself, most confident, most calm. Where were you then? If this is not accessible, imagine what it might feel like in your body to be in a space where you are most like yourself and authentic.
- Notice now what happens when we say the word *community*. Take some time to observe the sensations in your body. Are there images that show up? What memories and emotions take hold? Any words or thoughts that pop in?
- How do you define community? What are the features, qualities, and characteristics that you think a community should embody?
- Where do your ideas about community come from? Who and what informs your knowing? What do you think about this?

Seek Out an Anti-oppressive Community

We hold firm that communities can look many different ways and that our experiences sitting at the crossroads of multiple intersecting identities inform the way we know what feels good. What for one person may be a sacred space of belonging may not resonate for another. Part of what we have struggled with in some organizations and groups is that they inevitably center on Whiteness and privilege neurotypicality.

Often, then, it becomes a forced choice for many of us. We are asked to sacrifice some part of ourselves in seeking belonging. We compromise our whole authentic selves to find community. So often, our examples don't fit us and the many parts of our lived experiences. This does not mean we don't deserve community. Malika tells us, "I took my younger child to Cub Scouts, because I wanted to support him in his interests in the outdoors, exploration, and desire to be self-sufficient. In one of the meetings, I noticed how the colonization story of this country was whitewashed and presented to the kids. Later, I spoke to my child, explained that was not the whole story, and talked about what happened and continues to happen to Native communities. Our needs and values as a family were not in sync with the group. Questions my husband and I asked ourselves were what part of ourselves, our family identity, should we leave at the door? I asked myself, *Should I have said something in the meeting so all kids would have heard it, or would that have further ostracized my child? Should I have pulled the parent facilitators later and shared my observations? What will the impact of this be on my child? Should we just not be part of this group? What will the impact of that be on my child?*

"I speak to these tensions because this is the additional labor that parents of color raising kids who are neurodivergent are doing when building community for themselves and their children."

Many parents who lent their voices to this book shared their struggles in their search for community. One parent asked us, "How do I find a community that is anti-oppressive, so I can be seen fully in my authenticity? What do I look for in a space to know they are truly affirming of diversity?" We attempt to answer these questions here through a list of qualities we can look for in an organization that commits to upholding anti-oppressive values:

- A space that is intersectional honors that we do not live single-issue lives* and honors that people's identities are interlinked.
- Continuing with this idea that we do not live single-issue lives, representation matters in organizations and communities. Voices that embody the variety of lived experiences can be a force in shaping the direction of the group, attending to the needs of those in the group, and, most important, can begin to decenter privileged members and normative culture.

* Refers to the Audre Lorde quote "There is no such thing as a single-issue struggle because we do not live single-issue lives," which is from her speech "Learning from the 60s," given on February 1982 at Harvard University's Malcom X weekend.

- The space actively centers the voices of those most on the margins and calls on their wisdom and knowledge to shape the direction and momentum of the space.
- The community intentionally and stubbornly insists on examining the ways power plays out internally in the dynamics between members and externally as the organization relates to other groups.
- The group explicitly names that calling out and shaming (i.e., cancel culture) is a tool of White supremacy and practices accountability to heal those in the community together.

The Invitation

We ask you to review the above list and answer the following prompts:

- As you read through each characteristic, what arises for you? What do you notice in your body? What thoughts and feelings show up?
- What are you longing for that is not captured here? Can you give words, images, or songs to define it?

A Final Word on Community: It's OK to Be Done. It's OK to Take a Break.

Throughout our parenting journey, we have learned that when raising BIPOC neurodivergent children, the people around us show up as they can. All of us are at various stages of development around these identities. Our various communities may not support all the parts of our identity. A common example is unchecked homophobia and ableism in many communities of color. To not fit in with your people, or to have to split parts of yourself to belong, compounds the loneliness many parents already experience. In addition, many parents can feel desperation, unable to find safety and belonging in the larger society.

Having acknowledged that the people around us can offer what they can, we have also learned that, sometimes, you just need to cut and run.

The values between you and this group may not align, and you may be at a stage where you no longer want to try to fit in or squeeze yourself into something that does not suit you.

One parent shared a story of hiding their child's gender expansiveness in their Asian cultural spaces to maintain their connection to this group of people. Unfortunately, this parent's internal struggle of affirming their child's identity while finding support for themself is all too common.

Angela tells us about how some groups were too overwhelming: "Find the right support for yourself. For me, parent groups increased my anxiety, because the information they provided was overwhelming. Parents would ask me why I didn't try XYZ, and I would worry I had made a mistake, lose my confidence, and come back to it much later when I reconnected with my why. For me, connecting with select parents was more useful."

A village does not have to be static; it can shift and stretch according to the present needs, what feels accessible and what feels nurturing. Each village served its purpose at that moment, and we can learn from them all and cherish our times with them. And as we evolve, it makes sense that some communities do not fit us anymore. Trying to fit a narrow notion of a village in and of itself feels stifling. We ultimately long for people who see us, know us, and root for us.

The Invitation

Here are some questions to ask yourself to help decide if a particular community space is no longer serving you:

- What are the cues for you and your child when something is not working? First, notice how your body responds. Then, notice your thoughts and feelings.
- What keeps you from leaving a group or space? What are the internalized messages around quitting that inform your commitments?
- Think of a time you left a space that was not serving you or your child. What was it like to be in that space? What was hard? What was the result?
- What is the benefit and cost of staying for you or your child?

We invite you to remember that in creating our community, we are practicing a parenting love ethic, for ourselves and our children. A community can help our children deepen their sense of self in the presence of others; to be reflected back is one of the most fundamental human needs—to be mirrored is profound. For us parents, a community offers a sense of being held, known, and deeply supported. It can help you know you are not alone. Doing this intentionally, thoughtfully, and slowly is not a problem; it is the antidote. So let's commit to this healing for us, our children, and those who will walk long after we have gone.

12

A PARENTING LOVE ETHIC

An Invitation to Emancipation

Raising Black children—female and male—in the mouth of a racist, sexist, suicidal dragon is perilous and chancy. If they cannot love and resist at the same time, they will probably not survive.

—*Audre Lorde*

There can be no love without justice.

—*bell hooks*

At the core of parenting neurodivergent children of color is a delicate balancing act: honoring and affirming our children as they are while also teaching them how to navigate a world not designed with them in mind. We wrestle with teaching our children whether and how much to accommodate and contort within oppressive systems. We have to decide on how much to prepare and warn them that their spirits might take a beating as they morph to conform and squish themselves into a box. Maybe our children have already learned that. Or perhaps we won't tell them, and we will just be there to help them pick right back up, clean their wounds, love them, and reflect the truth we have always known: that they are inimitable. And most important, we will have to show them how to find pockets of communities and moments in time that allow them to return to their most authentic self.

The stories shared thus far in this book reveal the challenges and joys specific to parenting our neurodivergent children of color within inherently oppressive systems. Guided by bell hooks' love ethic, in chapter 2 we identified these four practices as core to a parenting love ethic—practices we see as the beginning of orienting toward parenting that is informed by liberation:

1. Giving *care.*
2. Being *responsible.*
3. Willingness *to (un)learn.*
4. Showing *respect.*

Here in our last chapter, we describe them again and share anecdotes from parents illustrating how these aspects of a parenting love ethic can look. Some of these may support many elements of the parenting love ethic, while others speak more specifically to one aspect. Wherever you choose to start and however you choose to engage with these practices, that is OK. Trust yourself. Finally, we offer an invitation to develop an emancipatory vision for you and your children. While this invitation concludes the book, we see it, not as an end, but as the beginning of unimagined futures. In charting a path forward, these stories remind us that raising our children offers an unparalleled portal through which we can uncover the layers of our humanity.

Giving Care

A parenting love ethic means cultivating a practice of *giving gentle care* to self. It is about making room for our feelings and trusting that what emerges holds important information about what we and our children may be needing. Holding ourselves with gentleness looks like:

- Accepting ourselves as imperfect human beings who are bound to mess up (and have capacity to repair!).
- Being conscious of the *shoulds* we place on ourselves that get in the way of our acceptance of self and generate fear.

Giving care to ourselves helps us move from fear to spaciousness and allows us to hold our children with the gentle care they deserve.

Finding Compassion and Forgiveness for Ourselves

Parenting our children means having compassion for ourselves and forgiving ourselves for how we may fall short. There will inevitably be times when we are not operating from a spacious, loving place. We may revert to fear and, in doing so, engage with our children more harshly than we intend. We may say unkind things. We may go into problem-solving mode. We may take our worries about how the world will see them and treat them and impose that onto our interactions with them, thereby creating more disconnection. And all of this will feel awful afterward, like nausea that lingers after a night of heavy drinking. And it will be tempting to punish ourselves for losing our cool. It can be easy to slip into a shame spiral and want to crawl under the covers.

Malika recounts times when she and her older child had fights over schoolwork and completing assignments: "I know I let my fear take over. I have taken in a narrow definition of what success looks like, coming from an Indian immigrant culture. As hard as I work to expand my thinking, there will be days when this old way of looking at the world will creep back in. And before I know it, I am engaged with them in unhelpful conversations about their future. After these conversations, there is a lot of regret for me breaking the connection and frustration with myself for slipping back into patterns."

We can't be perfect with our children. But we can own up, be accountable, and repair the harm. Malika shares a story of recovering from an argument with her child: "One day, kiddo and I were on a mom-and-child hike. As we made our slow ascent through old-growth forests I decided I needed to share my truth, be vulnerable with him, and begin the due apology. So, taking a defining breath, I begin, 'I want to share something with you, and I am hoping that it may offer you an explanation for where I am coming from.'

"'Um . . . OK, go on,' he offers tentatively.

"'I know I have been hard on you about your school and grades, and I have been thinking a lot about what that is about.' I explained my fears and provided insight into my upbringing and schooling. 'I love you so much, and want you not to struggle the way I did, that sometimes I end up pushing and inserting myself in ways I think are unhelpful.' He continues to listen silently, walking beside me, the rhythm of his breathing letting me know he is present with me. In deep—both in the conversation and the hike—I commit to both endeavors to come through the other side. 'I am learning now that my fear and anger are connected and about something bigger than what I can fix. I have also been angry with myself for not seeing it sooner. I am so sorry.'

"He hears my voice choke at this moment and leans over and hugs me. My child is not a hugger. At this moment, I feel the beginnings of a shift, as my body releases some of the fight I have been holding on to."

Being Responsible

A parenting love ethic is a practice of *being responsible*. We take responsibility for our own story and unhealed childhood wounds. We make time regularly to notice and reflect on our thoughts, feelings, and struggles (triggers, rigidities etc.) and meet them with gentle curiosity. Tending to our wounds, no matter how late, affirms that we are good and deserving. Being responsible for our own healing in this way can allow us to be more present for our children's, because we see them as good and deserving too.

Discovering Ourselves

While we focus on our children, their interests, aversions, and needs, we can quickly forget that we are people too. In raising our neurodivergent children of color, we are pushed to look in the mirror to better understand our responses to our children, including our fears, hopes, and doubts. Making the unconscious conscious, when possible, brings greater self-awareness, healing, and confidence to parenting in the present moment. So much of healthy parenting is reliant upon the internal self-development process we parents go through to show up for our children in the ways that they need.

Part of knowing ourselves is identifying the practices, hobbies, and interests that nurture our spirit. We may already have a self-care toolkit, but these practices can go to the wayside when the days bleed into each other and getting a good shower and scarfing down a breakfast bagel is the extent of our self-care. We feel like the world's weight is on our shoulders; we toggle between communicating with the teachers about the IEPs, making medical appointments, and ensuring that our kids eat a balanced meal of protein and carbs. We do this with love, in addition to the jobs we hold outside the home, the support we offer to elderly family, and the maintenance of running a household. So naturally, it can become very easy for us to forgo our interests in day-to-day chaos. But as the saying goes, we can't pour from empty cups. We need nourishment for our spirits too. So what are the things that nourish you?

Meena talks about finding her passions, like writing: "It was good to have my own thing away from autism and home and to find ways to be more grounded and centered." Deepti says, "For me, my love of music has been an important aspect of caring for myself. It hasn't been easy with my own neurodivergence, amidst the busyness of parenting and work, to integrate it into my life as a disciplined practice. But I embrace the spontaneous energy to play on my veena and to improvise on a raga.* I also often find myself accessing the instrument to express my emotions—a place where my words often take a backseat."

Valento shares how self-care for him is about persistence: "I am trying really hard for my life to not completely be wrapped around my kids, but it's hard. Sometimes I don't have time to myself, and it takes me six months to finish a movie in parts." In addition, his experience also speaks to how we need a community to remind us that we are in need of nurturing. "I do have a good set group of friends who have been trying to get me to do more myself. They invite me everywhere, knowing that I may not be able to, but they still offer out. They even offer to babysit."

These stories remind us to embrace—heck, celebrate—our imperfect selves, and in doing so, commit to creating joy—not *producing* joy, for production serves capitalism, while joy for the sake of creation serves love.

Trusting Our Intuition

In parenting our children, we are likely to seek outside counsel and receive input from doctors, educators, family members, and neighbors. While helpful, the information can also be overwhelming at times—deciding the best course of action can be even more complicated when there are multiple opinions. It is precisely at these times that it may be worth pausing and turning down the chatter of the voices outside, giving us the chance to hear the unspoken and unclaimed murmurs within us. Then,

---

* An Indian classical music term that is akin to a melodic structure.

we can lean into and trust what we know to be true and appropriate for our children.

Meena speaks about trusting her intuition when considering services for her child. For example, she says, "When asked to consider applied behavioral analysis (ABA) and speech and occupational therapy services, we researched all kinds of people who made all these claims that they can fix autism. So I stayed up reading a lot and browsing the web, considering the suggestion of forty hours of ABA. But it did not resonate with me, and luckily, I realized that that's not sustainable for me, not sustainable for the family, and I would just end up tiring myself out and then getting upset at him. And so very quickly realized that that's not for us, and I scaled back quite a bit."

Coming to Terms with Grief

When the reality of parenting does not match what we imagined for ourselves and our children, some of us experience grief. We grieve when we have experienced loss. In this case, the loss is not tangible, like with a pet or a beloved friend. Instead, it is *ambiguous*, where we are grieving ideas—of what healthy children look like, our knowledge of how to parent, and possibly most uncomfortable, our beliefs about how life should unfold. Raising neurodivergent children brings all of these ideas into sharp relief. Grief is multifaceted in that it encompasses many emotions, such as anger, hopelessness, guilt, and confusion. Grief is also layered, as our current grief rests upon grief we have experienced in the past, or upon chronic grief that people of color endure from living under oppressive systems that continue to perpetuate inequities and injustice every day. Grief for parents who are minoritized may not look like how it is portrayed in dominant culture. Sadly, there is no room for this experience in modern parenting, especially when parents are up against gigantic systems like the criminal justice system. In the urgency of having to fight for their child's life, parents of color are left with no space to engage with their feelings. Grief, then, gets bypassed to ensure survival.

In our clinical practices, we see the impact of neglected and silenced emotions. We see the impact of not giving ourselves time and space to move through the many ways grief shows up. Eventually, the anger, depression, and despair show up like uninvited party guests, claiming their space, and demanding attention. Grieving is a necessary step on our path to liberation, clearing the space for something new.

Let's hear from parents and their experiences with grief. Molly began to grieve even before her son was born. During the pregnancy, doctors identified that her baby had intrauterine growth. Her extensive research revealed that the chances of autism increased due to this pregnancy complication. She says, "There was a grieving process even during pregnancy. I was thinking about the possibility of autism during pregnancy itself. I knew signs and also had researched what could be predictors. I kept it to myself, hoping for the best and not wanting to be a worrywart. I especially did not want to worry my husband. After twenty weeks, we saw that the placenta was not growing. There was concern about his kidney and head. My husband was so excited about having a baby, and he was not registering the impact of these developments."

Social interactions with peers can surface feelings of grief. Seeing a friend's child do something with ease or sooner than our child can be a challenging moment. We may hold both the happiness for our friends as they revel in their child's development and also the sadness that our child is not quite there yet. Or perhaps, our grief overtakes us, and we struggle to share in our friend's joy. And as Dontea's story reminds us, not everyone has the luxury of expressing their emotions, and factors like race and gender make it harder for some to process. She tells us, "When everyone else's kids started hitting milestones, I felt sad for my child but could not express it." She adds that part of this is the added layer of being a Black woman and the societal expectation that she remains strong. She says, "When a White woman cries, the whole world cries with her, and when a Black woman cries, she cries alone."

Similarly, Valento names his sadness when he sees his daughter on the playground: "I still get sad when I take my daughter to school and see other kids playing at school and my child is spinning in circles with her mouth open to the sky—this takes a mental toll on me."

Willingness to (Un)Learn

A parenting love ethic is the practice of a *willingness to (un)learn.* We investigate our relationship to the systems of oppression within which we parent so that we can unpack ideas and values that our inner child and adult parent self have internalized. To do this we acknowledge and question the grip of systems of oppression on us and find small ways to deliver ourselves from its suffocating hold.

Adjusting Expectations

To parent our children means adjusting our expectations of ourselves as parents and who we think our children will be. So often these ideas about parenting and children come from what was taught to us by our families and society. Julie tells us about adjusting what she believes parenting is: "I did not think it was going to be peaches, rainbows, and unicorns." She had worked with kids with autism and knew about the importance of being warm and encouraging and setting appropriate boundaries. She says, "I did not understand that. In parenting, unlike teaching and tutoring, you get no breaks. Of course I can be on point when I am rested. Parenting a neurodivergent child is a marathon; it pushes you to limits you didn't even know you had."

And in recalibrating, we have to ask ourselves how we can like this child we love. For instance, Elizabeth tells us how she thought her child would be someone whom she would enjoy spending time with, imagining that they would do things like cooking and playing board games together. "My kid has not been enjoyable so far, and I have had to mourn that. I just don't want to do things with him right now."

For Janne, the last thirty years of parenting her son have taught her that she is the one who has to adjust, not her child. She says, "I had to remind myself that he is not my daughter. Just because my daughter did something at fourteen does not mean he will." Her story reminds us that we can't parent our children based on what we want or prefer; instead, we need to calibrate our parenting to what our children need.

Discerning Feedback

Parenting our children means being at the receiving end of unsolicited feedback that we get from other parents, teachers, aunts and uncles, and grocery store cashiers. Most often, unsolicited feedback, however well intentioned, has a harmful impact on us and our children. Comments like "Wow, he likes to speak loudly," "Your child did not take turns at the party and made the other kids upset," or "Your child needs therapy," no matter how factually true, can be untimely, inappropriate, and often shameful. These comments can make us feel small and unsupported. Such comments rightfully provoke feelings of sadness, anger, and disappointment in us. But what if the feedback also allows us to evaluate whether the standards used to judge our child are something we want to remain loyal to?

Reconsidering Our Models of Parenting

In parenting our children, we are faced with deciding whether the philosophy of parenting we grew up with still fits. We have to consider whether the advice we receive works for our children. And in assessing these models of parenting, we have to ask ourselves,

- Who is this decision for, and why am I doing something a particular way?
- Is it to appease family members or people around me so I can feel better about myself, or is it for my child?

Parenting philosophies are abundant, and there is no shortage of righteousness in promoting a particular approach. One such approach to parenting, and one that is conventionally accepted, is the idea that children should fit into the lives of adults, which encourages adults to continue with their lives and fold in their children. Sadly, when we fit our children into spaces that do not work for them, we power over them by ranking their needs against ours. There is a fine line between authority and control.

As Rupa offers, this is not to say that parents of neurodivergent children need to sacrifice their needs and interests. It means getting creative. Rupa talks about how they also imagined that parenting would mean that they would continue to live her life. Based on what they saw their cousin do as a parent and how their mother used to take the siblings across the country on trains, they too imagined taking their child everywhere, including restaurants and job interviews. However, after adopting their child, Rupa recognized that they could not parent the way they imagined; Rupa had to parent the child in front of them. "With our kid's needs, I had to ask myself, *How can we get on an airplane, or even go to the airport?*" They continue, "Two years ago, I would have insisted he had to do what we needed and maybe pushed him to go to a restaurant, because he needs to learn how to sit there. That is not the case anymore, and I needed to unlearn what I had learned from the people around me. Now, instead of forcing him to do what we want to do or have to do, we do not expect him to do unpleasant things for his sake and ours. It does not mean my partner and I give up on ourselves either. It just means that the things we do together intersect less."

Reimagining Hope

Parenting our children is about hope. Even before they are born, we hope that their experiences in the world are better than ours and that this next generation will make the world a better place. How we nurture our hopes and keep them from becoming expectations is a big part of this work of parenting. However, after we meet our children and come to learn of their neurodivergence, the hope we have becomes more complex. We hope that they will be safe, that they will have meaningful and purposeful lives, and that they will find community and belonging. The hope we have is a radical act of disrupting the systems of oppression.

We invite you to think about:

- Where do your hopes come from?
- What do you hope for?
- How much of your cultural upbringing and race inform what you hope for in a life for your children?

Showing Respect

A parenting love ethic is the practice of *showing respect.* We listen to our children deeply and lean in, committing to seeing them as worthy, whole, and competent. We take the bid when our children call us into their world, whether through nonsensical babbles, repetitive play, or long-winded storytelling. To join them in what looks incoherent may actually illuminate the path forward.

Advocacy

Parenting our children means being a fierce advocate. We are constantly called to defend and protect our children from well-meaning doctors, schools, aunts and uncles, and neighbors. We hope our kids grow up with a strong sense of identity and self-love, as the world keeps telling them they are not enough. Here, parents share how they advocate for their children.

Molly talks about how her first ob-gyn, a White woman, dismissed her, did not acknowledge her worries, and, worse yet, did not share with Molly that she had preeclampsia, putting her in immense danger. "The second time around, I advocated by seeking a provider of color and kept asking for what I needed. The worst thing I can do is ask again and then ask loudly."

Valento talks about his efforts in educating his extended family and neighbors. "I explained autism to my parents and in-laws and shared the reasons for my children's behaviors. I introduced myself to neighbors, told them about my kids, and told them, 'Here is my number. If you see my daughter around without me, please call me.'"

As parents, we advocate with our children's schools. A powerful example comes from Hana. During the end of her son's time in fifth grade, she could not provide the necessary support to him due to her work schedule, so she advocated for an in-classroom assistant. When the schools denied this, she pursued procuring appropriate support for her son by researching legal evidence for ADA (Americans with Disabilities Act) compliance. She says, "I fully support educators and know how hard it is. However, the school system relies on parents not knowing what to ask for or what they can push back on, because they are already strapped for resources so it is easier to say no. Teachers will say no, and administrators will say no."

Sometimes advocacy looks like removing our child from a situation. Valento recalls, "Just two days ago, I had to go inside the school because she was throwing a massive tantrum and no one could help her. Soon as I entered the school, I could hear her screaming all the way from the classroom into the hallway. The kids are all staring. The teacher is doing her best to not let the kids stare, but the kids are staring. I go into daddy mode and take care and get her out of the situation, but as a parent that still hurts me very, very much to see."

We also advocate with authority figures like the police. Dontea advocated with the police by taking her son to meet the local officers who patrol the neighborhood. Having her child meet them was important, because she did not want the police to see her child as a threat.

Accountability

Showing respect to our children also means holding them appropriately accountable. We can slip into excusing some behaviors as a manifestation of neurodivergence, and it is understandable that because the rest of the world is giving them so much feedback, we may be less likely to. Or on the other hand, if we are worried about how the world will see our children, we may overcorrect and hold them inappropriately accountable. Swinging between seeing our children as either infallible or incorrigible does not serve them in the long run. With the understanding that neurodivergent children of color will also make mistakes and can hurt people, we believe that accountability affirms their humanity, and that it can only happen when we can hold both the good and the bad with love and grace. What makes this especially challenging is teasing out when a behavior is about emotional regulation or communication versus when it is intentionally meant to hurt. Sometimes the reasons can overlap.

Finding Joy

Parenting our children means finding joy in the smallest packages. We learn that seeking happiness in blemish-free vacations, the highest grades, and the neatest homes will lead to more frustrations. Our days can be unpredictable and unexpected: a sensory-induced emotional tantrum, spilled juice, missed homework, a longer time to transition from the car, or the big feelings of losing a cherished teddy—these perceivably more minor things can change the course of a day. So instead of the big wins, we turn our attention to the magic inscribed into the present moment, where we might catch the invitation from our child to notice the unexpected, the extraordinarily ordinary, and the quickly passing changes within them. In tuning in, we can join our children in joy, however fleeting.

Molly shares, "Even though the joys can be fleeting, it's always wonderful to see when my son makes progress even in small ways. For instance, when he was able to tell his first simple joke, or when he showed us a new skill that I never witnessed before. It's wonderful to see this, because it shows how much he's grown at his own pace."

Sophia agrees. "It brings me joy that we get to have our personalized milestones! Every day brings the potential for a surprise breakthrough: a new word our kid acquires, a new skill, a new glimpse of their personality. Every little thing is a chance for celebration and achievement. Like the first time they eat a nonpreferred item spontaneously, when they teach themselves how to operate a toy, or when they say hi spontaneously. Never a dull moment in this family."

Meena says, "I think one of the constant and biggest lessons has been that the only way to cope with this whole journey is to live in the now—to live one day at a time. I was one of those people who always liked to have a plan and know what was coming. I wrote many lists, and I still do, but now it's about today."

An Emancipatory Vision

Being with our children, listening deeply to them, affirming their truth, and taking their lead to guide our development is the medicine we need. Their spirit, wisdom, play, emotions, and dreams are the way. We opened this chapter with quotes by Audre Lorde and bell hooks. If alive to speak, we wondered, what would they say to parents raising children at these intersections of race and neurodivergence? We imagine they would encourage us to sit with two critical questions:

- What does raising our children with a parenting love ethic look like?
- What would liberation for our children look like?

In imagining a more liberatory future for our children, we leave you with some questions that animate our thinking. These questions are the seeds of an emerging vision. We hesitate to provide an exact manifesto; it is not our place to say what or how. We believe that the answers are in the alchemy that results from struggle, resolve, hope, love, and joy. We invite you to join us in collectively envisioning and embodying a present and future where all of us experience true freedom, belonging, and safety.

- What if our children could show up in the world without an apology?
- What if we genuinely believed that our BIPOC neurodivergent child claims a rightful center space in the world?
- What if we could trust that our children have the wisdom to seek solutions?
- What if our children didn't have to perform for us adults constantly?

- What if we could see our children's beauty and love even when they are triggering us?
- What if we don't teach our children to adjust or conform to adultism but help them stand up to it?
- What if we had something to learn from our children?
- What if parenting was not about fixing but being, celebrating, and trusting?
- What if we didn't have to parent alone but could rely on a village to support us in raising our children?
- What if . . . ?

This book was born out of a desire for community. It is our hope that you felt the tug of the invisible threads connecting you to parents who lovingly shared their truth, inviting you into kinship with them. Maybe you found your story in theirs.

We hope you arrive here feeling a little more seen for the invisible labor of love you pour into your parenting every second. We hope you arrive here with a little more compassion and appreciation for yourself and the gifts you bring to your neurodivergent child/ren, every day. Because you deserve it, and so do your children.

ACKNOWLEDGMENTS

It is too easy to focus on the final form of this book, to strip it away from the process and community that helped bring it to life. While our names are listed as authors, this book would not be what it is today without the fierce and dedicated parents who contributed their stories, trusted teachers who steadily guided us, beloved friends and family who read early chapters and offered timely feedback, scholars and industry experts who readily offered their time to talk to us and broaden our understanding, and our loved ones whose unwavering support cheered us onto the finish line. It took not only time and hard work but also the loving embrace of a community far and wide to help realize the emancipatory vision of this book.

We acknowledge here all the people who supported and nurtured our vision for this book. The spirit of this book is about building community. From the beginning, we both knew that we had to have a community of people to love on us, champion us, and hold us accountable. Thank you, dear friends, family, and colleagues. We are eternally grateful.

We want to thank Eric Smith for identifying the need for this kind of parenting book and for accompanying us on the initial journey of writing a book proposal. Thank you to our friend Nidhi Berry, who heard the call for authors from Eric and generously connected the three of us—this is community embodied.

We are so grateful to Leticia Nieto, Agnes Kwong, Jamie Pearson, and Jannae Myers for being part of our elder council. You have lovingly and generously nudged us to think more deeply and provided insightful feedback to help us see what is in our periphery. A big thank you to Cheryl Poe for offering your expertise and enthusiasm in supporting us with identifying helpful strategies in dealing with the criminal justice and educational system. Our sincere gratitude also to Ujjayini Sikha for partnering with us and lovingly embodying the spirit of the book within your art. We appreciate your thoughtfulness.

We are grateful to Michelle Williams, our editor, who saw the possibility and the vision of this book and who patiently answered all of our questions, some of which we asked maybe three or four times. A big thanks to Devon Freeny and Frances Giguette for the meticulous and insightful edits. We also greatly appreciate everyone on Parenting Press's marketing, publicity, and sales teams who have worked so hard to get the word out about this book, including Lauren Chartuk, Valerie Pedroche, Candysse Miller, Melanie Roth, and Cynthia Sherry. Our heartfelt gratitude also to Jordan Alam, who supported us with promoting the book on social media and being our book doula, helping us birth this book into the larger world.

We give this line to honor those who did not want to be named and the parents out there who have yet to be heard.

Additionally, we are deeply indebted to the following contributors to the book: Blake Adams, Amber Naali Aelfgifu, Shubha Bala, Maggie Beneke, Rajiv Bharadwaja, Rafael Bocamazzo, Ashley Boulden, Daniel Brett, Nivi Brett, Athena Brewer, Shirley Chen, Emily Cherkin, Eve Crevoshay, Marilupe de la Calle, Kiara Dixon, Yarrow Durbin, Aparajita Durga, DeJesus Ellis, Patricia Gilbaugh, Ana Gomez, Liana Green, Zelon Harrison, Kristin Henning, John Hopkins, Meghna Jaradi, Sonora Jha, Janelle Johnson, Thejus Joseph, Jessica Joy, Raghav Kaushik, Kat Kerr, Elizabeth Kilmer, Jared Kilmer, Dalton King, Cynthia Landesberg, JC Lau, Maggie Locker, Meredith Macharia, Shelley Macy, Christina Malecka, Janne Mayes, Diana Mena, Michelle Morcate, Sangeeta Naidu, Prashant Nema, Yumiko Ogawa, Morénike Giwa Onaiwu, Calvin Osili, Jordan Pack, Trisha Pack, Nikita Pangarkar, Gia Parsons, Anjana Pawar, Liliana Perez, Stacey Prince, Tanya Ranchigoda, Sophia Rath, Gayle Shimokura, Danyale Sturdivant, Shirin Subhani, Ravi Subramanian, Savitha Subramanian, Maya Swaminathan, Sarah Valrejean, Daisy Vergara, Jeni L. Wahlig, Cassie Walker, Katherine Walter, Robin Wilson-Beattie, Patty Wipfler, Families of Color Seattle, and Open Doors for Multicultural Families.

Lastly, we want to thank our furry companions, Coco and Bagelz. They sat next to us patiently, offering us paws and drools as their encouragement, while we wrote and talked about the book. We promise to get back to our regular walking schedule now!

From Jaya

Nivi—You are not only my sister but also my friend. I may be older, but more often than not, I look up to you! I'm so glad you will always be part of the whole story, and there is no one else like you. Gina—You taught me that I needed to take extra diapers when I go out with a baby and how to make a mean pasta sauce. And you know me warts and all. I am forever grateful for your presence in my life. Sarah—It is a serendipitous blessing that we walked into the same grad school program and found each other. In our friendship, I find myself fully seen, challenged, loved, and understood. Gayle—I knew we would be fast friends when you congratulated me for quitting my corporate job to go back to school. You inspire me to see the good, to laugh heartily, and to use the public library more. And may you always be fed, my friend.

My heartfelt gratitude and love to my dear friends, family and teachers, Katherine, Stacey, Leticia, Meghna, Christina, Daniel, Jessica, Savitha, and Alexandra—thank you for reading the chapters, for encouraging me, for being a part of my process, and for believing in this book and me.

Avi, Rahul, and Nikhil—I love you three. Rohan and Taejas are lucky to have you as cousins.

All my love and respect for you, my dear friend Priya. There is no one else I could have written this book with. You have listened deeply, been incredibly patient with my wacky ideas, and shown me the gift of moving slower. The fact that this book didn't break us but only strengthened our friendship tells me we should write another one—just kidding!

From Priya

A heartfelt thank you to:

Maya and Pranav: For being here for me always, and for us being able to share the joys of parenting together. Raghav: For being a wonderful father to Ahir, and for sharing your love of cricket with him;

and to you and Chakku amma for squeezing Ahir extra while I wrote this book. Dilip: For all your lou. Kripa: For reigniting didi-hood. My extended family across the globe: For your love and blessings.

Aparajita, Blake, Brooke, Vanessa, Lauren, Michelle P.: For being my trusted listening partners and for allowing me to show up messy—what a gift! Rajiv, Raji, Arul, Kshama, Tapoja, Gigi: For always being able to count on your love and support. Athena, Krissy, Prashant, Michelle M.: For your friendship and nerding. I've learned so much in co-minding with you.

Cary, Yumi, Katherine E., Patty, and Lisa: For your invaluable teachings, and for believing in me. Your leadership and advocacy for children is a true inspiration. To my Hand in Hand parenting and Synergetic Play Therapy communities: For rocking me through this process.

Thejus: For seeing me whole, and for seeing beauty in hardship. Rohini and Rohit: For letting me into your beautiful world. It is no doubt colorful, rich, and unique because of you. Eliza, Joseph achen, and Teresa amma: For your loving, open arms. I feel lucky to have you all in my village.

Jaya, my twin! Life makes no mistakes. I knew we would be trouble together the moment we met. Thank you for being my second chicken and daring to dream big, for believing in me, and for infusing our friendship with a fierce love ethic. I couldn't shouldn't wouldn't this book without you.

APPENDIX A

Resources for Legal Considerations

Documentation Tips from Cheryl Poe of Advocating 4 Kids

- Most schools require both parent and child to sign a code of conduct, which states that certain behaviors are punishable. The code of conduct must not become a vehicle to unreasonably punish our children for their regulatory behaviors or any behaviors they may engage in due to their disability. As such, the following two statements can be written in on the code of conduct:
    - *I am unable to sign this document as I cannot guarantee that my child can abide by the code of conduct due to their disability [describe, if desired].*
    - *I do not allow my child to be disciplined or to be alone or speak with school resource officers and other enforcement figures without my physical presence.*
- If you suspect your child has a learning disability and they don't have an IEP or 504 plan, you may request a full comprehensive evaluation in writing, which triggers a diagnostic process.
    - A written email creates a record of your concern for your child's educational needs and of your interest in supporting them to be successful in school.
    - If a learning disability is determined, you will be able to use an IEP or 504 plan to your advantage, to document your child's learning needs and how best to support them as a team.
- Know the laws and your rights!
    - Understand your state laws around disciplinary actions at school: Education Commission of the States is a good resource.
    - If your child comes into contact with any form of discipline in school, under the Family Educational Rights and Privacy Act (FERPA), you have the right to access the following:
        - All written statements.
        - Reports (from school and police).

        - Witness statements.
        - Copies of any assessments or evaluations.
        - Your child's full education records.
- If this goes beyond the gates of the school and requires engaging with the judicial system, it is imperative that you continue to keep records of conversations with counsel, case workers, probation officers, etc. Request a copy of your child's full education records to share with your counsel. There may be information in the file that helps with your child's case.

Advocacy Suggestions for After an Arrest

- If possible, secure legal representation for your child. Additionally, the courts will likely assign a guardian ad litem* who will act as your child's legal representative in court.
    - Provide your child's counsel with all relevant information about your child's disabilities and access to necessary documentation that can be useful in supporting your child through this process.
    - When possible, find an expert who specializes in your child's disability. For example, if your child has ADHD, find an expert in ADHD to testify on your child's behalf or provide a written report about how your child's disability influenced their behaviors.
- Parents are the first line of defense in ensuring that all relevant information about their child gets to the key parties. Explaining your child's disability to legal counsel, probation officers, social workers, and judges can help them to understand how the neurotype of your child can impact their ability to grasp certain things or behave in ways deemed appropriate.
    - Know that if students have an IEP or 504 plan, the detention setting must implement those services. Getting this information to probation officers and counsel is essential.
- Parents can step in and advocate for their children by offering a safety plan to the judge and requesting that the judge enforce continuity in services the child received before arrest. Again, providing the plan in writing is highly recommended.
    - Parents, family, neighbors, and other community members can advocate by speaking about the child's strengths.

Police Training Considerations

We propose that police neurodivergence training:

- Be integrated into basic police training, not offered as short adjunct training, and happen regularly after that.
- Be conducted by neurodivergent BIPOC adults, with input from our children.
- Cover in-depth neurodevelopmental experiences and needs of children.

---

* A guardian ad litem is a person who is appointed by the court to protect the interests of someone who can't take care of themselves.

- Cover the topic of internalized race and ability bias and how to counter it actively.
- Be hands-on, preferably in interaction and relationship with neurodivergent children of color.
- Be uniform and consistent across police departments in the United States.
- Include assessment tools to discern if police presence is even necessary on the scene of calls.

APPENDIX B

Our Community Members

WE INVITED PARENTS to participate in this book through many different forums, including Twitter, Facebook, Instagram, LinkedIn, and personal connections. We were overwhelmed by the responses and the generosity of our parents. In all, we interviewed more than thirty parents from diverse backgrounds and experiences. They are Black, Latinx, Afro-Caribbean with indigeneity, Asian, South Asian, and biracial; their experiences speak to raising children diagnosed with autism (speaking and nonspeaking), ADHD, learning challenges, intellectual and developmental disabilities, and giftedness. Parents were provided a small honorarium and offered a support group to connect with other parents for their participation and contributions to this book.

Though we reached out through many avenues, the book is missing the voices of parents who have Indigenous heritage here in the United States. This profoundly saddens us, as we did not want our book to be complicit in the erasure of Indigenous voices, especially as the production of this book is under a settler-colonial context. We are also missing the voices of parents who have a Middle Eastern background and those who are undocumented parents. Furthermore, in response to our call for parent participation, we mainly heard from those with kids with ADHD and autism. We did not receive stories from those with Tourette's, OCD, bipolar disorder, or other expressions of neurodivergence. Possibly telling, most of the parents we spoke with self-identified themselves as mothers. Only three participants self-identified as dads. And thus we have an imperfect book.

With more time and resources, we would have loved to narrow our gaps, knowing that there will always be room for *more, better,* and *perfect.* Perhaps within our vulnerability in presenting an imperfect creation lies our strength in standing up to notions of *perfection.* Perhaps imperfection is where we must start, with ample room for further conversation with you. And maybe our imperfection is enough.

Below, we provide background information of each of our parent contributors. All details are accurate at the time of writing this book. Here and throughout the book, their names have been replaced with pseudonyms, and some identifiable characteristics have been removed or changed to protect privacy.

Anamika

Anamika is an Indian woman who is raising two kids with her husband. Living in the Pacific Northwest, she identifies as a cis immigrant woman of color with education and class privilege. Her older child has been diagnosed with speech delays and autism.

Angela

Angela is a South Asian first-generation immigrant who came to the country with the hope of a better promise for her autistic daughter's care and future. She is a single mother of two adult children, one of whom is nonspeaking with high access needs. Angela and her children live together on the West Coast.

Arica

Arica is Black, disabled, and Jewish. She has one child who is biracial and trans and who has a diagnosis of autism, ADHD, and giftedness. Arica is an educator and lives on the West Coast.

Carmen

Carmen is a cis Black woman who identifies as Christian and works in the arts. She is a single mother who is raising twin kids, one of whom has ADHD. She lives on the East Coast.

Corey

Corey is a cis Black man who is a single father currently raising a daughter with autism and other medical conditions. He does not identify as neurodivergent and owns a school. Corey lives on the East Coast and has two other adult children.

Deepti

Deepti identifies as a cis woman to a neurodivergent preteen daughter. She is a first-generation neurodivergent Indian immigrant living in the Midwest. She holds class and caste privileges.

Dolores

Dolores identifies herself as a first-generation Chinese Indonesian, an adoptive mother of a Latinx neurodivergent (ADHD) child, and a wife. She was raised Catholic and identifies her family as multicultural. Dolores is a mental health therapist.

Dontea

Dontea is a Black, heterosexual woman who is a single parent to a child with autism. She and her ex co-parent their child. Dontea lives on the East Coast with her son.

Elizabeth

Elizabeth is multiracially Black and queer and does not identify as neurodivergent. Partnered, Elizabeth is raising an adopted child who is multiracial Latine. An educator, she lives with her family on the West Coast.

Hana

Hana is a mother to two multiracial kids, one who has a diagnosis of ADHD and another who has not been formally diagnosed with giftedness but presents very much so. She is an Asian American cis woman who does not identify herself as neurodivergent. Living on the East Coast, Hana is active in her children's education as a homeschooling parent.

Janne

A mother of two grown children, Janne is Black and possibly neurodivergent herself. One of her children is autistic and suffers from a brain injury resulting from a suicide attempt. Married, she is a former teacher who has lived internationally.

Jasmine

Jasmine is a Black single mother raising a child with ADHD and anxiety. She works in health care and is currently going back to school to pursue a master's degree. She identifies as a Christian and a survivor of abuse and trauma.

Josefina

Josefina identifies as a Hispanic woman and mother of a nonspeaking adolescent with cerebral palsy. She lives on the West Coast.

Joshua

Joshua is biracial and identifies as a first-generation Nigerian American. He is queer and neurodivergent. He co-parents with his children's other parents. Joshua is in a polyamorous partnership. For the interview for the book, his partner (**Minnie**), who is a White woman, joined for parts. In some places, both Joshua and Minnie are attributed.

Joy

Joy is a Black cis woman who is neurodivergent and also disabled with chronic illness. She is married to her husband, with whom she is raising an autistic child. Joy and her family live on the East Coast.

Julie

Julie is Taiwanese American and identifies as first-and-a-half generation, having migrated as a young child. She is a cis woman who holds class and education privileges. She does not identify as neurodivergent. Married, Julie is parenting two children, one of whom has intellectual disabilities.

Kim

Kim is Korean American and adopted. She does not identify as having a disability. Married to her husband, Kim is raising three children who were adopted from Korea. Her oldest has a formal diagnosis of ADHD and autism. Their second child does not have a diagnosis but could be neurodivergent as well. Kim and her family live on the East Coast.

Leela

Leela is part of the Indian diaspora and a cis woman raised in the United States. In an interracial marriage, Leela is raising two kids. Her younger child has a diagnosis of autism, and her older one has not been identified as neurodivergent. She herself does not identify as neurodivergent. Living in the Pacific Northwest, Leela enjoys spending time with her family and dog.

Luisa

Luisa identifies as a Hispanic and Latinx Cuban American mother, a second-generation immigrant, and neurodivergent. She is raising two neurodivergent children. She lives with her husband, children, and furry family members on the East Coast.

Malika

Malika is a first-generation Indian American woman who is neurodivergent and is raising two neurodivergent children. She is married and works in health care. She has educational, caste, and class privileges.

Mary

Mary is an immigrant from China who is married and raising two neurodivergent children. She is not neurodivergent and has class and education privileges. She is a stay-at-home mother who lives with her family on the West Coast.

Meena

Partnered, Meena is the mom of two kids, fifteen and eleven. Her oldest child has a formal autism spectrum diagnosis (ASD) and ADHD diagnosis, and her youngest has qualified for pervasive developmental disorder (PDD). Meena identifies as South Asian and lives in the Pacific Northwest. Meena identifies as a cis woman of color who is nondisabled and an immigrant of the Hindu faith.

Min

Min is a first-generation Chinese Guamanian woman who is a single mother to two kids, one of whom has an ADHD diagnosis. She comes from a big family and identifies as middle class. Min is an educator.

Molly

Living on the West Coast, Molly is an Asian immigrant cis woman. She is partnered with her husband and raising two kids, one of whom has a diagnosis of autism and ADHD. Molly works in the health care field.

Mumbi

Mumbi is a first-generation East African American who does not identify as neurodivergent herself. She is the mother to twins, both multiracial and Hispanic. One of her kids has a diagnosis of ADHD, and the other has a diagnosis of autism. Mumbi lives on the West Coast.

Rupa

Rupa is of Indian descent and identifies as queer, genderqueer, and nondisabled and is in an interracial partnership. As an activist, they are partnered with someone who is autistic.

They grew up in Canada and live on the East Coast. Rupa and their partner have adopted a Black child who has a diagnosis of autism.

Sanvi

Sanvi is a Sri Lankan woman who is in an interracial marriage and raising two kids. One of her children has a diagnosis of dyslexia. Sanvi identifies as a cis woman who is non-neurodivergent. Raised as a Buddhist, she holds both class and education privileges.

Serena

Serena is a first-generation Chinese American woman who is raising two kids, one of whom has a diagnosis of ADHD and OCD. She does not identify as neurodivergent and has class and education privileges. Serena works in the medical field.

Sophia

Sophia is a single mom of two multiracial kids, one who is eight and another who is six. Both children are identified as being on the autism spectrum, and one of them has a co-occurring diagnosis of ADHD. Sophia identifies as an Afro-Latina from the Dominican Republic. She has traced her ancestry to all continents with the exception of Australia.

Valento

Valento is a father to three kids. He is a cis Black man who is partnered. Growing up he was the youngest in his family. He is a stay-at-home dad and does not identify as neurodivergent, but two of his kids have been identified as such. His oldest has a diagnosis of autism and more recently ADHD and dysgraphia. His second-oldest child has a diagnosis of autism. He and his family live in a multigenerational home.

Zion

Zion identifies as a Black woman, a single mother to eleven children, and a grandmother to many. She lives on the West Coast. While they are not seeking out a formal medical diagnosis, her youngest child was born prematurely and struggles with sensory processing and has other difficulties with learning.

NOTES

A Note on Language

the word profound has also been used: Alison Singer, "It's Time to Embrace 'Profound Autism,'" *Spectrum*, October 27, 2022, https://www.spectrumnews.org/opinion /viewpoint/its-time-to-embrace-profound-autism/.

1. The Framework

"Because the intersectional experience is greater": Kimberlé Crenshaw, "Demarginalizing the Intersection of Race and Sex: A Black Feminist Critique of Antidiscrimination Doctrine, Feminist Theory and Antiracist Politics," *University of Chicago Legal Forum* 1989, no. 1, https://chicagounbound.uchicago.edu/cgi/viewcontent.cgi?article=1052 &context=uclf.

"The Disability Rights movement simultaneously invisibilized": Patty Berne, "What Is Disability Justice?," Sins Invalid, June 16, 2020, https://www.sinsinvalid.org/news -1/2020/6/16/what-is-disability-justice.

A disability justice framework is built on: Patty Berne and Sins Invalid, *The Ten Principles of Disability Justice*, Sins Invalid, tinyurl.com/DJ10Principles.

"A disability justice framework understands": Patty Berne, "Skin, Tooth and Bone—The Basis of Our Movement Is People: A Disability Justice Primer," *Reproductive Health Matters* 25, no. 50 (May 2017), 149–150.

"Neurodiversity is a natural and valuable": Nick Walker, "Neurodiversity: Some Basic Terms & Definitions," Neuroqueer, accessed July 31, 2023, https://neuroqueer.com /neurodiversity-terms-and-definitions/.

shows that the ongoing connectedness: Nicole Lezin, Lori A. Rolleri, Steve Bean, and Julie Taylor, *Parent-Child Connectedness: Implications for Research, Interventions, and Positive Impacts on Adolescent Health* (Santa Cruz, CA: ETR Associates, 2004).

Another unique feature: Gilda Morelli, "The Evolution of Attachment Theory and Cultures of Human Attachment in Infancy and Early Childhood," in *The Oxford Handbook of Human Development and Culture: An Interdisciplinary Perspective*, ed. Lene Arnett Jense (Oxford: Oxford University Press, 2015), 149–164.

2. Standing at the Intersections

Sonya Renee Taylor writes about how: Sonya Renee Taylor, *The Body Is Not an Apology: The Power of Radical Self-Love* (Oakland, CA: Berrett-Koehler, 2021).

"white supremacy is not a shark": Kyle "Guante" Tran Myhre, "How to Explain White Supremacy to a White Supremacist," in *A Love Song, A Death Rattle, A Battle Cry* (Minneapolis: Buton Poetry, 2018).

We refer to the work of Kenneth Jones and Tema Okun: Tema Okun, White Supremacy Culture, https://www.whitesupremacyculture.info/.

"Racism and capitalism emerged": Owen Jones, "Ibram X Kendi on Why Not Being Racist Is Not Enough," *Guardian* (US edition), August 14, 2019, https://www.theguardian.com/world/2019/aug/14/ibram-x-kendi-on-why-not-being-racist-is-not-enough.

We do not consider whether they want to be touched: Jenny Marder, "The Case Against Tickling," *New York Times*, July 13, 2020, https://www.nytimes.com/2020/07/13/parenting/kids-tickling.html.

not only historical but also intergenerational: Resmaa Menakem, *My Grandmother's Hands: Racialized Trauma and the Pathway to Mending Our Hearts and Bodies* (Las Vegas: Central Recovery, 2017).

A powerful antidote to this was the mutual aid practices: Dorothy Hastings, "'Abandoned by Everyone Else,' Neighbors Are Banding Together During the Pandemic," *Nation*, April 5, 2021, https://www.pbs.org/newshour/nation/how-mutual-aid-networks-came-together-in-a-year-of-crisis.

"presupposes that everyone has the right": bell hooks, *All About Love: New Visions* (New York: William Morrow, 2018), 87.

3. The Map Is Not the Territory

Children, however, are wired to depend: Larissa Hirsch, "Nervous System," Nemours KidsHeath, July 2022, https://kidshealth.org/en/parents/brain-nervous-system.html.

Lisa Dion, founder of Synergetic Play Therapy Institute: Lisa Dion, "How Trying to Be Calm Gets in the Way of Regulation," Synergetic Play Therapy Institute, July 1, 2022, https://synergeticplaytherapy.com/how-trying-to-be-calm-gets-in-the-way-of-regulation.

Nadine Burke Harris, founder of the Center for Youth Wellness: Nadine Burke Harris, "Adverse Childhood Experiences," Burke Foundation, https://burkefoundation.org/what-drives-us/adverse-childhood-experiences-aces/.

"A central premise of the neurodiversity movement": Kathy Leadbitter et al., "Autistic Self-Advocacy and the Neurodiversity Movement: Implications for Autism Early Intervention Research and Practice," *Frontiers in Psychology* 12 (April 2021), https://doi.org/10.3389/fpsyg.2021.635690.

Based on observations with gifted children: "Asynchronous Development," National Association for Gifted Children, http://dev.nagc.org/resources-publications/resources-parents/social-emotional-issues/asynchronous-development.

theory of multiple intelligences: Howard Gardner, "Are all Intelligences Equal? An Issue Raised by Cormac McCarthy's Recent Novels," author's personal website, January 17, 2023, https://www.howardgardner.com/howards-blog/are-all-intelligences-equal-an-issue-raised-by-cormac-mccarthys-recent-novels.

These models were developed by White men: Hanna Bertilsdotter Rosqvist, Nick Chown, and Anna Stenning, eds., *Neurodiverstiy Studies: A New Critical Paradigm* (London: Routeldge, 2020).

As a result of variability in structure: Nanda Rommelse, Jan K. Buitelaar, and Catharina A. Hartman, "Structural Brain Imaging Correlates of ASD and ADHD Across the Lifepsan: A Hypothesis-Generating Review on Developmental ASD-ADHD Subtypes," *Journal of Neural Transmission* 124, no. 2 (December 21, 2016): 259–271, https://doi.org/10.1007/s00702-016-1651-1.

Studies have shown a strong correlation: Koen Luyckx, et al., "Personal Identity Processes and Self-Esteem: Temporal Sequences in High School and College Students," *Journal of Research in Personality* 47, no. 2 (April 2013): 159–170, https://doi.org/10.1016/j.jrp.2012.10.005.

We reject this conflation and, in fact, argue: Leah Lakshmi Piepzna-Samarasinha, *Care Work: Dreaming Disability Justice Work* (Vancouver: Arsenal Pulp Press, 2018).

quickly learn to code-switch: Courtney L. McCluney, Kathrina Robotham, Serenity Lee, Richard Smith, and Myles Durkee, "The Costs of Code-Switching," *Harvard Business Review*, November 15, 2019, https://hbr.org/2019/11/the-costs-of-codeswitching.

Kieran Rose, an autistic advocate: Amy Pearson and Kieran Rose, "A Conceptual Analysis of Autistic Masking: Understanding the Narrative of Stigma and the Illusion of Choice," *Autism in Adulthood* 3, no. 1 (March 18, 2021), https://doi.org/10.1089/aut.2020.0043.

Numerous articles and literature by neurodivergent: For example, Ann X. Huang et al., "Understanding the Self in Individual with Autism Spectrum Disorder (ASD): A Review of the Literature," *Frontiers in Psychology* 8, no. 1422 (August 22, 2017), https://doi.org/10.3389%2Ffpsyg.2017.01422; Viktoria Lyons and Michael Fitzgerald, "Atypical Sense of Self in Autism Spectrum Disorders: A Neuro-Cognitive Perspective," in *Recent Advances in Autism Spectrum Disorder*, vol. 1, ed. Michael Fitzgerald (IntechOpen, March 6, 2013), https://www.intechopen.com/chapters/41296.

a neurodivergent brain will likely take longer: Mark Wheeler, "Autistic Brains Develop More Slowly than Healthy Brains, UCLA Researchers Say," UCLA Health, October 20, 2011, https://www.uclahealth.org/news/autistic-brains-develop-more-slowly-than-healthy-brains.

Gabor Maté, author of Scattered: Gabor Maté, *Scattered: How Attention Deficit Disorder Originates and What You Can Do About It* (New York: Plume, 1999).

"an instinctive, automatic resistance": Gordon Neufeld and Gabor Maté, *Hold On to Your Kids: Why Parents Need to Matter More Than Peers* (New York: Ballantine, 2006), 74.

they are likely to experience: Erin O'Brien, "The Youth Mental Health Crisis: Supporting Patients with ASD and ADHD," *Psychiatric Times*, June 10, 2022, https://www.psychiatrictimes.com/view/the-youth-mental-health-crisis-supporting-patients-with-asd-and-adhd; Amanda Kirby, "Is There a Link Between Neurodiversity and Mental Health?" *Psychology Today*, August 26, 2021, https://www.psychologytoday.com/us/blog/pathways-progress/202108/is-there-link-between-neurodiversity-and-mental-health.

typical mental health issues resulting: Michael P. Dentato, "The Minority Stress Perspective," Psychology and AIDS Exchange Newsletter, American Psychology Association, April 2012, https://www.apa.org/pi/aids/resources/exchange/2012/04/minority-stress.

4. Building the Model

Many parents experience the absence: Joanna Mang, "The Myth of the Postpartum Love Rush," *Outline*, October 24, 2018, https://theoutline.com/post/6441/post-partum-hormones-love-myth.

data reveals that becoming a parent: Jennifer Glass, Robin W. Simon, and Matthew A. Andersson, "Parenthood and Happiness: Effects of Work-Family Reconciliation Policies in 22 OECD Countries," *American Journal of Sociology* 122, no. 3 (November 2016): 886–929, https://doi.org/10.1086/688892.

5. Uncovering Vibrant Playgrounds

Author Dr. Stuart Brown defines play: Stuart Brown with Christopher Vaughan, *Play: How It Shapes the Brain, Opens the Imagination, and Invigorates the Soul* (New York: Avery, 2009), 17.

The UN High Commissioner for Human Rights: "UN Convention on Right to Play," Playing Out, https://playingout.net/why/childrens-right-to-play/un-convention-on-right-to-play.

Author adrienne maree brown reminds us: adrienne maree brown, *Pleasure Activism: The Politics of Feeling Good* (Chico, CA: AK Press, 2019).

There are four therapeutic powers: Mary Anne Peabody and Charles E. Schaeffer, "The Therapeutic Powers of Play: The Heart and Soul of Play Therapy," *Play Therapy*, September 2019, https://cdn.ymaws.com/www.a4pt.org/resource/resmgr/magazine_articles/2019-20/Peabody_&_Schaefer.pdf.

the "second chicken" effect: Lawrence J. Cohen, *The Opposite of Worry: The Playful Parenting Approach to Childhood Anxieties and Fears* (New York: Ballantine, 2013).

we could attempt to perceive aggression: Lisa Dion, *Integrating Extremes: Aggression and Death in the Playroom* (Lake Placid, NY: Aviva, 2016).

Research in the field of play therapy: Brandy Schumann, "Effectiveness of Child-Centered Play Therapy for Children Referred for Aggression," in *Child-Centered Play Therapy: The Evidence Base for Effective Practice*, eds. Jennifer N. Baggerly, Dee C. Ray, and Sue C. Bratton (New York: John Wiley, 2010), https://onlinelibrary.wiley.com/doi/10.1002/9781118269626.ch11.

can have its own constructive purpose: Lisa Dion, *Integrating Extremes: Aggression and Death in the Playroom* (New York: Aviva, 2015), 137.

"attention vitamins": Patty Wipfler, *Listening to Children: How Children's Emotions Work* (Palo Alto, CA: Hand in Hand Parenting, 2006), 13.

tickling induces forced laughter: Marder, "The Case Against Tickling."

6. Standing in the Doorway of Adulthood

girls as young as eleven or twelve are: Jamilia J. Blake and Rebecca Epstein, *Listening to Black Women and Girls: Lived Experiences of Adultification Bias*, Initiative on Gender Justice and Opportunity, Georgetown Law Center on Poverty and Inequality, https://genderjusticeandopportunity.georgetown.edu/wp-content/uploads/2020/06/Listening-to-Black-Women-and-Girls.pdf.

The acceleration of puberty cannot be separated: Jessica Winter, "Why More and More Girls Are Hitting Puberty Early," *New Yorker*, October 27, 2022, https://www.newyorker.com/science/annals-of-medicine/why-more-and-more-girls-are-hitting-puberty-early.

Reaching puberty earlier means: Louise Greenspan, "Why Are Girls Starting Puberty Earlier?" *U.S. News & World Report*, April 6, 2017, https://health.usnews.com/wellness/for-parents/articles/2017-04-06/why-are-girls-starting-puberty-earlier.

"disabled people have been culturally desexualized": Kim Sauder, "Issues of Disabled Sexuality and Consent: When Parents Get Involved in Their Children's Sex Lives," *Crippledscholar*, July 9, 2017, https://crippledscholar.com/2017/07/09/issues-of-disabled-sexuality-and-consent-when-parents-get-involved-in-their-childrens-sex-lives/.

an absence of sex education catering to the needs: *Neurodiversity and Gender-Diverse Youth: An Affirming Approach to Care 2020*, National LGBT Health Education Center, Fenway Institute, https://www.lgbtqiahealtheducation.org/wp-content/uploads/2020/08/Neurodiversity-and-Gender-Diverse-Youth_An-Affirming-Approach-to-Care_2020.pdf.

increased risk of being sexually victimized: Nicholette Zeliadt, "Girls with Autism at High Risk of Sexual Abuse, Large Study Says," *Spectrum*, May 14, 2018, https://www.spectrumnews.org/news/girls-autism-high-risk-sexual-abuse-large-study-says/; Patricia M. Sullivan and John F. Knutson, "Maltreatment and Disabilities: A Population-Based Epidemiological Study," *Child Abuse & Neglect*. 24, no. 10 (October 2000): 1257–1273, https://doi.org/10.1016/s0145-2134(00)00190-3; "How Common Is Child Sexual Abuse?," Joshua Center on Child Sexual Abuse Prevention, accessed July 20, 2023, https://uwjoshuacenter.org/how-common-child-sexual-abuse.

"how much one is similar to, or different": Terra Vance, "The Identity Theory of Autism: How Autistic Identity Is Experienced Differently," NeuroClastic, October 17, 2021, https://neuroclastic.com/the-identity-theory-of-autism-how-autistic-identity-is-experienced-differently/.

speaks poignantly to the transformation: Kristin Henning, *The Rage of Innocence: How America Criminalizes Black Youth* (New York: Pantheon Books, 2021).

Many psychological benefits for our youth: Anne C. Montague and Francisco Jose Eiroa-Orosa, "In It Together: Exploring How Belonging to a Youth Activist Group Enhances Well-Being," *Journal of Community Psychology* 46, no. 1 (October 17, 2017): 23–43, http://doi.org/10.1002/jcop.21914.

Peer rejection has a strong correlation with anxiety: O'Brien, "Youth Mental Health Crisis."

7. Parenting at the Edge of Understanding

combined annual revenue of upwards of $100 billion: Daniel Ku, "Which Social Media Platforms Make the Most Revenue?" PostBeyond, August 3, 2021, https://www.postbeyond.com/blog/revenue-per-social-media-user/.

they are played by people for a variety of reasons: For instance, some people play chess online to improve their skills, and for athletes, playing a simulation via a video game can improve their skills. For example, Rory Smith, "How Video Games Are Changing the Way Soccer Is Played," *New York Times*, October 13, 2016, https://www.nytimes.com/2016/10/14/sports/soccer/the-scouting-tools-of-the-pros-a-controller-and-a-video.html.

Many teens have connected with long-distance: Monica Anderson and Jingjing Jiang, *Teens' Social Media Habits and Experiences*, Pew Research Center, November 28, 2018, https://www.pewresearch.org/internet/wp-content/uploads/sites/9/2018/11/PI_2018.11.28_teens-social-media_FINAL4.pdf.

social media can be a way: Gerrit I. van Schalkwyk et al., "Social Media Use, Friendship Quality, and the Moderating Role of Anxiety in Adolescents with Autism Spectrum Disorder," *Journal of Autism and Developmental Disorders* 47 (June 14, 2017): 2805–2813, https://doi.org/10.1007/s10803-017-3201-6; Naseem Alhujaili, Elyse Platt, Sarosh Khalid-Khan, and Diane Groll, "Comparison of Social Media Use Among Adolescents with Autism Spectrum Disorder and Non-ASD Adolescents," *Dove Medical Press* 2022, no. 13 (February 1, 2022): 15–21, https://doi.org/10.2147/AHMT.S344591.

especially with the use of tone tags: Ezra Marcus, "Tone Is Hard to Grasp Online. Can Tone Indicators Help?," *New York Times*, December 9, 2020, https://www.nytimes.com/2020/12/09/style/tone-indicators-online.html.

video games are an essential way: Raffael Boccamazzo, Take This, phone call with authors, April 14, 2022.

can improve these skills: Li Li, Rongrong Chen, and Jing Chen, "Playing Action Video Games Improves Visuomotor Control," *Psychological Science* 27, no. 8 (August 2016): 1092–1108, https://journals.sagepub.com/doi/abs/10.1177/0956797616650300.

video games provide education benefits: Mark Griffiths, "The Educational Benefits of Videogames," *Education and Health* 20, no. 3 (2002): 47–51, http://irep.ntu.ac.uk/id/eprint/15272/1/187769_5405%20Griffiths%20Publisher.pdf.

When we spend time exploring digital worlds: Elizabeth Kilmer, Take This, phone call with authors, April 7, 2022.

Data confirms that depression and anxiety: Kirby, "Neurodiversity and Mental Health?"

autistic youth report higher rates of depression: *Research Brief: Mental Health Among Autistic LGBTQ Youth*, Trevor Project, April 2022, https://www.thetrevorproject.org/wp-content/uploads/2022/05/Autistic-LGBTQ-Youth-Research-Brief.pdf.

One study correlated the rise in smartphones: Jean M. Twenge, "Have Smartphones Destroyed a Generation?" *Atlantic*, September 2017, https://www.theatlantic.com/magazine/archive/2017/09/has-the-smartphone-destroyed-a-generation/534198/.

a whistleblower leaked an internal Facebook document: Sofia Ongele, Sam Schmir, and Zach Praiss, "Instagram Is Bad for Teen Mental Health—We Want to Know All the Data," *Teen Vogue*, October 26, 2021, https://www.teenvogue.com/story/facebook-instagram-teen-mental-health.

A healthy sense of self is protective: Michal Mann et al., "Self-Esteem in a Broad-Spectrum Approach for Mental Health Promotion," *Health Education Research* 19, no. 4 (August 2004): 357–372, https://doi.org/10.1093/her/cyg041.

confirms not only that people on the sites: Erin Vogel et al., "Social Comparison, Social Media, and Self-Esteem," *Psychology of Popular Media Culture* 3, no. 4 (2014): 206–222, https://doi.org/10.1037/ppm0000047.

50 to 80 percent of autistic youth: Luigi Mazzone et al., "The Relationship Between Sleep Problems, Neurobiological Alterations, Core Symptoms of Autism Spectrum Disorder, and Psychiatric Comorbidities," *Journal of Clinical Medicine* 7, no. 5 (May 3, 2018): 102, https://doi.org/10.3390/jcm7050102.

Unlike real-life bullying, cyberbullying: According to the School Climate and Safety Report, approximately 135,200 individual allegations of harassment or bullying based on sex, race, sexual orientation, disability, or religion were reported during the 2015–2016 school year. "School Climate and Safety," US Department of Education Office for Civil Rights, May 2019, https://www2.ed.gov/about/offices/list/ocr/docs/school-climate-and-safety.pdf.

the connection between dopamine and ADHD: Nora D. Volkow et al., "Evaluating Dopamine Reward Pathway in ADHD: Clinical Implications," *JAMA* 302, no. 10 (September 9, 2009): 1084–1091, https://doi.org/10.1001/jama.2009.1308.

hallmark features of ADHD include impulsivity: Bob Seay and Nancy Ratey, "The ADHD-Dopamine Link: Why You Crave Sugar and Carbs," *Attitude*, January 21, 2023, https://www.additudemag.com/slideshows/adhd-obesity-link/.

one study found that constant stimulation stemming: Gabriel Arantes Tiraboschi et al., "Associations Between Video Game Engagement and ADHD Symptoms in Early Adolescence," *Journal of Attention Disorders* 26, no. 10 (January 25, 2022): 1369–1378, https://doi.org/10.1177/10870547211073473.

introduced by blogger Jay Geiger: Candace Osmond, "Clickbait—Origin & Meaning," Grammarist, accessed July 21, 2023, https://grammarist.com/new-words/clickbait/.

Their contents are random and unknown: James Close and Joanne Lloyd, *Lifting the Lid on Loot-Boxes: Chance-Based Purchases in Video Games and the Convergence of Gaming and Gambling*, Gamble Aware, 2021, https://www.begambleaware.org/sites/default/files/2021-03/Gaming_and_Gambling_Report_Final.pdf.

62 percent of the videos watched by children: Déjà Rollins et al., *Who Is the "You" in YouTube? Missed Opportunities in Race and Representation in Children's YouTube Videos*, Common Sense Media, 2022, https://www.commonsensemedia.org/sites/default/files/research/report/2022-youtube-report-final-web.pdf.

"videos from the gaming YouTuber VuxVux": Rollins et al., *Who Is the "You."*

over 80 percent of video game creators: Johanna Weststar et al., *Developer Satisfaction Survey 2021: Summary Report*, International Game Developers Association, September 13, 2021, https://igda-website.s3.us-east-2.amazonaws.com/wp-content/uploads/2021/10/18113901/IGDA-DSS-2021_SummaryReport_2021.pdf.

Representations of BIPOC characters are: Nadine Dornieden, "Leveling Up Representation: Depictions of People of Color in Video Games," Independent Lens, PBS, December 22, 2020, https://www.pbs.org/independentlens/blog/leveling-up-representation-depictions-of-people-of-color-in-video-games.

it is vital for those who hold marginalized : JC Lau, video call with authors, April 22, 2022.

"Racism is a social determinant of health": Maria Trent et al., "The Impact of Racism on Child and Adolescent Health," *Pediatrics* 144, no. 2 (August 2019), https://doi.org/10.1542/peds.2019-1765.

Black and Brown kids may experience online: Xiangyu Tao and Celia B. Fisher, "Exposure to Social Media Racial Discrimination and Mental Health Among Adolescents of Color," Journal of Youth and Adolescence 51 (January 2022): 30–44, https://doi.org/10.1007%2Fs10964-021-01514-z.

alarming stories of people being exposed: Noah Smith, "Racism, Misogyny, Death Threats: Why Can't the Booming Video-Game Industry Crub Toxicity?" *Washington Post*, February 26, 2019, https://www.washingtonpost.com/technology/2019/02/26/racism-misogyny-death-threats-why-cant-booming-video-game-industry-curb

-toxicity/; Patricia Hernandez, "Playing Red Dead Online as a Black Character Means Enduring Racist Garbage," *Verge*, January 15, 2019, https://www.theverge.com/2019/1/15/18183843/red-dead-online-black-character-racism.

8. The Halls of Medicine

we are subject to derogatory and/or condescending: Irene V. Blair, John F. Steiner, and Edward P. Havranek, "Unconscious (Implicit) Bias and Health Disparities: Where Do We Go from Here?" *Permanente Journal* 15, no. 2 (Spring 2011): 71–78, https://www.ncbi.nlm.nih.gov/pmc/articles/PMC3140753/.

"Many times trauma in a person decontextualized": Resmaa Menakem, "Restore Reclaim and Resource: A Weekend with Resmaa Menakem MSW" (Professional training seminar attended by author, Bastyr University, Kenmore, WA, June 21–23, 2019).

trauma can alter the expression: Rachel Yehuda and Amy Lehrner, "Intergenerational Transmission of Trauma Effects: Putative Role of Epigenetic Mechanisms," *World Psychiatry* 17, no. 3 (October 2018): 243–257, https://doi.org/10.1002/wps.20568.

largely impacted Indigenous, Black, Latinx, and disabled people: Emily Medosch, "Not Just ICE: Forced Sterilization in the United States," Immigration and Human Rights Law Review, May 28, 2021, https://lawblogs.uc.edu/ihrlr/2021/05/28/not-just-ice-forced-sterilization-in-the-united-states/.

Black people were subject to medical trials: Harriet A. Washington, *Medical Apartheid: The Dark History of Medical Experimentation on Black Americans from Colonial Times to the Present* (New York: Anchor, 2008).

These experimentations have a long history: Allison C. Meier, "Grave Robbing, Black Cemeteries, and the American Medical School," *JSTOR Daily*, August 24, 2018, https://daily.jstor.org/grave-robbing-black-cemeteries-and-the-american-medical-school.

identified by the following symptoms: American Psychiatric Association, *Desk Reference to the Diagnostic Criteria from DSM-5* (Arlington, VA: APA, 2016), 60.

DIR Floortime: "What Is DIR®?," International Council on Development and Learning, accessed July 21, 2023, https://www.icdl.com/dir.

music therapy: Eileen Reynolds, "'What Can Music Do?' Rethinking Autism Through Music Therapy," New York University, July 22, 2016, https://www.nyu.edu/about/news-publications/news/2016/july/autism-and-neurodiversity-at-nordoff-robbins-center-for-music-th.html.

dance/movement therapy: Michele C. Hollow, "For Some Children with Autism, Dance Is a Form of Expression," *New York Times*, November 19, 2019, https://www.nytimes.com/2019/11/19/well/family/autism-children-dance.html.

play therapy: Robert Jason Grant, "Play Therapy and the Neurodivergent Child: A Parent's Guide," AutPlay Therapy, July 27, 2021, https://autplaytherapy.com/play-therapy-and-the-neurodivergent-child-a-parents-guide/; "Dr. Robert Jason Grant: AutPlay Therapy—Working with Neurodivergent Children & Their Families," Synergetic Play Therapy Institute podcast, February 14, 2023, https://synergeticplaytherapy.com/139-dr-robert-jason-grant-autplay-therapy-working-with-neurodivergent-children-their-families/.

animal-assisted therapies: Roslyn Malcolm, Stefan Ecks, and Martyn Pickersgill, "'It Just Opens Up Their World': Autism, Empathy, and the Therapeutic Effects of Equine Interactions," *Anthropology & Medicine* 25, no. 2 (2018): 220–234, https://www.ncbi.nlm.nih.gov/pmc/articles/PMC6199690/.

More so, there are minimal support systems: Jamie N. Pearson, et al., "Meeting FACES: Preliminary Findings from a Community Workshop for Minority Parents of Children with Autism in Central North Carolina," *Journal of Autism and Developmental Disorders* 50 (November 15, 2019): 1–11, https://doi.org/10.1007/s10803-019-04295-4.

the misdiagnosis-to-prison pipeline: Devon Frye, "The Children Left Behind," *Attitude*, March 31, 2022, https://www.additudemag.com/race-and-adhd-how-people-of-color-get-left-behind/.

According to Dr. Cort: Frye, "Children Left Behind."

at least three years of delay: John N. Constantino et al., "Timing of the Diagnosis of Autism in African American Children," *Pediatrics* 146, no. 3 (September 2020): https://doi.org/10.1542/peds.2019-3629.

9. Unlearning the Script

The impacts of boarding schools or residential schools: Associated Press in Anadarko, OK, "Native American Elders Recall Abuse at US Government Boarding Schools," *Guardian* (US edition), July 9, 2022, https://theguardian.com/us-news/2022/jul/09/native-american-elders-us-government-schools-oklahoma.

This modern segregation, due to practices like redlining: Sequoia Carrillo and Pooja Salhotra, "The U.S. Student Population Is More Diverse, but Schools Are Still Highly Segregated," *Morning Edition*, NPR, July 14, 2022, https://www.npr.org/2022/07/14/1111060299/school-segregation-report.

the current special education laws state: "Sec. 300.114 LRE Requirements," May 3, 2017, Individuals with Disabilities Education Act, https://sites.ed.gov/idea/regs/b/b/300.114.

children of color and children with disabilities: National Council on Disability, *IDEA Series: The Segregation of Students with Disabilities*," February 7, 2018, https://ncd.gov/sites/default/files/NCD_Segregation-SWD_508.pdf.

"students from nondominant groups tend to be overrepresented": Federico R. Waitoller, Alfredo J. Artiles, and Douglas A. Cheney, "The Miner's Canary: A Review of Overrepresentation Research and Explanations," *Journal of Special Education* 44, no. 1 (May 2010): 29–49, https://doi.org/10.1177/0022466908329226.

inclusive education for all children: Down Syndrome International, "A Brief History of the Concept of Inclusive Education," YouTube, 4:04, March 23, 2022, https://www.youtube.com/watch?v=Ed9Nc4ayQ-A.

There is strong evidence that inclusive education: National Council on Disability, *IDEA Series*.

"When I get emails, they're only in English": Moses Perez, Munisha Kaur, and Joy Y. Sebe, *Family Feedback Report on Language Access in Schools*, Open Doors for Multicultural Families, January 2021, https://www.multiculturalfamilies.org/wp-content/uploads/2021/01/2021-ODMF-Family-Feedback-Report-on-Language-Access-1.pdf.

even when teachers do not directly bully kids: Aaron Kupchik, *The Real School Safety Problem: The Long-Term Consequences of Harsh School Punishment* (Berkeley: University of California Press, 2016).

Cheryl Poe, founder of Advocating 4 Kids: Quotes from Cheryl Poe in this chapter are from interview with the authors, October 13, 2023, unless otherwise cited.

Children of color with neurodivergence are more likely: National Center for Learning Disabilities, *Significant Disproportionality in Special Education: Current Trends and Actions for Impact*, 2010, https://www.ncld.org/wp-content/uploads/2020/10/2020-NCLD-Disproportionality_Trends-and-Actions-for-Impact_FINAL-1.pdf.

to discipline is to teach: Dionne Grayman, "Opinion: 'Punitive Discipline Makes School Feel Like a Prison, Not a Community,'" *Hechinger Report*, April 25, 2019, https://hechingerreport.org/opinion-punitive-discipline/.

refusal to attend school: "School Refusal," Stanford Medicine Children's Health, accessed July 31, 2023, https://www.stanfordchildrens.org/en/topic/default?id=school-refusal-90-P02288.

What is more frightening than our children's: Linda Kryvoruka, "Back to School Can Be a Challenging Time for Neurodivergent Students," Alliance Against Seclusion and Restraint, August 28, 2022, https://endseclusion.org/2022/08/28/back-to-school-can-be-a-challenging-time-for-neurodivergent-students/.

The crisis of school shootings has perpetuated: Kupchik, *Real School Safety Problem.*

It has been a long-standing act of social resistance: Amaarah DeCuir, "Inequality Has Long Driven Black Parents to Pull Children from Public Schools," *Washington Post*, February 24, 2022, https://www.washingtonpost.com/outlook/2022/02/24/inequality-has-long-driven-black-parents-pull-children-public-schools.

"unique opportunity to step away from systems": Earl Stevens, "What Is Unschooling?" Natural Child Project, https://www.naturalchild.org/articles/guest/earl_stevens.html.

"an act of resistance": Iris Chen, "Unschooling as an Act of Resistance," Alliance for Self-Directed Education, October 18, 2021, https://www.self-directed.org/tp/unschooling-as-an-act-of-resistance/.

10. Dismantling the Pipeline

The data shows that most of these children: "Youth Involved with the Juvenile System," Youth.gov, accessed July 21, 2023, https://youth.gov/youth-topics/juvenile-justice/youth-involved-juvenile-justice-system.

SROs are armed police officers placed in schools: Stephen Sawchuk, "School Resource Officers (SROs), Explained," *Education Week*, November 16, 2021, https://www.edweek.org/leadership/school-resource-officer-sro-duties-effectiveness.

the incarceration of parents gravely impacts: Eric Martin, "Hidden Consequences: The Impact of Incarceration on Dependent Children," *National Institute of Justice Journal* (March 1, 2017), https://nij.ojp.gov/topics/articles/hidden-consequences-impact-incarceration-dependent-children.

It destroys families within a generation: Kristin Henning, *The Rage of Innocence: How America Criminalizes Black Youth* (New York: Pantheon, 2021).

the logic of elimination has dictated policing: Raghav Kaushik, "On Community Control of Police: An Interview with M Adams," Countercurrents.org, September 8, 2020, https://countercurrents.org/2020/08/on-community-control-of-police-an-interview-with-m-adams.

more Indigenous people die at the hands of the police: Teran Powell, "Native Americans Most Likely to Die from Police Shootings, Families Who Lost Loved Ones Weigh In," WUWM, June 2, 2021, https://www.wuwm.com/2021-06-02/native-americans-most-likely-to-die-from-police-shootings-families-who-lost-loved-ones-weigh-in.

Policing expanded during slavery to control Black bodies: Connie Hassett-Walker, "The Racist Roots of American Policing: From Slave Patrols to Traffic Stops," *Conversation*, June 2, 2020, https://theconversation.com/the-racist-roots-of-american-policing-from-slave-patrols-to-traffic-stops-112816.

slave patrols, a group of self-appointed White men: "The Origins of Modern Day Policing," NAACP, https://naacp.org/find-resources/history-explained/origins-modern-day-policing.

the Black codes, which limited the freedoms: Nandra Kareem Nittle, "The Black Codes and Why They Still Matter Today," ThoughtCo, December 21, 2020, https://www.thoughtco.com/the-black-codes-4125744.

Jim Crow laws, which denied civil rights: Hassett-Walker, "Racist Roots of American Policing."

the overcriminalization of petty offenses: "Policing," Prison Policy Initiative, https://www.prisonpolicy.org/policing.html.

Today, disabled people of color are overrepresented: Vilissa Thompson, "Understanding the Policing of Black, Disabled Bodies," Center for American Progress, February 10, 2021, https://www.americanprogress.org/article/understanding-policing-black-disabled-bodies.

Data from the American Civil Liberties Union: Amir Whitaker et al., *Cops and No Counselors: How the Lack of School Mental Health Staff Is Harming Students*, American Civil Liberties Union, https://www.aclu.org/sites/default/files/field_document/030419-acluschooldisciplinereport.pdf.

a nine-year-old Black girl, handcuffed: Janelle Griffith, "'You did it to yourself,' Officer Tells 9-Year-Old Girl Pepper-Sprayed by Police in Newly Released Video," *ABC News*, February 12, 2021, https://www.nbcnews.com/news/us-news/you-did-it-yourself-officer-tells-9-year-old-girl-n1257630.

a "disturbing national trend": "School-to-Prison Pipeline," ACLU, https://www.aclu.org/issues/juvenile-justice/juvenile-justice-school-prison-pipeline.

A staggering 250 preschoolers are suspended: Molly Kaplan, "How to End the Preschool to Prison Pipeline," *At Liberty Podcast*, ACLU, https://www.aclu.org/podcast/how-end-preschool-prison-pipeline-ep-172.

Zero-tolerance policies, an artifact: Libby Nelson and Dara Lind, "The School-to-Prison Pipeline, Explained," *Vox*, October 27, 2015, https://www.vox.com/2015/2/24/8101289/school-discipline-race.

a Black child with a developmental delay: Ny Magee, "Florida Teacher Accused of Assaulting Special Needs Black Student," *Grio*, January 21, 2022, https://thegrio.com/2022/01/21/florida-teacher-accused-of-assaulting-black-student.

it cannot but reinforce a perception: Jen Wight, "Cultivating Resilience: Developing a Sense of Purpose," Balance Health & Healing, June 24, 2020, https://balancehealthandhealing.com/cultivating-resilience-developing-sense-purpose/.

Nick Dubin offers a significant limitation: Nick Dubin, *Autism Spectrum Disorder, Developmental Disabilities, and the Criminal Justice System: Breaking the Cycle* (Philadelphia: Jessica Kingsley, 2021).

"So that parents can avoid finding": Quotes from Cheryl Poe in this chapter are from Poe, interview, unless otherwise cited.

the Autism in Black podcast has an episode: Maria Davis-Pierre, "IEPs, 504s, Due Process, and More with Shemica Allen," *Autism in Black Podcast*, July 17, 2020, https://www.autisminblack.org/podcast/ieps-504s-due-process-and-more-with-shemica-allen.

In such an environment, our children: Silvia Molina Roldan et al., "How Inclusive Interactive Learning Environments Benefit Student Without Special Needs," *Frontiers in Psychology* 12 (April 29, 2021), https://doi.org/10.3389/fpsyg.2021.661427.

Nick Dubin emphasizes the paramount role: Dubin, *Autism Spectrum Disorder*.

research reveals that the presence of SROs: Corey Mitchell, Joe Yerardi, and Susan Ferriss, "When Schools Call Police on Kids," Center for Public Integrity, September 8, 2021, https://publicintegrity.org/education/criminalizing-kids/police-in-schools-disparities.

the reality is that school shootings: Kendrick Washington and Tori Hazelton, "School Resource Officers: When the Cure Is Worse than the Disease," ACLU of Washington, May 24, 2021, https://www.aclu-wa.org/story/school-resource-officers-when-cure-worse-disease.

SROs contribute to pushing students of color: Washington and Hazelton, "School Resource Officers."

Morénike Giwa Onaiwu, an autistic self-advocate: Elissa Ball and Jaclyn Jeffrey-Wilensky, "Why Autism Training for Police Isn't Enough," *Spectrum*, November 26, 2020, https://www.spectrumnews.org/news/why-autism-training-for-police-isnt-enough.

the Office of Juvenile Justice and Delinquency Prevention's: "Juvenile Justice System Structure and Process," Office of Juvenile Justice and Delinquency Prevention, US Department of Justice, https://www.ojjdp.gov/ojstatbb/structure_process/case.html.

diversion programs informed by restorative justice: Impact Justice, "What Is Restorative Justice Diversion," March 10, 2021, YouTube, 1:00:32, https://www.youtube.com/watch?v=S43efMiSzjM&t=36s.

Appendix A: Resources for Legal Considerations

Documentation Tips from Cheryl Poe: Maria Davis-Pierre, "Protecting and Preparing Back to School Edition with Cheryl Poe," *Autism in Black Podcast*, August 19, 2022, https://www.autisminblack.org/podcast/protecting-and-preparing-back-to-school-edition-with-cheryl-poe.

Education Commission of the States: See Bryan Kelley, Carlos Jamieson, and Zeke Perez Jr., "School Discipline Policies: State Profiles," Education Commission of the States, May 17, 2021, https://www.ecs.org/school-discipline-policies-state-profiles; Bryan Kelley, Carlos Jamieson, and Zeke Perez Jr., "50-State Comparison: School Discipline Policies," Education Commission of the States, May 17, 2021, https://www.ecs.org/50-state-comparison-school-discipline-policies.

ABOUT THE AUTHORS

Jaya Ramesh, MA LMHC, is a psychotherapist in private practice in the greater Seattle area, specializing in supporting BIPOC neurodivergent individuals and couples in having more authentic relationships. She also runs a DEI consultancy, coaching leaders at organizations on creating antiracist culture in the workplace.

Priya Saaral, MSW, LICSW, RPT-S, is a neurodivergent mama, a play therapist, and a parenting coach in the greater Seattle area, specializing in the emotional well-being of neurodivergent children and parents by helping them reconnect to their playful spirit amid personal and structural adversity.

Visit them online at **https://www.parentingattheintersections.com/**.